Gateways
to the
Otherworld

Gateways to the Otherworld

The SECRETS BEYOND

the FINAL JOURNEY,

From the EGYPTIAN UNDERWORLD

to the GATES in the SKY

PHILIP GARDINER

best-selling author of *Gnosis* and
The Ark, the Shroud, and Mary

New Page Books
A division of The Careeer Press, Inc.
Franklin Lakes, NJ

GATEWAYS TO THE OTHERWORLD
EDITED AND TYPESET BY KARA REYNOLDS
Cover design by Lucia Rossman/Digi Dog Design NYC
Printed in the U.S.A. by Book-mart Press

To order this title, please call toll-free 1-800-CAREER-1 (NJ and Canada: 201-848-0310) to order using VISA or MasterCard, or for further information on books from Career Press.

The Career Press, Inc., 3 Tice Road, PO Box 687,
Franklin Lakes, NJ 07417
www.careerpress.com
www.newpagebooks.com

Library of Congress Cataloging-in-Publication Data
Gardiner, Philip.
   Gateways to the otherworld : the secrets beyond the final journey, from the Egyptian underworld to the gates in the sky / by Philip Gardiner.
      p. cm.
   Includes bibliographical references and index.
   ISBN-13: 978-1-56414-925-1
   ISBN-10: 1-56414-925-0
   1. Future life. 2. Parapsychology. I. Title.

BL535.G37 2007
130--dc22
                                                        2007020748

I dedicate this book to my parents, John and May, for being caring, loving, and at all times understanding. I am blessed to have known you.

Acknowledgments

o book written can evade acknowledging the work of others. To list the names of all those wonderful individuals who have influenced me on this road would take another book. The bibliography at the end of this book is a testament to many of them, and I acknowledge every author in that list for their hard work and efforts. But more than these, there have been those who have spoken words of wisdom and guided me toward places and moments of truth, and I wish to thank them all. My thanks go to Crichton Miller, a man on a mission of a lifetime with an ancient secret of profound importance. Warren Croyle, a mentor and good friend. Tim Wallace-Murphy, my Sufi friend; Kay Sturgis; Dominic O'Brien; Henry Hopking; and so many more.

Thanks also to the following people for their inspiration and help, whether directly or indirectly: Hamish Miller, Gary Osborn, Steve Mitchell, Kara Reynolds, Kirsten Dalley, Anna Franklin, Dr. Gebbie, Matt Clark, O.H. Krill, my wife, Harald S. Boehlke, and Dr. John Jay Harper.

Contents

Introduction

any years ago I decided that there were still truths to be discovered that humankind had sidelined into the world we know as the paranormal. Mysteries of the material and esoteric worlds still cried out to be revealed. One of these mysteries is, even now in the 21st century, the answer to whether there is life after death. And yet, I knew that there must be simple and scientific answers to this most profound of riddles. But, more than this, there was another question, related to our lives here and now: Is there another realm of existence, often spoken of throughout history?

In my search for the truth I discovered that there had indeed been answers to these profound questions for thousands of years, cloaked in the language of religion, belief, and myth. The language of our ancestors had understandably been based around a pantheon of deities and ancestor worship—the words expressing the understanding of the time.

Now, in the 21st century, we have a new language—the language of science. It is still a belief system, with its own inbuilt flaws. Science is an ever-evolving process of objective, and sometimes all too often subjective, experimentation. We are told that asbestos is safe, only to then discover that it is really a killer. We are told that global warming is the worst thing to hit the planet in the modern era, to then be told by other scientists that the warming of the planet is nothing more than a cyclical and natural phenomena. Just like the myriad of religions, we end up believing in one or the other, or none at all.

I believe, from my research, that a situation spoken of by the ancients is far more crucial to a proper understanding of the reality of life—*balance*. If we assume, as is often the case today, that ancient wisdom is no longer required for our modern lives, then we shall lose a great deal of insight. On the other hand, if we refuse to try to understand the modern religion of science, then we shall be like the bastard son of a virgin. It is an impossible situation. This is why we attempt to understand the wisdom of thousands of years of human thought, *in balance with* the resultant science of modern humankind.

This book is my attempt to provide such a balance, and by doing so to provide answers to the most profound questions humankind has been asking for as long as there has been consciousness. I am not the first to do so, and shall not be the last. Many have developed philosophies, created religions, or even found the darkness and void of total atheism. I, on the other hand, do not wish to be anybody's messiah; I am no great philosopher and I have no concept of a belief system for myself, whether for God or against. My thoughts have

sprung up from a well that has been filled through the years by a great many people, experiences, and emotions. If any writer is honest, he or she will admit that the words he or she writes are formed from the amalgamation of other people's input, and I am no different. Without Einstein, Jung, Freud, Tesla, Schumann, and whole host of visionaries, scientists, historians, mystics, sceptics, and people I have met in the pub, this book and all others would not have been possible. And that is partly the point of this book—that life itself is only possible because we are part of the whole, like cells within the body, needing the next cell to pass on information in order to know what to do. This book is not my theory, not my creation; it is my understanding of all those who came before and some of those still present today. Yes, I have also discarded some information that I have found to be, for me, incorrect, and the reader may wonder why. The truth is that some information would lead me into dispute where it is not required, and some is just simply not scientifically provable. There are some things in this book that may not yet be provable, but I have included them because I believe that one day science will catch up with our intuitive ancestors.

We will find that on this journey of thought, many theories and statements will challenge our way of thinking. A great deal will challenge our inbuilt view of nature and evolution. Moreover and more importantly, it will challenge our "external phenomena," as the Buddhists like to call them. These "external phenomena" are the beliefs we have learned from others and from life's experiences—the exoteric; such things as

our understanding of what God is or even how humankind evolved. These beliefs and more are inside us not from the totally archetypal world of Jung's unconsciousness, but also from our parents, peers, and especially today, the media. I myself have held certain opinions, and even put them in writing, only to then discover that there was no scientific basis, that the theory had been proven incorrect, or, more worrisome, that certain elements of it were dangerous. More than ever, today's beliefs are created inside of us from the technological world around us—from television, the Internet, radio, and all manner of visual and oral devices. These are the new Cathedrals of belief. These are the new stained glass windows of propaganda that we see, hear, touch, and give credence to.

My way of working is to smash these windows of manipulation with the stone of hard research, and to see what lies behind them more clearly. If I throw enough stones, then eventually the window will break and the sun will shine through.

In this way I have worked hard at ignoring the interpretations of each generation of historians, philosophers, scientists, and religious exponents. I have listened to their secret languages, which have been created to evade questions that I wished to ask. And I have brought together the underlying truths from each and every generation of human endeavor that has been dormant for thousands of years.

Every generation, whether living under the oppressive Catholic Inquisition or the Age of Enlightenment, has thirsted for the answers to the questions I pose here today. Each time they believed they knew the reality. But what I have discovered is a constant across time and space. It is a belief, an understanding, and an often hidden process, which has been at the core of each and every generation, and is still alive today. In order to view this constant we need to understand the thoughts of each period of man's illusive history, and test this thread against modern objective science. When we discover that the same psychological system has been at the root of each generation, and is the origination of each and every religion, then we will be astounded by the universal nature of the process. But, more than this, we will be amazed at the scientific evidence there is for this constant, and that it now, in light of ancient wisdom and modern science, can be proven to be the answer to the questions we posed at the start of this introduction—is there life after death, and another realm to explore in this life? The answer, as we shall discover, is yes, but not as we know it—and, I guarantee, not what you may be expecting.

Chapter 1

Gateway: What Do We Mean?

 he word *gateway* can summon up all manner of ideas in our mind. In the Western Christian world it could be the Gateway to heaven, guarded by St. Peter, who balances the lives of those wishing to enter, as did Thoth and Anubis in ancient Egypt, who weigh the souls of prospective entrants against the feather of Maat. To Pagans it could be the portal to the world of Annwyn—the Celtic Underworld, with its myriad deities and heroes. To clairvoyants we could be talking about the Gateway to the spirit realm, just like the Shaman who induces trance states to see the parallel world of dead ancestors and Earth spirits. To scientists and theoretical physicists we could be discussing the quantum world of parallel or holographic universes, or even the psychologists' altered states of existence.

All these countless beliefs are linked together through time and space in a way never before realized. They are all evolved methods of the very same process, which we shall discover was at the root of all religions and is implicated in the origin of consciousness. There is an answer and a good reason for them all, as we shall discover, and that answer is the constant we discussed in the introduction.

However, to clearly express the true concept of a Gateway we need to try and understand what it truly means in as simple a manner as possible. Keeping the concept straightforward we can break it down into two distinct parts.

depending on how good or bad we have been. Similar concepts are discussed in other religions, but with minor alterations. Many do not believe in a hell, for instance.

Heaven is generally the dwelling place of God and angels or the pantheon of gods. It is the ultimate destiny of humanity, to rest eternally with the chosen God. This place is conceived of as being high above

Ancient burial crypts beneath the ground at St. Paul's Catacombs in Malta.

Life After Death

Firstly there is the Gateway after physical death into the realms known by Christians (and others) as heaven or hell,

the Earth or on top of the World Mountain or Tree, but is accessed often through a tomb or cave where we are laid to rest. The Islamic heaven is a paradise, and often takes the form of a garden (al-jannah). It is full of beautiful trees, flowers and plants, wonderful rivers and lakes, and is enclosed

and sheltered all around. This place is thought to be so wonderful that no man can imagine its beauty.

From at least the 11th century an enigmatic group known as the Assassins emerged in Persia. They take their name from Hashish (hashish-in, hashish or Cannabis takers), a trance-inducing drug thought by many to help the leaders control the minds of the subverts, and used as a derogatory term. In one famous statement, Hasan, son of Sabah, the Sheikh of the Mountains, said to an official of an emperor's court: "You see that devotee standing guard on yonder turret-top? Watch!" Hasan clicked his fingers and the adherent jumped to his death. This was true control, even if it was later propaganda, but how did the sheikh do it?

It is known that there was a physical paradise built within the compounds of the main Assassins Citadel, which was hidden from ordinary eyes. The new initiate would be drugged and led into this paradise where sweet water ran and beautiful ladies would produce a strong desire in the initiate to return. This psychological game was powerful; so powerful that the adherent would die without question upon the command of his superior, knowing he was going to a much better place *after* death—but one that he had already experienced through drugs in this life. This, of course, shows the belief that the Otherworld could be accessed while still alive.

This was a psychological paradise built within the mind of the individual via physical means. It was playing upon a belief system that was thousands of years old and deeply entrenched in the minds of the

An ancient portal to the Underworld: Cresswell Crags, England.

people. All it needed for total and utter control was a little added incentive of drugs and lust.

In Christianity there was a merging of many beliefs in the concept of heaven. From the Judaic Sheol and Paradise to the Hellenistic Hades and Celtic Otherworld. This was due in part to the fourth century council of "bishops" at Nicea. According to standard Christian propaganda, this was the first ecumenical council of the Church called by Emperor Constantine to settle doctrinal dispute. However, the truth is that this was really a meeting between the disparate religions of the time in order to finally create the new empirical Paganism of Christianity. The council drew together

Christ being laid in the tomb for access to the Otherworld, in Kykoss Monastery, Cyprus.

"Bishops" from across the religious spectrum, including the followers of the Roman Mithras, the Eastern Buddha, and Krishna (Christna), as well as wealthy Judaism, obstinate Celtic Druidism, and the riotous Dionysius/Bacchus to name a few. This is the real reason that Christianity can be unfolded into all these other creeds—because it was a Holy Grail mixing bowl of their beliefs. This is also why the heaven and hell of Christianity are as diverse as the hell of Hades and the heaven of the Celtic Otherworld.

We will time travel into these various beliefs later on to uncover the deeper meanings that they hold within their grasp. However, I said there were two distinct parts to the concept of the Gateway, and in this second element we discover a truer meaning to these notions.

The Otherworld Now

It is all well and good having a paradise or heavenly home that we disappear to after physical death, but many of us would like to experience this Otherworld now, to know for ourselves that there is a better place awaiting us. There may also be aid to be gained from this Otherworld—such as healing and prophecy from the deities or spirits that reside there.

I will lay down a general concept of this age-old belief in order to better understand the idea in as simple a fashion as possible, understanding that there are as many strands to this thread as there are branches on a tree. I am specifically trying to keep all of this as simple as possible, as much of the detail given in this book will build into a very complex system. Suffice it to say that the reader may turn to my other books (*Gnosis: The Secret of Solomon's Temple; The Ark, The Shroud, and Mary*) for more background evidence.

Legends, myths, and fables are still alive today with the beliefs of the Otherworld or Underworld of ancient Pagan times, in which great warriors enter and emerge renewed, or the universal and archetypal Shaman goes to bring back healing, prophecies, and messages from the spirit realm. This Otherworld is the place of the spirits—whether ancestors, demigods, or nature spirits. Somehow the Shaman, or, more modernly, priest, enters into this realm via various processes we shall discuss later in light of scientific evidence.

It is a world of magic, mystery, and often madness. It is a place of the mystic, who appears different in some way from the rest of his logical, thinking counterparts. Because there is a drug or meditative introduction into this mystical realm, the visualizations, which are brought back and portrayed in literature and art, are almost impossible for ordinary people to understand—you have to experience the process to fully conceive the portrayal. In this way, *this* Otherworld becomes—and comes from—the mind of man, which is, through its in-built imaginative processes, good *and* evil. Hence, we have a place of terror, torment, and darkness, or peace, serenity, and beauty. It is a polarity, created from within the polarity of the mind. It is also archetypal, as the images and notions expressed are innately human and worldwide. However, there is a third explanation, more universal and more profound, as I will explain in later chapters.

This Otherworld contains the cauldrons and tools to better ourselves and to improve our lot here on Earth now, not in some afterlife. It is also, though, the place from where our tormentors emerge—the place of trickery and deceit. This Otherworld concept can easily be shown to be the origin of the first part—the heaven or hell to which we go after death. The beauty and splendor of our imaginings and the dark demons of our mind are the angels and demons of heaven and hell. These places, both before and after death, were the same thing to our ancient ancestors.

These inner concepts of the mind evolved through vast periods of time and through hundreds of wonderful and mighty civilizations into anthropomorphic resonances that remain with us today. The archetypal figures of these hidden worlds were brought out of the mind for all to see as the sun, moon, and stars; as the spirits of the trees and animals around us; as the sibyls of the underwater realms and the ghosts of the mountains. In the same respect, these everyday natural objects were taken inside and given life as human figures.

Today we see these inner spirits in tales from the Mabinogion or the Gilgamesh Epic, in the Arthurian legends and alchemical mutterings, in biblical revelations and Greek philosophies. All can be drawn back to this inner working of the mind of man. All can be shown to have emerged from the Gateway of the human mind into the Otherworld of our existence.

But can the Gods really have emerged from within our own minds? Have we really created in vast periods of time the one God who is the manifestation of all those that went before? Is there no spirituality of real worth? And if there is, can it be described using modern scientific language?

Scientific Reasoning for God

Humankind has a strange place in the annals of history as the only species that can supposedly touch God in its prayers and meditations. But is this true? To answer such questions we have to ask another one. Does God exist? The answer to this age-old question may indeed lie inside the brain itself, and not on some esoteric trip of the light fantastic.

The Gateway to Heaven for the Christians of Whitby, England.

Simply put, the brain is an organic computer with electromagnetic neurons firing across it at an amazing speed—as we shall see in later chapters, some information actually travels faster than the speed of light. Internally there are yet further parts that release hormones dependent upon the neurons that are fired. Why these neurons are fired depends upon the activity we are currently undertaking—be that making a cup of coffee or praying—or the effects of the world around us, such as electromagnetic impulses from solar activity. Every activity or thought creates a different set of "sparks" that release hormones in different ways and in varying amounts—the mix being a kind of alchemical wedding and seemingly beyond comprehension at present. However, as science furthers humankind's knowledge of itself, we discover through reductionism the various elements that make up the whole. This then gives us a picture, so that we can now put the puzzle together.

But what science neglects are the spiritual aspects and the interconnected natures of the universe as a whole. Just like us, the earth and the universe have electromagnetic energies, which also release effects on a universal and global scale. Things such as tectonic plate movement cause electromagnetic activity in the atmosphere, which in turn cause storms or other atmospheric effects.

The universe also has strange "neurons" that fire constantly across it, called neutrinos, among many other kinds of interactions. These neutrinos come in threes and

are only now being understood to actually affect the Earth and us (not to mention the universe). All of this, as we shall discover in the holographic and quantum universe, shows the unique interconnectivity between us—as evolved elements *of* the universe—and the universe itself.

Let's look at a simple example of this ordered interconnectedness.

The universe theoretically began with a big bang approximately 15 billion years ago. The process will slow down until one day it will also theoretically turn in on itself and we will have a big crunch—at which point it will start all over again. The sun goes up and comes down each day. We rise in the morning and sleep in the evening. We breathe and even blink to a rhythm or cycle. The pump inside of us we call the heart is repeating a cycle also. Even down to the smallest atom (and even smaller subatomic particles), we have these universal cycles—they are the things that give energy and life. They are a constant, and we are part of that constant. Even the waves of the sea are the same as the waves of sound or light. In this way, and in more complex ways, we are connected to the waves, particles, and cycles of the entire universe. This wave constant has been called *resonance*, and is a key to unlocking the secrets of humankind's place in the cosmos.

Through certain kinds of meditation, fasting, prayer, the use of drugs, and dancing (dervish), humankind can actually affect his own electromagnetic "wave resonance" and make it similar to that of the earth/universe—something akin to F-sharp, as we shall see. This resonance is found throughout the ancient world in megalithic monuments, pyramids, Shaman texts, and elsewhere. This is the *God resonance*, which aids in the cause of "illumination" inside the mind of man, so that he believes he is in contact with God, whereas he is truly in tune with the resonance of the universe. God is simply a human visualization of the effect—like seeing a face in a cloud; a kind of archetype, which alters as you move through various cultures. Some archetypes remain the same the world over, such as snakes or spirals. For instance, somebody in North America may see the shape of Jesus in a cloud phenomenon, whereas in India they may see the same cloud formation, but will visualize it as Krishna. It is the same part of the universe that the two humans perceive—they are just visualizing it in their own unique cultural ways.

Now, I believe we will prove for the first time that ancient humans understood their place in the vast resonant universe more than we currently give them credit for, and it is for this reason that they placed certain buildings and objects around the globe. Why? Because at these points upon the globe (and points that are within the universe and ourselves), we have discovered convergence points where lines of energy cross—these points have distinct relation to the universal and human wave resonance of electromagnetism. When people journeyed upon pilgrimages to these places, they were joining with God (universe/earth) and visualizing the effect.

This, in short, is the journey to God and the creation of the Gateways to the Otherworld.

Mary and the infant Christ in the upturned crescent moon upon the cross; a perfect union of opposites, revealing the enlightened child, in Rome.

This emptiness is nothing more than the space within the atom—the majority of the atom in fact. You see, the truth is that all things are made up of atoms and all atoms are basically empty—they contain an emptiness, which is little understood. The same can be said of the universe, which is also made up not of what can be seen, but by what cannot be seen. A true ancient symbol of this very fact is the dot within a circle—a symbol that is thousands of years old that represents the sun and also the polar axis, as my good friend and author Crichton Miller explained to me. However, it is not only the external sun, but the internal enlightenment, beautifully associated with the vacuum.

You may have heard or read about the so-called akashic records—a realm within our collective unconscious where all the information of the universe is supposed to be recorded and stored. Again, this abstract realm can only be what the eastern mystics refer to as the absolute—the very center of consciousness, which is also the dot at the center of the circle.

In order to better understand the "original concept of the Otherworld," we must now move into an esoteric world of understanding. And, in order to discover the true Gateways to this Otherworld, we must try to discover the beliefs of the ancients with regard to the modern psychological term for it—*the vacuum.*

Akashic Records

The word *akashic* derives from the Sanskrit *akasha*, meaning "the fundamental and etheric substance of the universe." This etheric substance is thought to fill all space and to link all things together. Because this mystical substance connects everything to everything else, then a vast record of knowledge is built up, and it is into these akashic records that we can supposedly tap. In the West we call these records the book of life, a location where

the full extent of our lives is recorded, awaiting our ascendancy to heaven.

So let's think about this for a moment. The akashic records are where all the information of the entire universe resides, and the word itself means the "substance of the universe." So the substance of the universe holds the records of everything from all time.

If this is true, then the vacuum within the atom, the "empty" space of the universe and even the supposed junk DNA of the human, could really be all interconnected like some great internet, passing information to and fro. Adding to this the fact that the ancients claimed they were able to go into these records and see them for themselves, then we have the supposed ability to enter into the vacuum consciously.

This can all sound quite mad upon first reading, and it is for this reason that I have joined ancient mythology with modern science—so that we may have a modern language (science) to be able to comprehend what our ancestors were telling us.

So, who was it that first claimed the ability to be able to enter this emptiness? And can we discover more truth from understanding their ways? In the next chapter we will travel back in time to uncover who these people were.

Chapter 2
The Shaman: Our Guide?

In the last chapter, we discovered that the Gateway was a method of entering what we shall call the vacuum—a portal to the Otherworld. We discovered that this involved understanding the nature of empty spaces.

But what kind of person is capable of firstly discovering this vacuum, and secondly mastering it? Whoever it is, he or she must be dedicated, have a spiritual grounding, and have been through an extremely long training period. This last requirement, I found, was essential to a "soft landing" on the pathway to the Gateway.

It's simple really, in that by using drugs only, the expectant traveler would simply come down with a bump. The trained traveler had been through the process gradually, and with practice, knew how to land.

There is much dispute concerning the minor technicalities of the term *Shaman*, and the methods used to reach the Otherworld. These disputes come from the fact that there are many ways of the Shaman and many ethnic variances. There is no difference between them and, let us say, the Christian Church, which has Protestants, Catholics, and all manner of orthodox and evangelic in-betweens. They

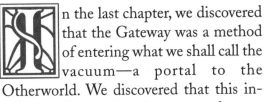

are, however, all still Christian, and all emerged from the same basic belief systems. The same can be said of the Shamanic world. They are called "primitives" due to fact that they are original sources of religion, magic, and medicine.

worldwide existence: Either they were part of an ancient and universal system of knowledge and religion, or the very beliefs and methods are archetypal and held within each and every one of us. Other explanations that have often been put forward are that ancient humans had a special kind of ESP such that they could understand the thoughts of others across the globe, or the more incredible alien technology explanation. We shan't be going down that last path, but we will find that there is truth within the ESP route. People seem to have to choose one or the other of these explanations. However, it could easily be that several of them are correct at the same time.

If the effect of entering the Gateway to the Otherworld is archetypal, as the evidence shows, then we could easily imagine that the phenomena could have erupted universally, worldwide, without outside influence. Added to this the emerging scientific fact that ESP could now be proven, then the archetype could simply be coming from the collective mind of these "entangled" (via quantum entanglement, as we will discuss later) and superconscious individuals.

Stone altars in Mnadjra, Malta, used during ceremonies to contact the Otherworld. Jacob laid his head upon a stone pillow and was taken to the seventh level of heaven.

Shamans are a worldwide phenomena, appearing in Asia, the Pacific, North and South America, Siberia, Russia, Scandinavia, and Europe. There can be only two or three explanations for this

However, with the fact that much of the ritual is similar, as we will show, then we have a peculiar occurrence. Different cultures, if already established, would surely

have produced rituals that also differed, and in some cases they do, but only ethnically—the basic ritual structures are the same. The fact remains that from the earliest possible times, in any culture discovered, the Shamans are always there, in remarkable similarity. Added to this the clothing, instruments, symbols, and especially etymological similarities the world over, it becomes ever more peculiar, and seems to have been a process that emerged from the very beginning of humankind's spread across the globe. These Shamans seem to be a spreading religious impulse, nomadically moving from one continent to another within the tribes of the prehistoric world. These people, men and women (and especially women, early on), as humans enlightened to the internal sun and acutely aware of the movements of the exoteric sun, were the original "Shining Ones" of humankind, which is why we find the etymology of the Shining Ones in every culture of the world: The Atlanteans, the Lemurians, angels, and fairies were all Shining Ones, today but a folk memory of some lost time and lost knowledge. Was this enlightenment the spark in the cycle of human consciousness? Did the consciousness of humanity come from within our attempts to enter trance? And thus it spawned the global trek and establishment of seemingly similar religions around the globe?

Although technically the term *Shaman* is only from central and arctic Asia, the actual practices and images are found universally. The Eskimo Shaman is known as the Angakok, which is phonetically similar to the Annakim and Anannage—names given to the Shining Ones of Sumer, where the *An* comes from the chief "shining" deity Anu.

The aim of the Shaman was to free his thoughts from his physical body. In the same way that Buddhists and Hindus try to achieve this, the Shaman attempts to "remove the obstacles" or crush the chaotic serpent. To become an Angakok he must call down the positive power of god from within the Otherworld—the solar divinity, the sun within and without. Just as the spirit touched the Christian apostles and flames licked above their heads, so too this powerful spirit comes upon the Shaman and is called *gaumanek*, which means "illuminated" or "shining." The Shaman literally becomes the Shining One on earth.

The universal nature of these beliefs is also seen in the very basic concepts—dealing with the spirits on behalf of the mortals. A comparison with the priests of Egypt will highlight how this process developed and became mainstream and orthodox.

The Egyptian priest of the dead was the one who would contact the Otherworld through magical incantations and would make the way or path easier for the soul of the deceased—thus removing the Shamanic obstacles. This is exactly one of the processes of the Shaman. The priestesses of Isis or Hathor conducted the souls of the deceased to the Duat, one of the Otherworlds of Egyptian myth, as psychopomps (one who escorts the living or newly dead into the afterlife), just like the Shaman. In Shaman ritual the soul/spirit or Egyptian Ka/Ba would be left in the Otherworld to the devices of the spirits, who would then conduct them further.

However, in Egyptian myth, the priestess continues to officiate and leads the deceased through the house of the Tuat/Duat. These rituals last for approximately 70 to 72 days, which is a number associated with the transition of the zodiac—hence the Duat is mirrored again in the heavens above; the great cycle in the sky. There are still similarities here though, as this process is the same as the preparation that the deceased undergoes before being taken by the Shaman, which itself is copied by the Egyptian priests. The Egyptian priest would also wear the Leopard's Skin, as would the Shaman, who would take on the skin of a wild animal in order to gain the power of the animal spirit. In essence, the Egyptian priesthood was nothing more than an evolved Shamanic brother/sisterhood. The complexities added into the initial Shaman rituals are just those, complex additions. The basic underlying principles of the Gateway to the gods are the same.

In the ancient Sumerian religion, the Queen of Heaven, similar to Mary the mother of Jesus and Isis the mother of Horus, went through a descent and ascent ritual that is remarkably similar to the Dance of the Seven Veils that Salome undergoes in the Old Testament. In the Trial of the Shaman, or Gilgamesh in the Sumerian literature (the oldest on the planet), we have exactly the same process. The Shaman prepares by putting on various articles of clothing, such as a headband, a beaded collar, and copper and silver armbands, which mimic the Irish Luada of the Silver Arm, another Otherworldly deity. Inanna then, the Queen of Heaven 7,000 years ago, did exactly the same, and then at each Gate into the Underworld

was forced to remove one item of clothing, until at the seventh Gate she was completely naked—like Salome and like the Shaman, having removed the obstacles to illumination. The element of the number 7 in the realm of the Gateway mythology is of extreme importance, and we shall return to it again. For now, we do know that it is exactly the same as, and therefore related to, the seven levels of heaven in the biblical and Islamic context. All of these are ultimately related, as can be shown and will be shown with the connections between Isis, Kali, Salome, Inanna, and others. We will also note that these queens are always connected with the serpent (electromagnetic energy), which rises up the axis mundi or World Tree that was so enlightening to the first woman, Eve, which itself means "female serpent." Note here also that Eve is the one who gives the fruit of knowledge to Adam, the man—was she the psychopomp Shaman who brought back the knowledge for the man?

At the center of the Sumerian process Inanna is judged by the Annuna, the judges of the Underworld, and punished or beaten and then crucified. This is not just the same as the later Christian crucifixion, but also the same as the ancient Shamanic process wherein the Shaman enters a tomb or womb. This tomb may be a man-made mound or cave in which the Shaman is fastened to a pole or joist in mock crucifixion, mimicking the solar deity that dies three days each year, and connecting themselves to the point that itself connects to the "light."[1] This is the Shaman enacting the outer and inner sun in symbolic fashion and achieving a heightened state through pain, isolation, starvation, and

dehydration—bringing on a trance state. This sensory depravation brings on forms of madness and mystical experience so often associated with the Otherworld. Eventually, the Shaman returns as a savior of the community, having confronted all their contemporaries' darkest fears.

from the tomb/womb of the Mother Goddess following his death on the axis. This mixture of myrrh and aloes is well known as a purgative, and would have supposedly purged Jesus of the poison of Gall (snake venom) and vinegar (wine) he had been fed while on the cross. Jesus was the

The author at the pope's "gateway" to heaven, St. Peter's, Rome.

In the same way, Inanna returns after three days and three nights. She was in fact "rescued" by two flies, commanded by Enki, the Lord of Flies. The flies brought with them the Food of Life and Water of Life, which resuscitated Inanna. In the same fashion, in John 19:39, Joseph of Arimathea "was joined by Nicodemus, who brought with him a mixture of myrrh and aloes, more than half a hundredweight" to rescue Jesus

symbolic sun god and archetypal Shaman, voyaging into the Otherworld on our behalf to deal with the spirits in exactly the same fashion that the Shaman still does today.

These similarities can be shown to be universal, and it is these methods, found from the Americas to the Middle East, that show that the Shaman process was much more than archetypal phenomena. However, there is so much more of interest, including symbols that have stood the test of thousands of years and are at the very center of modern secret societies.

The Five-Pointed Star

One of the world's most mysterious symbols, utilized more recently by Christian propagandists against the Pagan and Wiccan world, and yet probably one of the most holy of symbols ever to have been created, is the pentacle. The very term itself is revealing, in that *pen* can mean either "five" or "head/first"—indicating a connection with the process seen and understood to be enacted within one's own head.

The pentacle as a five-pointed star was used in ancient times extensively as a talisman actually *against* Witches, in a stark reversal of our modern perceived usage. It was often worn in the folds of a turban or headdress to protect the "subconscious mind" from demons and conjurations.

> And on her head, lest spirits should invade,
> A pentacle, for more assurance, laid.
> —Ludovico Ariosto, *Orlando Furioso*

Its usefulness is thought to have emerged from the fact that it is made up of three triangles; a trinity within a trinity—the most holy of numerical concepts. There is also the idea that it symbolizes the figure of a man with outstretched arms, like the crucified Shaman, and the fact that it is a symbol of eternity in that it can be drawn in one endless line, let alone that this also contains the mystical number 9 (three triangles).

In later Christianity it came to symbolize the five wounds of Christ and was the emblem that Sir Gawain of the Arthurian romances had painted on his shield for protection. It was much later that Christianity utilized the symbol in an inverted position as a sign of the devilish arts.[2]

Getting back to its origins, the sign was extensively used in Sumeria. From this moment on its associations are profound. It is known as *ub*, which is related to *ob* (which became one of the Kabbalistic dualities in conjunction with *od*), and means, not surprisingly, "serpent." It also means "corner," "angle," "nook," a "small room," "cavity," or "hole," from whence serpents were said to emerge. This will become apparent and more important when we move on to discover the importance of caves and "holes." This is also the cavity of the mind, or the womb of the World Mother, from whence we are reborn into and out of the Otherworld, as emergent serpents like Moses (whose name means "emergent serpent"). Indeed, in Pythagorean thought the pentamychos was very similar, and means "five caves." These were the ab(ob)-addon—the caves where the initiate went through the rituals, and which later became the lower region of the Hebraic hell or the Greek Tartaros—the ab(ob)yss or place of destruction, which simply meant being killed before being born again, and was in actual fact a positive process. We have to go to hell before we can experience true heaven—we have to overcome the "obstacles."

The Shaman: Our Guide?

In Turkish, the word *uber*, which is related, means "sorcerer," as *ubaur* does in Bulgarian, coming probably from the Tartar *uba*, which is a name for a Shamanic idol. *Obeah* is "voodoo" and also "sorcerer," and in the Hebrew Kaballa *ob-Aur* is "crown" (of the head), which closed after the creation of the cosmos—implying that at creation the skull or cave of the mind was open. In Slavic Russian, *upir* is the word for "vampire," which is a term for one who is neither alive nor dead—they are instead in the "in-between" state or Gateway. This is the superconscious Gateway and is a term for a Shaman.

Ob, *ub*, and *up* probably (nobody knows for sure) come from *oph*, meaning "serpent" and related to the basilisk, the serpent of the sun and ancient deity of Africa. Many Africans ended up in America, especially the Ashanti, whose name for their religion ended up as Obeah or Voodoo. These Ashanti Shamans are no different from other Shamans, and claim the ability to fly and leave their own bodies. There are definite uses of drugs here also: "The Obeah poured a warm tea-like broth into two small bowl-shaped cups without handles. He took one and gave me the other, gulping down the liquid while motioning me to do the same. He asked me what I liked about Jamaica. I told him things like the weather and the people. Then he asked again what I liked about Jamaica. But now I wasn't able to answer. It was like my mind had grown so huge that trying to focus on something as minuscule as a few words to string together into a sentence had become an impossible hardship."[3]

So the word, as shown in its history (or etymology), is universal, and with the travel of Africans as slaves to the United States of America, we can see how these beliefs can easily spread, now, as in the distant past. But there are older examples too, which are very telling in their use.

In Greek mythology one had to cross the River Styx to enter the Underworld. The Styx was therefore the dark or void-like watery Gateway. In order to cross this Gateway one would have to pay the ferryman, Charon, one Obolos, which was one sixth of a drachma.

Obolos or *obolus* came from *obol*, which is related to the the terms *ob* and *up*, as in sorcerer and Shaman. In this respect the hidden language is telling us that we must pay or take one Shaman in order to enter the Gateway. Actual obols exist in many museums, and show, remarkably, another link to the pentacle other than that of etymology. On each that I have seen there is on one side Apollo—the archetypal sun god and Shaman, and on the other the Shaman's steed accompanied by a pentacle.

The coin carried on in European usage right up into the medieval period. There is even a strange story of Belisarius (AD 565), a great general of Justinian who was supposedly accused of conspiring against the emperor and had his eyes put out. He was said to have then begged in the street for obolus. There is no historical foundation for this story; however, it may relate to the suffering one has to endure to enter the Gateway—a votive offering of eyes for the sin he has committed in payment for the obolus—or the closing of the external

33

The author in Roman tombs or portals to the Otherworld on Cyprus.

eyes in order to open the inner ones. Either way it is the overcoming of the Shaman obstacle. It is this very concept that gave rise to coins being placed over the eyes of a laid-out corpse, in an offering to the ferryman.

It is interesting to note that Shaman idols were called *uba*, which also related to worms or serpents—an indication that the "irrational" idols (in Italian *uba* means "irrational fear") of the Shaman were seen as serpentine, an idea that archaeology often backs up. Many of these Uba, especially those of the Asian Turko-Tarter origin, actually made their idols stick out of the ground—half in and half out (like the worm), and it was this that gave them the

title *Juan-Juan*, which means "wriggling worms." These uba, worms, or serpents, were therefore in the in-between state, which of course is known as the Gateway.

Other etymology helps us with tracking down the Shamans of Europe. The sorcerer concept used in association with the Shaman also gives rise to the Sanskrit term *vidya*, which means "wisdom," "knowledge," or "science." The vidya were possessors of knowledge, and are often called *nabhaschara*, which means "to fly," or "to move in the air," like the Shaman. They were often considered tricksters, as were the early Shamans and later Witches. In fact, this is the link, as *vidya* is the root of *Wicca* or *Witch*.

So the root of our European Witches lies in the vidya, who were Shamans from Asia—a direct link, even without the other and more obvious associations of flying, healing, and contacts with the spirits or familiars. The link can be confirmed by the world's most famous of Witches from the Bible: the Witch of Endor. She was a necromancer, sorceress, and potion maker. Moses said that her like were born obic, or with forbidden knowledge, and her name was Bahalath-Ob—Bahalath the Shaman or serpent.

There is also another connection we must raise at this point: The Witches of Europe were said to practice the "black arts"—the magician's cloth being black. This black art was also the role of the medieval alchemist. But why the idea of black? It could be that they were said to practice at night under the dark sky. It could be that their art was seen as mysterious, and therefore we were in the dark. However, there is a deeper reason, one more pertinent to the role of the ancient archetypal Shaman: The Otherworld that these special people were accessing and mastering was the void—it was blackness, and therefore to master it, one was the master of the black art.

There are further etymological links between the various cultures: In Ireland the queen of the Otherworld was Babd, whose name means "crow" (as in flight of the black bird) or "demon." In Welsh, Bod was a kite—also flight. In Turko-Tartar, Boga was a Shaman; in Mongolian, Bogdo was holy; in Celtic, a Bog woman was a sorceress or Witch; and all relate to the modern bogeyman slang with which we still frighten our children (well, I do).

We also find that the Finnish word *noita* means "witch," and originally referred to the people who practiced the technique known as *lovi*, which means "trance" or "state of ecstasy." It also means "hole," and is the term used for the void between heaven and earth, an obvious allusion to the "in-between" state or Gateway. This then links the Shaman to the Witch, and is the reason that the pentacle also has a similar meaning as a cavity or hole itself—it is therefore the key to the Gateway. There can now be no wonder that these pentacles were created upon the ground over vast expanses by people such as the infamous Knights Templar.[4]

Serpent Shamans, Sevens, and Trees

The Magyar people have a name for the highest initiation available to the Shaman: *tethatu*, which translates as "one who talks with dragons." Dragons or serpents (the terms are interchangeable) are, they say, the strongest helpers on the spiritual path, and I believe relate to the energies or electromagnetic resonance I shall be discussing in later chapters. These are serpent spirits, seen by most Shamans in their Otherworld experiences. In connection with tree spirits we can see, especially in the originally Sumerian Eden story of Eve and the serpent, that the Tree of Knowledge only released its wisdom with the aid of the Shamanic serpent energy (or energy/information as we shall see). This serpent is also seen in the tale of the Midgard Serpent of Norse mythology, in which the World Shaman, Odin, is sacrificed on a tree that represents the fixing of the energy—wherein "fixing" means to determine a point on the planet (or indeed body) of special or sacred nature or energy. The snake is the medium for the information exchange—like an information/energy wave.

We have already seen how the number 7 was important to the ancient Shamans (a term we are using for the universal aspect of the primitive cultural religion). In fact, it is a characteristic feature of the entrance or Gateway to the celestial Otherworld, as we saw with Salome, Inanna, and Isis—the great queens of heaven—the female psychopomp Shamans. This number is also closely associated in the same way with the ascent to heaven or Otherworld on a tree, ladder, stairway, or mountain. In Eurasian Shamanic lore the Gateway is accessed by ascending the cosmic pillar or axis—a structure represented the world over by pyramids, mountains, trees, and megaliths.

According to Mircea Eliade in *Shamanism: Archaic Techniques of Ecstasy*: "The Altaians conceive the entrance to the underworld as a 'smoke hole' of the earth, located, of course, at the 'Centre' (situated, according to the myths of Central Asia, in the North, which corresponds to the Centre of the Sky; for as we know, the 'North' is assimilated to the 'Centre' through the whole Asian area, from India to Siberia). By a sort of symmetry, the underworld has been imagined to have the same number of levels as the sky." Eliade goes on to point out that "the Altaic Shaman successively passes through the seven underworld 'obstacles.'"

Of course, this central location is wherever one fixes one's location via the angle of the sun on Earth. In this way it does not matter where you are on Earth; it is always the center that we are aiming for. The fact that the ancients pointed upward to the sky and transliterated their internal dialogue into the macrocosm of the cosmic world is fascinating, but it avoids the inward journey that the Shaman was most interested in. This inward journey, they knew, related entirely to the constants we are seeing in regard to relationships between all things in the universe.

The upwardly thrusting axis mundi, the center, was also called *soma* in the *Rig-Veda*: "He who is the pillar of the sky, the well-adorned support, the full stalk that encircles all around, he is the one who by tradition sacrifices to these two great world-halves." Soma was also a god, associated mostly with the moon, but also the sun, showing the polarity of beliefs again—the red and the white. There has been much debate as to the true nature of soma: whether it is a mushroom, which is possible, or a plant extract, or even a mixture of venom and blood. However, there is no problem with any of these ideas, as we have constantly found ancient beliefs to be multilayered. The idea that there were seven spots on the amanita muscaria (or fly agaric) mushroom, and the hallucinogenic properties it holds, are obvious reasons for seeing it as a method of entering the Gateway into other dimensions, so long as practiced by a trained Shaman. It brought on a trance state and hence access to other parts of the mind.

These drug-induced effects cause supposed time warps in the mind, much akin to the natural meditative effects caused over long periods of meditation, starvation, and pain or ecstasy—these are the physical Shamanic obstacles we see again and again alluded to in myths and traditions.

Those entering the Otherworld believe that their stay there is short, when those in the material realm say that the participant has been gone a long time. Such examples can easily be found in legendary literature—even such European stories as the Arthurian romances and the Voyage of Bran. This is in effect the same mental process that alien abductees go through, though often in reverse. Therefore the phenomenon is an internal, mental process, and not the result of aliens from Mars. It is, in a way, a voyage through the Gateway of the mind, which is why so many alien stories are archetypal.

Often, these experiences are psychotropic, with soft glowing lights and beautiful unearthly music. The luminosity is often overwhelming and remembered strongly—giving rise to the "shining" title. These experiences, of the Shaman, Witch, drug-taker, or alien abductee, are all rooted in the same mental process. The true differences are in the fact that only the Shaman and Witch are prepared, similar to the Egyptian priest who prepares the deceased. This enables the ascent or descent into the Otherworld to be controlled and manipulated, rather than a confused and abstract experience, as that of the drug-taker or alien abductee. This does not mean that the Shaman does not take drugs to enter the trance; he certainly does: drugs such as

The Eye of God at the center of this Masonic set quare and compass, in Salisbury.

amanita muscaria, for instance. But it does mean that he controls the usage and is almost conscious of what he is doing.

The creative force of the number 7 is seen strongest on the seven-headed serpent of many myths. Baal, the ancient sun god, destroys the seven-headed Lotan in a Canaanite myth, and this serpent is probably one of the originators of the biblical Leviathan, which encircles the Earth and is no different from the ouroboros. The mystical number 7 is symbolic of the greater universe—the celestial seven. This is the divine spark that continues the cyclical process—as the Leviathan encircles the Earth like an ouroboros.

The Shamanic method is a controlled process, developed in thousands of years and held secret or sacred by millions of Shamans. It is the complex result of an internal process, visualized and imaged as only humans know how. As ever, this sevenfold process, seen all around the world, in relation to a universal world axis, is further evidence that the ancient, serpent-related Shamanic process was more than a mere archetypal emergence. It was the result of a worldwide, primitive, and prehistoric nomadic religion.

So far, we have learned that the female Shaman enters the Otherworld realm and acts as a dominant force, whereas the male Shaman can enter, but does the bidding of the spirits—and often the bidding of the female. This is seen throughout history and religion, and is well known to the Shamanic world.

Virgin Divine, nothing remains in this life, that can tire me or frighten me. Nothing will be new to me, or that I have not foreseen. I am prepared for every kind of suffering. All I ask of you, since it is here, it is said, that the Entrance to the Underworld and the Lake of Acheron begins, let me come to see my beloved Father. Here is the Gate if you will show me the Road and be my Guide.

—Virgil, *Aeneid*

This ancient, primitive religion we are terming "Shamanic" shall therefore be our guide, as he or she was the guide in times gone by. The wisdom, traditions, and folklore of the Shaman will guide us through the various elements of the world of myth, history, and science, and shall be as the most original of all beliefs, the ultimate guardian of the Gateway to the Otherworld.

Chapter 3
Serpent Realm

In my constant search for the truth, the most important thing I discovered was the existence of a huge, worldwide serpent cult or belief system. This ancient and profound worship of the serpent existed in just about every country and every period of man's history. In *Secrets of the Serpent* I found that this belief system spawned all the major religions on the globe, and that the basic rituals and beliefs of this organism could still be revealed within each of them.

An indication of this most ancient of beliefs is still to be found in modern Egypt as snake charmers and magicians still maintain a method of hypnotizing a viper by compressing its head and making it appear like a rod. Quite a remarkable feat, and one still practiced today by snake charmers elsewhere.

This brings to mind the resurrection rituals of the serpent being pinned to a tree. This image was not from my own imagination; it was a registered fact, seen earliest in Africa, but carried on in the resurrection deities of the rest of the world. Odin, the great Norse god was pinned to a tree, with the Midgard serpent gnawing at the roots. Christ was seen as a serpent on a tree or pole by the Gnostics. Moses held aloft the Brazen Serpent on the Tau cross. The serpent on the Tree of Knowledge in the Garden of Eden supposedly tempted Eve. These, and many more images of the serpent and the tree, are linked across thousands of years and hundreds of nations.

The image of the magician-prophet-Shaman holding forth the rod of the snake brings to mind a magical scene on a Graeco-Egyptian papyrus from 200 BC (currently on display at the Royal Museum of Natural History in Leyden, Holland) in which the figure is holding two magical rods to either side. It must also bring to mind the various hillside figures found in Great Britain (the "Long Man of Wilmington," for instance), which are remarkably in the same stance—the same stance, incidentally, as that taken by the now-famous Minoan Snake Goddess figure, and the ancient images of Hathor from Egypt still to be seen in the Louvre in Paris. This image, I found, was prevalent in many other cultures, with thousands of images of the same device being utilized.

The remarkable Minoan Snake Goddess is only 34.2 centimeters in height and holds out to either side two writhing snakes, as if about to cast the great magic power with which they endow her. She is thought to be a "mother goddess" or "World Mother," associated with serpents. She is, more to the point, the feminine Shaman who controls the energy of the spirits, seen here as serpents. She is controlling from the center, between the two earth energies, fixing the location on the earth that she has found

conducive to accessing the Otherworld. Another snake appears coming from the head of the goddess, bringing to mind the Uraeus serpents of the Egyptian deities, and showing her ultimate aspect as a true illuminated one. This is the serpent seen within the mind during trance states—during access to the Otherworld.

It is clear that the Minoans borrowed much of their culture from their Egyptian trading partners, as numerous Egyptian artifacts have been discovered on Crete. Sir Arthur Evans, an archaeologist, linked this Minoan goddess with Wadjyt, the cobra goddess of lower Egypt, and the snake found in Aphroditopolis (City of Aphrodite), where the insignia of the city is the feather (balance) and the serpent (energy). This goddess can also be easily linked to Asherah, the serpentine "mother goddess" found hidden beneath Judaic texts and in the Temple as the Asherah Poles (the axis mundi, pinpointing the earth energy).

It seems, therefore, with the linkages we know about, that the wielding of the serpents—straightened as rods or writhing—were images of the wands of magic. They gave the power to perform great magical tricks, such as bringing people back from the dead. And as I have pointed out previously in other works, religion comes from magic. The added image of the feather, from Aphroditopolis, was simply the measurement or weighing device for the souls of the dead—or even the living—who wished to enter the Otherworld. This too is an image seen in hundreds of other cultures across the planet, always in association with the serpent, and always associated with balance.

In the Fitzwilliam Museum in Cambridge, there is a remarkable wand in the shape of a twisting bronze serpent, straight in the middle for holding. It is an authentic piece of Egyptian magic, similar to several I have seen in the Louvre in Paris. The link between the entwined snakes and the tree with the wand are the real origins of the magician's wand. The magical mini-staff of the serpent power is the guardian of the secret and the wielder of the power—in other words, one who knows the location of and how to access the Otherworld.

This idea of the tree or staff of the serpent issuing power is seen starkly in the imagery of the Rod of Aaron, which, when thrown down, became a snake. This is an ancient and widespread symbol of the power of the snake, symbolizing earth energy. This caduceus or Aesculapian staff later goes on to save the Israelites by parting waters (waves), bringing plagues upon Egypt, and drawing water (waves) from rock. It was even believed to be so sacred that it was one of the objects hidden within the Ark of the Covenant. The Ark, of course, opened up a Gateway wherever it was.

Often, the tree or axis pole with the serpent is seen with the orb of the solar divinity—the sun. This, however, is more than just the sun we see every day in the heavens. It is also the inner sun of the enlightenment experience. This sun-like feature is almost always shown at the top of a caduceus. The winged globe or eye is a prominent feature there, because it also symbolizes the skull.

In a normal caduceus, the snakes or serpents, known in the East as the *ida* (female or negative pole) and *pingala* (male or positive pole), spiral around the one staff in both directions. This is a subtle indication that the doorway to other levels of consciousness is located at the center, and between the two polarities, symbolized by the two snakes or serpents—and often by two pillars. In other words, this "doorway" or "Gateway" to other dimensions or realities is found between these opposites, and neither side is good on its own. Instead we must walk in balance *between* the opposites, *between* the pillars (it is, after all, obvious that one cannot enter by walking *into* a pillar). In essence, both the snakes and the tree are required; we must pin the location where the earth energies cross in balance and neutrality.

This symbolic doorway reveals the beliefs of the Shaman—that a technique exists by which we can all journey to "other realities" that exist within us. It also shows us that the ancient Egyptians, and others, knew of this technique, and that the initiates who understood this Shamanic knowledge and technique were able to access this "space."

And now we can understand some of the deeper meanings behind the enigmatic images and symbols left for us by our ancestors, such as the Long Man of Wilmington, carved into an English hillside c. AD 1545. This late date makes no difference, as someone, or some group of people, may have known that this hill was possibly the location of a special energy. At Wilmington the man holds a staff in each hand, representing the opposites. He stands serenely between these opposites, in balance and on the location of access. This shows us the ancient belief that man

holds within himself the Gateway between dimensions and realities.

So we can now see that the Minoan Snake Goddess, and other depictions of the World Mother, who are shown holding a serpent or snake in each hand, convey a more direct allusion to the concept of the caduceus. The esoteric meaning behind these figurines is evident: It shows that the Gateway is the point between the opposites. But there is nothing new in this; it has been spoken of by Sufis and other groups for centuries. All we are trying to do here is understand with modern eyes and minds.

Our ancestors used the sun as an incredible link between ourselves and the universe, because they knew perfectly well that all life and all energy on our planet comes from the external sun, and that the energy we hold within ourselves via this amazing enlightenment process also derives from the real sun, as well as the energy of the earth. No wonder that the rays of the sun were often seen as writhing serpents, and that the etymology of snakes, serpents, and even dragons is linked with the sun.

No matter how far back in history or prehistory we go, we seem to always find this link between the sun and the serpent. We must now realize that this link is also an internal dialog between the perceived balancing serpents and the internal shining sun of the so-called ultimate enlightenment process. The superconductor of this psychical effect cannot be overemphasized—it is something that we will discover to be perfectly scientific and human. As we shall discover, these

Otherworlds that the Gateway of the serpent allows us to enter are always dual in nature. On the one hand they are dark and eerie, and on the other they are bright and shining. These are the dual natures of the inner man coming out and being represented in images produced by the various mystics of times gone by.

Ancient Serpents and Mother Goddesses

In ancient Mesopotamia the early Sumerians described themselves as constantly nourished by the milk of Ninkhursag—the great mother goddess. She was also known as Ninlil, the consort of Enlil—who were later to become Adam and Eve, and were known as Shining Ones and serpents. It is strongly believed by many scholars that Ninlil is probably the source of most mother goddesses. She was also known as Ki or Ninti/Nintu, and was a double-headed or double-eyed serpent goddess of the earth. She has been linked with Ashtoreth (Asherah), the Phoenician goddess of love, whose symbol was also the double-headed serpent. She merged with her daughter Anath to become the wife of Jehovah as Matronit or Shekinah. This was a goddess of health and fertility, and was worshipped by Sarah (Sarasvati), Abraham's (Brahma's) wife. The Syrians knew her as Atar Gatis, the Mermaid, because she was seen here as half in the water (or Otherworld) and half out. In Egypt, Ninkhursag was called Isis, the ultimate mother of the messianic line, and in Greece she was Demeter, the goddess of

the Otherworld. According to some, Ninkhursag gave the most potent of all life forces, which was venerated as "star fire."

The fact that Isis is Ninkhursag, the double-headed serpent goddess, explains why there are many images of her feeding the pharaohs, sons of gods, her sacred milk.

None of these goddesses were real people. They were anthropomorphic images of the World Mother, the great guardian and overseer of the Otherworld. She allowed access to the realms via her intrinsic power—the power of the earth. Always associated with serpents and the Otherworld, she was the original concept of the Shamaness—the feminine Shaman who could control the Otherworld spirits.

As the snake she was Tiamat or the Leviathan, which became so many other serpent gods and goddesses through time. Ninkhursag's womb was the very place of the Otherworld, a place that shone like the cosmos—similar to Mary, the mother of Jesus, as the "light bearer." In Babylon, as we shall see later, the gateways of the sanctuary were seen as the entrance to this womb of the Mother Goddess—the Otherworld, often depicted as two pillars. These pillars symbolized duality and balance, and to enter between them, one was enacting the sacred balance required to enter the Otherworld. More often than not, these pillars were wrapped around by spiraling serpents and capped by the lotus flower—a symbol of the enlightenment within the mind, and from whence the Hindu Agni, the Shining One, was born. Of course, this also makes sense of the twin pillars of the modern Freemasons. The pillars are therefore not important; it is the space between, the hidden location on earth, that is.

In Hindu literature the great Shining One himself, Agni, is said to shine from within the mother's eternal womb, and so we have a perfect allusion to the place from whence the shining arises—the Otherworld. This is not some place to be discovered after death, as became the paramount belief in later years. It was instead a place that could be accessed now, in this world, as the fabled Jesus told us.

The Sumerian Shining One An, or Anu, whose glyph was a pillar (he being one half of the duality), was the great god of the sacred city on high, where the exalted gods dine, filled with radiance and awe. He was the inner sun and an original solar divinity. His city was wherever the sun rose. An emerged, as did Agni, from the womb or Otherworld of the serpent Tiamat, and is the progenitor of the Hindu myths—he is therefore the symbol of the location on earth where access to the Otherworld may be gained. His symbol was that of the inner four-way sun—the cross—and was the origin of the cross of the Christian anointed one: Christ. The cross is a perfect device for fixing a location. This four-way symbol was known as *saru*, a wind that radiated from An/Anu, the Shining One or sun. Wind was the breath of life, the word and logos of later Christianity, and was the Holy Spirit, which brought wisdom, knowledge, and strength, and was feminine in aspect. (It is another way of expressing the quantum wave-particle that opens up for us the science of the Gateway, as we shall see later.)

This solar city of An, the womb of Tiamat and the Otherworld of the Shaman, was where the waters emerged, showing the link that we shall find with water and serpents in later years. The Vase of An was the Mother Goddess's womb, called the "place of the flowing forth of the waters which open the womb." Note that here the waters are opening the Gateway to the Otherworld, something that in later myths elsewhere in the world shall become of great importance.

Many other elements of the Gateway journey are also to be found in this Sumerian Shining One. For instance, An/Anu was shown to be standing upon "the illustrious mound," a symbol of the World Mother and womb or Gateway to the Otherworld. In later years, mounds across the world would be associated with the serpent and the Otherworld. An/Anu was also the Horned One, a progenitor of the horned gods of Europe and elsewhere, especially Osiris, who himself is nothing more than the archetypal male Shaman. In the Satapatha Brahmana, a "Hindu" (as all Pagan religions were dubbed by the Christians who discovered them) religious text dating from roughly 300 BC, we find that the word for "horn" actually means the "womb of the primeval genesis." This is the symbol of the creative process: You need to shine to enter and remain inside. No wonder, therefore, that horns, especially those of the solar bull, were used as altars and encapsulated the solar orb. Indeed, we are also told that the earth itself shall be the altar—a subtle indication of the portals that were created all over the world.

The same text also tells us that "The black deer's horn is the same as that womb. The priest touches it with his forehead close over the right eyebrow," saying, "thou art Indra's womb." This issue of the black deer is very telling so early on, as the emptiness was symbolized as blackness, as we shall discover in the Black Madonnas of medieval Europe.

We find in the mythology of the same continent, India, that tantric skull cups encapsulate the power of the inner Gateway, with their horns emerging from energized skulls. These skulls would merge with other beliefs and myths to become the Holy Grail. All represented the womb or Otherworld of the Mother Goddess. But Chretien de Troyes, the masterful writer of the Arthurian tale *Parzival* said also that the Grail as a chalice *represented the goddess's womb*. Note that he says *as a chalice*. This is because the enlightenment aspect of the Grail was imaged as a chalice or cup, which is linked throughout etymology and myth to the skull. And again, not surprisingly, this skull cup was always linked back to the serpent: The skull is our cave, our way to the Otherworld.

In later years Christianity would encapsulate these ideas in the baptismal font, which represented the watery womb of the Mother Goddess, where we are submerged in death to be reborn anew. Mary, as the great Mother Goddess of Christianity, was said to be "igne sacro inflammata"; that is, fecundated by the sacred fire of the male—bringing the divine union we need of water (female/negative) and fire (male/positive) to balance the earth energies and enter the Gateway. No wonder then that

around the fonts of Europe there are strange images of serpents, dragons, and even bulls and horns. Taken to the extreme, we see the female, lunar aspect of the horns, surrounded by the male serpent in many images of the mother Mary—especially those of Our Lady of Guadeloupe, in which the upturned crescent (horned) moon is beneath her, entwined with serpents. In all the images of this device I could find I noted the way radiant lights were emerging from behind Mary, who stands within the oval shape of the Vesica Piscis, an almond shape created by the intersection of two circles. *Vesica Piscis* means "bladder of a fish," and has been a holy or sacred symbol for thousands of years.

The union of the serpent and the bull is seen most starkly in the Greek mythology of Ceres and Proserpine, in which a great secret is communicated to the initiates: "Taurus Draconem genuit, et Taurum Draco," meaning, "The bull has begotten a serpent and the serpent a bull." This may explain the sometimes confused element of the male and female aspects of the bull and serpent. In the thousands of years that these two images have been associated with each other, there has often been confusion between the sexes of each symbolic device. Sometimes the bull is the solar creative principal, and sometimes the horns of the bull are seen as the crescent, upturned moon, and therefore feminine. Originally, the serpent was more often than not the mother of creation, later still to be stolen by patriarchal domination of the religions. The answer to these riddles is not just in the battle between the sexes in the control of religion. It is to be found in the union of the opposite principles required

to enter the Gateway to the Otherworld—our control of our own psychological opposites, the opposite energies within the body, and the understanding of the twin earth energies at specific locations. This is the reason that, early on, gods are goddesses—or both. The concept of becoming androgynous is the whole point. Unite the powers within the mind; do not let them battle. The serpent and the bull are, and rightly should be, seen together.

In Egypt, Sumeria, and elsewhere, the horns of the bull were of immense importance. As the bull was universally a symbol of the sun, so too An/Anu was the bull killed or mastered by the serpentine Gilgamesh, the originator of so many Judaic and Christian myths, and the one who can control, pin, and balance the earth energies to access the realm of the deities.

In a Sumerian hymn, the Hymn to Adar (adder/snake), there is a remarkable reference to the a bull in association with some kind of early Grail vessel:

(Men) altogether have proclaimed his name (Adar [adder/snake]) for sovereignty over them.

In their midst, like a great mild bull, has he lifted up his horns.

The Shu Stone, the precious stone,

the strong stone, the snake-stone and the mountain stone,

the warrior—the fire stone too—their warrior carries away to the cities.[1]

All the elements required for the Otherworld access are hidden in this one excerpt. Men proclaim the name of the

Christ crucified at Golgotha, Kykoss Monastery, Cyprus.

great serpent—it being the inner process of balance and energy. This lifts up the horns of the bull—the energy process and enlightenment. This creates the strong stone or vessel, enabling access to the Otherworld—similar to the Stone of Destiny, which gave kings the right to rule via the power of the Otherworld—the original stone of the Holy Grail. The ruler (one who could rule/measure) would know the time of year and day (via the heavens), and could fix the energies of the earth in specific locations.

We also find clues in the name of the bull in the heavens—Taurus. This is yet another union of the shining principles

required—Tau and Ru(s). Tau is the cross or symbol of Tammuz and various other solar and messianic divinities. It is also the base of the Egyptian Ankh, which was used by the gods and pharaohs to give life-breath or wind—again the wind seen issuing from the cross of An/Anu, the Shining One. The Ru as the oval was placed above the Tau cross to form the Ankh, and was originally a serpent eating its own tail, a symbol of eternity, immortality, and the cyclical patterns of the heavens, as Crichton Miller points out. It is the symbol of the Gateway and became the oval Vesica Piscis of Christianity, through which Mary and Jesus are often seen emerging in rays of life.

We also find in Sumerian myth and language that the word for "heart" is no different from that of "womb" or "vulva." A prominent concept was *An Sa Ta*, or the "heart of An"—the center of being, the center of the place of An the Shining One. We also find indications of physical representations of the stone or rock from which it was believed access to the Otherworld could be gained. This can be no different from the rock from which Mithras (who struggled with the bull) was born, and is indicative of the cave—just as Jesus himself would emerge from a cave. This will become extremely important as a guide along the path to discovering real physical artifacts and locations that were seen as Gateways.

So, in reflection, we have the Otherworld as the womb of the Great Mother Goddess (earth), who was symbolized as a serpent. She is brought into union with the male creative aspect of the bull or other device (fixing the location). This gives us the fertile rains enabling enlightenment (trance) and access to the Gateway. These beliefs are still with us today in the Holy Grail, the Eucharist chalice, and the baptismal font.

Lazarus: The Christian Shaman

In the Christian Bible, Jesus raises a dead man after four days of lying dead in a tomb (cave). This man is named Lazarus, and there is much debate as to the origin of this fabled individual.

Firstly, we must try to alter our perceptions slightly. Many reading this book will either believe that the Bible holds some literal truth, or that it does not. There are truths in the Bible, for sure, but not many literal ones. Most of the characters spoken of were not real individuals. For instance, let's take the most famous man, Jesus. There is absolutely no literal truth of a real Jesus Christ in the Bible, or elsewhere for that matter. There is, however, truth, in that what he stood for symbolically was truth. On one level of understanding Jesus represented the sun. His mother/wife Mary was the moon, as is shown in the etymology of her name being linked to both the moon and the sea (mer). Mary is the Mother Goddess, as was Isis, and Jesus is the solar god, as were both Osiris and Horus. Horus, similar to Jesus, is both the Son of God and God. In fact, there are easily more than a hundred similarities between Horus and Jesus. Here are few of the most important:

- Horus was born to the Virgin, the Queen of Heaven, Isis-Meri, on December 25, in a cave. He was even announced by a star.
- Horus had 12 disciples and was baptized at age 30.
- Horus walked on water, delivered a sermon on the mount, and was transfigured. He was the Way, the Truth, and the Light.
- Horus was called the messiah, God's Anointed, and "KRST" was often found written upon mummies as a word of anointing and blessing from Horus. He was KRST/Christ, and the Word made flesh.

Such mysteries as the Trinity, the Incarnation, and the Virgin Birth, the Transfiguration on the Mount, the Passion, Death, Burial, Resurrection and Ascension, Transubstantiation and Baptismal Regeneration, were all extant in the mysteries of Amenta with Horus or Iu-em-Hotep as the Egyptian Jesus.[2]

So, the creeds associated with Jesus go back thousands of years before his supposed existence, and are related strongly to those of Horus, the deity of the horizon—the place between heaven and earth. He is also the deity of time, as "hour" comes from *Horus*. But note the elements of the Jesus myth: Transfiguration on a mount,

for instance, is simply the shining enlightenment of the Christ upon the world mountain, which is simply the womb or Gateway of the Mother Goddess to the Otherworld. This is Jesus having become the Christ—the anointed and therefore Shining One. He dies upon the solar cross, is buried as a dead man within the womb of the Mother Earth, and is risen again to empowered life like the sun and the Shaman who copied the process of the outer sun to obtain the inner sun.

Jesus as the sun then has a wife, Magdalene the moon, and the 12 disciples are the zodiac. He is the solar divinity, the KRST ("Karast"/Christ) or anointed, just as Krishna (Christna) was, who was also crucified. Jesus was the ultimate Shaman and serpent king, being the serpent sacrificed on the tree for our benefit. The whole mythos of the Christian religion is a merging of the various religious groups to form a unifying empirical religion. As we have previously mentioned, this occurred at the Council of Nicea in AD 325, where the very first utterance of the unified name, Jesus Christ, was heard.

Prior to the Fourth Century, there was frequent and general mention of "Christos," and his worship to the east of Rome. But nowhere can be found any authentic mention at that time of a Jesus Christ. It was not until after the Council of Nicea that the name Jesus Christ was ever known to the world.[3]

This "Christos" was not the Christ we know of today. It was instead a Gnostic ideology of the inner sun, and the method

of locating the access points to the Otherworld. The Council of Nicea was not just a gathering of Christian Bishops and dignitaries, as previously thought, and as put forward by the manipulative historians of the Christian Church. Instead, it was a gathering also of the followers of Apollo, Buddha/Krishna, Dionysus and Bacchus, Janus, Zeus, Demeter/Ceres, Oannes, and, more importantly, Osiris and Isis.

It seems then that, quite simply, Christianity is at best a mixed bag and at worst a manipulation of propaganda of the highest order. The most interesting part is that most of this can be traced back to ancient Shamanistic practices, and to that greatest of archetypal Shaman, Osiris, who epitomizes the very nature of the journey to the Otherworld.

As if to prove that the Bible was a culmination of ancient beliefs, we now discover that none other than the infamous Lazarus of the Bible is also linked with the Egyptian Osiris. If Jesus is Horus—the Son of God, then he must somewhere in the Bible raise Osiris from the dead, just as Horus, the son of Osiris, did in Egyptian myth. In the ancient Egyptian religion, Horus calls into the cave where Osiris lays, telling him to rise and come forth. Jesus did the same to Lazarus. This cave is none other than the womb of the Mother Goddess (earth), where the great Osiris has gone—it is the Otherworld. Note the use of caves in ancient traditions as "portals" or "gateways" to the Otherworld—it will become of paramount importance in later chapters when we try to discover the real, physical Gateways to the serpent realm. Also note that Osiris, as a male, needed Isis, the female, to aid in his resurrection.

However, Lazarus and Osiris are distinctly different names, and so cannot be related. Although, there is still much debate on the exact etymology, many believe that there is a proven link. How?

The ancient Egyptian designation for "Osiris" was *Asar* or *Azar*. When the Egyptians spoke of their Gods they used the article "the," and so we would have had "the Azar." This article "the" also meant *lord* or *god*, similar to the Greek word for "God": *The-os* or *Theos*. One of the Hebrew terms for "Lord" was *El*, and was applied to their many deities, such as El-Shaddai or El-ohim. So when the Hebraic writers included Osiris in their myths, they put him in as *El-Azar*—"the Lord Osiris." In the later Latin this translation was changed to *El-Azar-us*, the use of the "us" being the way masculine names ended in the Roman language. In fact, in Arabic, "Lazarus" is still spelled El-Azir, without the "us." In this way, the Egyptian, or should we say much older mythos, became the literal truth of the biblical record.

This story of Lazarus's resurrection should more accurately be said to have happened not just within a cave, but from a mountain or hillside. We find confirmation of this fact when we realize that Bethany, where Lazarus was raised, was actually situated on the summit of a hill overlooking the Dead Sea and the Jordan. Not only that, it is also said that the place was known as Anu. This struck me as important, because An/Anu was the Sumerian Shining One who lived on the lofty heights, which was none other than the Otherworld. Lazarus then was raised from the Otherworld—from within the womb, and we are given its specific location.

And, not only that, he was raised from the cross, as this was the symbol of Anu. In astrological terms, Anu was also the pole star (a perfect device for locating places on earth), the axis, and was worshipped as such. It was from Anu, the great god, the place on high above the floodwaters, that the kings of earth derived their power—they were kings by the powers of the Otherworld.

Lazarus's story is connected to an ancient and universal process on initiation and illuminative ceremony. With the biblical story of Lazarus lying at the gate of the rich man, we have an indication of pent-up energy lying sick and dying. He is covered in sores, an indication of his need to be risen physically and mentally. Dogs—representatives of Anubis, the dog-headed embalmer of Osiris—come to lick his sores. Lazarus is both being embalmed and shown the way to the Otherworld—he is being prepared; the dormant earth energies need balancing out for true resurrection to occur.

In the biblical story, the rich man dies and goes to hell. He was not prepared, and had not the balance required. Lazarus, on the other hand, had been made ready, and went to heaven, which is the Otherworld of the superconscious (or trance).

Lazarus was also said to have "rested in the bosom of Abraham." I already knew from previous research that Abraham was akin to Brahma the Indian deity. In the Koran (6:75) we also find that Abraham's father was called Azar! As Azar was Osiris and his son was Horus, this can only mean that Lazarus was resting in the bosom of Horus, or Heru-Ur, as he is more properly known—Heru of Ur—Lazarus/Azar/Osiris's own son. We also know that Abraham was said to have come from Ur of the Chaldees (Sumeria). It seems all these so-called individuals are nothing more than part and parcel of the same myth, which has been mixed up and confused in the translation.

There is yet more backing for this claim. In the Bible, Abraham's father is named as Terah, and Ausar/Azar in India was also known as Tarah. They are in fact one and the same—Abraham's father was Osiris, and therefore Abraham was Heru from Ur. Ur then is yet another location of the earth energies required to achieve trance and access the Otherworld. Horus ruled over the heart of man, and therefore Lazarus rested upon the bosom or heart of Horus—he rested in the heart of Ur, the Otherworld.

The heart kept coming up throughout my research. In Sumerian literature the heart was symbolic of the "womb" of the Mother Goddess—"womb" and "heart" being the same word. In etymological terms the word for "heart" simply meant to quiver or jump. In Christianity it was the sacred heart of Christ, or denoted Christ when displayed with wings or on the bared breast. In Irish Celtic myth Meich was the son of Morrigan, and was said to have had 'three hearts,' each one containing a serpent, something seen often in later alchemical images. This in relation to the ancient concept that the heart, along with the head, was one of the seats of the cosmic fire or life essence, must have been a good reason for the use of the symbol. Not to mention that it was related to "womb" in etymological terms in Sumeria. The heart, in balance

with the mind, is therefore the central location where one could enter trance (quiver or jump) and the Otherworld.

The heart, throughout time, has been a symbol for the *center* of the being, both physically and spiritually. It is where the divine presence is felt—the very reason Lazarus was to rest upon the center of his own/father/son's being. With the head being the center of reason, and the heart being the center of emotion, the coming together of the two concepts is no different from the coming together of the dualistic male/female, light/dark aspects of balance required to attain enlightenment, illumination, and the Gateway to the Otherworld. This symbolism is seen worldwide, from the Aztec to the Celt, from the Egyptian to the Chinese.

The Practical Use of the Snake

As I discovered in *Secrets of the Serpent,* there was often more to the symbolism of the ancients than met the eye. I was amazed yet again to discover that the physical reality of the snake was indeed implied even in such symbolic language. Many authors and researchers have proven that the uses of hallucinogenic drugs were involved in the myths of the ancient world. These include opium from poppies and even the fungi ergot and Soma.

Serpents were associated with scenes of religious and ritualistic revelry. The worshipers of Dionysus or Bacchus were often depicted on walls and pottery holding or playing with snakes as they danced toward the ecstasy or enlightenment. These serpents appear frequently in ancient art and coins. In many representations, the worshipers or deities were shown clearly to be bitten by the snake.

I believe that it is highly likely that the snake was used in this way to induce the enlightenment experience, and this is one of the reasons that the serpents were associated with the deities involved. To this end, under medical supervision, I ingested neurotoxic snake venom bought from the Far East. To my surprise, instead of my gastric juices destroying the venom's strength, the venom actually made me very light-headed, as if I had been fasting—something the ancient Shamans also did. This light-headed effect made my vision blur, and I started to see shadows around objects such as trees and animals. These shadows then became auras, and I was almost in an alternate world of vision. Because I had not taken a heavy dose, the effects wore off quickly, and I have not attempted this process again—and would not recommend it to anybody.

Joseph Campbell, in his book *Transformations of Myth Through Time*, gives some insight into the meanings of initiation and the potency of snakes as spiritual symbols when speaking of a beautiful ceramic piece from Athens showing a woman initiating a man by turning herself into a snake, just as in marriage in which the woman is said to be the "initiator." The reason for this is that the woman is deemed to be closer to nature (earth energies) than the man, and knows its deepest secrets. The man, on the other hand, is coming purely for illumination. In the case of this particular piece, the two people are Thetis and Peleus, the mother and father of Achilles, and it is indeed a marriage:

Thetis was a beautiful nymph with whom Zeus fell in love...the text tells us that when he went to take her in marriage she transformed herself into a serpent, into a lion, into fire, into water, but he conquered her. Well, that's not what you see here at all. She has power that is symbolised in serpent and in lion....

The serpent sheds its skin to be born again as the moon sheds its shadow to be born again. The serpent, therefore, like the moon, is a symbol of lunar consciousness. That is to say, life and consciousness, life energy and consciousness incorporated in a temporal body-consciousness and life engaged in the field of time, of birth and death. The lion is associated with the sun. It is the solar animal. The sun does not carry a shadow in itself; the sun is permanently disengaged from the field of time and birth and death, and so it is absolute life. These two are the same energy, one disengaged, the other engaged. And the goddess is the mother personification of both energies.

One serpent is biting the youth between the eyes, opening the eye of inner vision, which sees past the display of the field of time and space. A second serpent is biting under the ear, opening the ear to the song of the music of the spheres, the music, the voice of the universe. The third serpent is biting the heel, the bite of the Achilles tendon, the bite of death. One dies to one's little ego and becomes a vehicle of the knowledge of the transcendent—becoming transparent to transcendence.

Certain venom is neurotoxic in that it affects the nervous system and causes mental effects leading to the enlightenment process, which, if dealt with correctly and in the proper ritual, would create the same effect in everyone undergoing the process. My self-inflicted experiment also reveals this to have some scientific truth.

Carl Kauffeld, in his book *Snakes: The Keeper and the Kept*, tells us:

As I brought my hand up to free the rostral shield with thumb and forefinger I must have hooked the snake's right fang into the base of my thumb on the inside. I felt not so much as a pinprick of pain, possibly because of the analgesic nature of cobra venom. The first indication I had that anything was amiss was a trickle of blood running down my hand...a tingling began in my arms, and a pins-and-needles sensation in my lips, which I interpreted correctly as the onslaught of the classic neurotoxic symptoms of cobra envenomation. I had no pain or swelling at the site of the wound....

[After 6 or 8 minutes] I was beginning to lose awareness. I was sinking into a state that could not be called unconsciousness, but one in which I was no longer aware of what was going on about me. My gaze was fixed on the end of the keeper's alley, and the walls, floor, and ceiling gradually darkened and enclosed, more and more, a square of light at the far end of the corridor. I felt no anxiety; I felt no pain; it did not even strike me as strange that the darkness was closing in on the light. I am certain

that I did not lose consciousness entirely at any time; I only felt a complete and utter lassitude in which nothing seemed to matter—not at all unpleasant, if this is the way death comes from cobra poisoning.

This, I believe, alongside the thousands of pieces of evidence uncovered in *The Serpent Grail*, proves that snakes were seen as part and parcel of the trance states—the road to the Holy Grail and immortality, as perceived by the ancients.

It seems, then, that not only is the snake part and parcel of the religions of the ancient world, but that it is a physical key to unlocking the Gateway to the serpent realm. No wonder, in my eyes, that from the very primitive Shaman to the most modern Priest, the serpent is of paramount importance. No wonder that the serpent is the key to knowledge. It was and still is the symbol of the mental energy required to achieve illumination.

In the next chapter we shall investigate the science behind this amazing aspect of human history and discover for ourselves the technical abilities of the ancients.

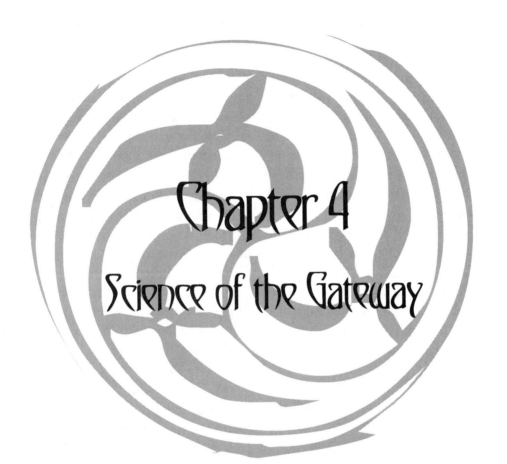

Chapter 4
Science of the Gateway

here are those who believe that introducing science into a metaphysical concept is wrong. I, on the other hand, am of the opinion that it has been wrong of humankind to separate these things for so long. Our ancient ancestors would be laughing in their burial mounds if they could hear us today—arguing such pointless semantics. To them, nothing was divided. The planets, the sun, the moon, and our earth were all part of a greater entity called God. All the many wondrous miracles, such as childbirth and the morning glory of the sun peeking over the horizon, were all part of this too. There were explanations for why things ran downhill and why it rained in autumn more than it did in summer, but these were not separate, divided explanations; these were inclusive in the whole. Indeed, only now are we beginning to realize that this is so. Now, in the 21st century, we understand that the moon does in fact affect the seas—and even deeper than that, she also affects our own inbuilt human fluidic cycles.

My own view of God has always been a scientific one. I imagine God, if he exists, as not so much a being, but a universal power in the ether; something interconnected with everything and able to know everything because of these purely particle connections—a quantum connection, empowering change through love, thought, and word. To me, the expression "Christ is all and in all" meant that he, as the Word, the empowering being, was in touch with all of nature via the basic physics of particle matter. But my opinion has developed and changed the more I learned of this wonderful interconnected world, and now I have come to some stark conclusions (laid out in this book).

You see, we have developed throughout millions of years to arrive where we are today, and even now we are not yet at the pinnacle of evolution, should there be such a thing. Regardless of whether there is a God, simple human knowledge of self, rationality, and emotions all contributes to our present evolutionary pace. And yet, we still need to answer the most fundamental question of where we come from with the idea of God. Perhaps we should try to look at the whole thing in a different way.

To understand the beginning of space and time, our perception of beginnings, ends, and what came before, must be challenged. There are many theories within this arena, some more acceptable than others. For thousands of years our views of where we came from were basically religious. From the Middle Eastern "Word of God" creation to the myriad Hindu beliefs that claim that existence is but a dream in the mind of the creator, all religions have certain common themes, but with local ethnic differences. The teachings of the hermetic sects claim the creation to be God's artistic side coming out, although he gets so involved, he can no longer separate himself from his creation. As we will see, it is quite within the laws of quantum physics for thought to have created the universe, and even more amazingly, it is possible that this concept of being unable to separate from the greater whole answers many questions. Indeed, with quantum theory, it is possible for anything to occur—even for a universe to come into existence on its own.

On the face of it, there does not seem to have been much of a challenge to these faith-oriented beliefs until the enlightened age of philosophy. This was the time when people challenged all ideas, even their own. The early philosophers required their students to assume that what they were being taught was wrong and to come up with their own ideas. However, people were challenging the assumptions of life long before the existence of the classical philosophers.

We can see from ancient writings and structures that people have understood, or found the need for, a clear beginning and end. A cycle of life emerged, and with it came a religious copy of this cycle, more complex and intuitive than we could ever imagine. Recently emerging data has put the beginning of civilization further back in time, and has proved that there was greater knowledge among early peoples. With every passing day we find new evidence for the purpose of megalithic structures: the secret resonance, the effects of radiation causing lights in the sky, the planetary alignments, earth energies and pathways, the symbolism of life and death—all these things are coming under closer scrutiny, and many are being proven correct.

The fact that our ancestors knew so much about the cycles of life is partly the cause of the difficulty in understanding our beginning. These beliefs in life cycles lasting many thousands of years, and our own inbuilt cyclical nature, will not allow us to comprehend anything without a start and finish. That is, unless we can step outside of this box and be in the place between the cycles—at the point of beginning and end, the alpha and omega.

Our whole lives are based on cycles. The element of time causes cycles to come into existence. Without time there are no cycles; without cycles there is no time. Man created deities to control these things. On a simple level, cycles are about birth and death, sunrise and sunset, the waxing and waning of the moon, the changing of the seasons, the tides of the sea, the reproductive cycle of females, and waking and sleeping. All these are inextricably linked with the entire universe. The difference between our ancient ancestors and us is that we have forgotten about these links, and their whole lives revolved around this understanding. Our ancestors understood that the universe and everything within it revolved around a massive repetition of cycles.

We are only beginning to understand the harmony in which we have lived and the disharmony we are causing with our constant damage of our finely balanced environment, which has taken the last 15 billion years to achieve. Just as our immune system sends out warrior cells to attack cancer, so too will the universe put a stop to that which causes it harm—humankind should be warned.

The earth has subtle energy waves, which some incorrectly call "ley lines," and which the Chinese call "feng shui" or "dragon paths." (These forces are scientifically proven to exist, although many blatantly unscientific claims are made for them by certain New Age sects.) When we alter the environment, we alter the balance of these paths, and in turn the subtle balance of the earth and the universe. We are also beginning to understand the effect we are having, not only on the environment, but also on our own psyches: The energy of our surroundings does have an effect upon our minds. For example, some people suffer from seasonal affective disorder (SAD) as a result of the lack of sunlight in the winter. This recently discovered cyclic problem affects us all to some extent. If we can suffer from problems because of a loss of sunlight (which is in the electromagnetic spectrum), then we could, in theory, suffer other problems caused by imbalances in electromagnetic radiation.

Our ancestors have shown that they understood these subtleties. They placed clues for us to find. All of their rituals, religions, cults, gods, demigods, and lives were linked to the cycles of the universe.

Without cycles, there would be no life. The entire universe would be one great chaotic soup. And according to scientists, this is how it all began. In the course of billions of years the universe settled down into regular patterns. Thermodynamics shows us that when two systems come together (for example hot and cold), an equilibrium is naturally achieved, albeit dependent upon many factors, such as environment, velocity, mass, and much more. This follows through from the universal scale right down to our own bodies and lives, which find equilibrium with the rest of the universe. Taking into account all the factors that affect us—solar wind and flares, electromagnetism, gravity, heat, radiation—we still manage to come into balance with these things. This in itself ought to teach us a universal truth: that if we are to truly connect with and understand our wonderful existence and universe, then we have to allow this balance to come to fruition.

It is our understanding of this fact that has altered. We have come through thousands of years of beliefs, through a hundred years of rationalism, and this perception has been lost, or overgrown by capitalist lust.

Electromagnetism

Electromagnetism has a striking and profound effect upon us. First, let's start with what they are.

Electromagnetic radiation waves are produced by the acceleration, or oscillation, of an electric charge. These waves are both electric and magnetic. The frequency of the waves can range from high to low. Visible light is a small part of the electromagnetic spectrum, as are X-rays, gamma rays, ultraviolet radiation, infrared radiation, and micro and radio waves. Add to this quantum physics, whereby particles also exist, and we have a complex and universal energy in everything. Now, we must also understand that we see only part of this wonderful wave-particle dimension: light. We hear sound waves, and we only see these other areas of the spectrum by use of special machines. In truth, there are whole new dimensions out there, all around us, similar to the "Force" in *Star Wars*—you can almost feel it and touch it.

Hamish Miller is a white-haired and bearded Scotsman who has, for many years now, been dowsing these energies, and he is a remarkable man—something akin to Gandalf from *The Lord of the Rings*. I want to use Miller to make a little point about our ancestors, whom we know to have dowsed.

I was at a conference recently in sunny Cornwall in the southwest of England giving a speech about serpents in mythology, and Miller came on before me to give his lecture about energy. At the start of the lecture he got out his dowsing rods and found a center of energy, right where the speakers stood. What he found were 10 lines of energy running off from the central point. Now, who knows whether there were 10 lines of energy? I don't. But something told me this guy was truthful and had no reason whatsoever to lie.

At the end of the lecture Miller now asked the fairly large audience to concentrate on the spot where he had dowsed, and after a short while he retraced his steps with his little rods—this time discovering 18 energy lines. Miller told us that this was because the earth was so "excited," in energy terms, by the mental connection, that it was opening up new lines of communication. I would like you to remember this for a few reasons: firstly that Miller's technique is nothing new. With the greatest of respect to this wonderful man, and I mean that truly, he is following in an ancient tradition. This tradition goes back thousands of years and to a people who were what we know as Pagan—which simply means people of the countryside. These are the people who respected the earth, loved it, worshiped it, and gave back what they took. In short, they were nothing like us. The second point of this is the scientific element: What Miller was revealing to us was quite startling. In truth, we may be seeing man's connection unconsciously to the electromagnetic spectrum. This may be another way of perceiving the wave-particle phenomena rather than with our eyes (light) and our ears (sound). The truth of this will become very apparent in later chapters. Now, we must move on.

Electromagnetic waves need no medium for transmission. They can travel through almost anything, including space. Virtually everything gives off electromagnetic radiation, including the sun, the moon, stars, and the Earth.

Caling electromagnetic radiation "waves," however, does not account for all the properties discovered. Max Planck showed that radiation occurred in finite quanta of energy, and was therefore also particles, as I explained earlier. We now understand radiation in two ways, particle and wave, and they react together; the quantum theory can now be brought into line with electromagnetic radiation. A wave-particle soup is bombarding us daily, and we have almost no idea what it is doing, nor the effect it has on us.

In geophysics, we study the phenomena of Earth's electromagnetic field, the heat flow, seismic waves, and the force of gravity. We also look into the outer-space activity that can affect us, such as solar

Aboriginal photons? Taken from an Aboriginal musical instrument used in rituals of ancestor worship and Otherworldly activity. Note the similarity to modern images of photons.

winds and manifestations of cosmic radiation that affect the Earth's own radiation.

In terrestrial magnetism (magnetohydrodynamics or hydromagnetics) we have found that the Earth's magnetic field is related to the motion of fluid, which conducts electricity within the Earth. The rotation of the Earth within the gravitational pull of the moon and sun periodically imposes gravitational effects upon the Earth (the changing ocean tides and solid earth tides), which in turn alter the electromagnetism of the planet. All these things happen cyclically, and all these things affect us.

Every time a volcano erupts, the Earth's magnetic field changes its orientation and strength. The depth of the mantle increases or decreases the conductivity of the electromagnetic wave. When a solar wind approaches, the Earth forms a magnetic sheath, called the magnetosphere, which acts as a giant natural dynamo more than 60,000 miles across. When the high-energy particles of solar radiation penetrate this sheath and enter the radiation belts, we see the beautiful phenomenon known as the aurora.

Electromagnetic waves possess energy according to wavelength and frequency. This energy is imparted into matter when the radiation is absorbed, something that Michael Faraday realized when he said that the electromagnetic field was the lowest form of physical reality.[1] The resonance caused by the various frequencies of the particle waves affects the molecules within our bodies. Every molecule in our bodies is held in place by various methods, and when we are bombarded daily with fluctuating and cyclic electromagnetic radiation these molecules are moved—including those in our brains. We have lived with this bombardment since life began. It must have affected our evolution, and we must retain some natural and deep link with this phenomenon.

A better understanding of these effects could be gained by research into such phenomena as Kirlian photography. This was discovered by Semyan Kirlian in 1939 when either he or another person (it is disputed) received an electric shock while undergoing electrotherapy. The shock caused a spark, and Kirlian wanted to see what would happen if he put light-sensitive material in the path of the spark. After much experimentation Kirlian managed to photograph an aura around his hand. Dr. Victor Inyushin of the Kirov State University in Russia, a biophysicist, concluded that the photograph showed the existence of what

he called biological plasma. This concept relates to healing powers, in that better photographs have been achieved using the hands of healers.[2] Plasma, in this context, is the name given to the collection of positive and negative ions, and is not solid, liquid, or gas. It has no charge because it contains equal amounts of positive and negative ions; plasma is in equilibrium, or is neutral, and it is this aura that I saw when ingesting neurotoxic snake venom.

The Foundation for the Study of Cycles found that sunspot activity is intimately related to the reaction of large groups within both the human and animal populations of the world. Research that stretches right back to 500 BC has shown that every 11.1 years the sun flares, and major upheavals, unrest, and wars arise. It brings a whole new meaning to the various religious beliefs about the controlling God of our lives that manifests as the Light.

So what effect is all this radiation having upon us? Will Kirlian photography ever escape the paranormal shelves in bookstores? What effect have the radiation and cyclic patterns had upon our evolution? The complexities of the formulae and ingredients are immense, and too much for any computer model to predict.

And yet, ancient humans would have us believe that they understood the subtleties of this complex world by altering the state of their own consciousnesses. Could it be that, as wildlife flees from an oncoming tsunami by their own connection to the electromagnetic resonance of the world, we too were once able to know and understand so much more? To find the answer to this question you must read a little more,

but before we move on we must touch upon the word *energy*.

Energy

We now need to visit the term *energy* and its relationship to the Gateway. *Energy* is simply a term often used by both scientists and mystics, but in different ways, and neither would necessarily agree with the other about the use of the term. For the purposes of this book I have decided to look at both sides to see if there is a common ground between them, and hopefully discover the truth somewhere in between.

This energy, as I am calling it, is nothing more than the serpent fire, solar force, or pranic energy of the serpent-worshiping mystics of the world—the earth energy we call electromagnetism. It is the power base and drives the whole process forward. And yet, what is this energy? And have scientists ever discovered it? Or even looked for it?

Throughout the course of human history, as we have seen, there have been thousands of individuals who have claimed to have experienced the enlightenment or illumination, giving rise to the term *shining*, as far back in our history as we care to go. If it is true that humankind, across the world and across time, has been having these experiences, and if they are real experiences, then it is true to state that they must be brought on by some kind of energy. This energy, as we shall see, is both the electrical charge within the nervous system to the brain, and the chemical and biological reactions within our brain brought on by numerous methods of meditation, prayer, and dervish. The connection to the Gateway into

another mental dimension is also often found to be at specific locations on the Earth with special energy alignments or properties.

These ancient methods and locations were discovered throughout the course of tens of thousands of years, and have been perfected by initiates and adepts of many cults and creeds. The methods do work; they do create altered states of awareness via the electrical, biological, and chemical reactions that they generate. The question we have to ask for ourselves is whether there is anything real (in the true sense of the word) to these trance states. Humankind certainly believed they were accessing a higher realm or a new dimension. This book will show that understanding of and union with the energies of the earth, and therefore universe itself, is required to gain the understanding claimed by our ancestors.

There are many more terms for the illumination, but the point is that the energy is universal, that humankind has discovered this energy at specific locations, that we have tamed it and controlled it and given it names that relate to our gods—and in fact it was our god. We have even then gone on to abuse it, as seems to be a common theme for humanity. In all cases this energy, or Holy Ghost, which is part of our naturally evolved makeup, is said to be our guide and key to access other worlds, through what we now know to be quantum entanglement and zero point energy.

There are issues with the brain to which we must turn before we proceed. These issues have been pointed to by those among us who reason away the enlightenment experience as a purely hormonal or emotional reaction. In order to discuss these "issues," we must understand what we mean when we use the term *consciousness*. As Dr. Peter Fenwick put it, "By consciousness, I mean the appearance within me of an experiencing self that is able not only to know itself but also...to differentiate a group of experiences which clearly are not part of itself or part of the body to which it belongs,...they come from the outside world."[3]

Consciousness is not as clear as we may have believed. There are, in fact, according to psychiatrists, two kinds of consciousness. On the one hand we experience our *self*, and on the other we interpret the *outside world*—but we do this according to our *self*, so one element of consciousness (the *self*) affects the other. In this way our experiences of the outside world should differ around the world, due to localized influences, and it does. This gives rise to differences of opinion in many subjects, causing conflict between individuals, and even cultural conflicts whereby the outside world is experienced collectively.

Most importantly, the reality of the inner self (that is the experience of our own "self" consciousness) remains a universal constant, just as the ancients believed— Christ is all and in all.

We can see this in the test results of altered states of consciousness experiments that scientists have been doing for the last few decades, and it is something we will look at shortly. For now it is sufficient to understand that the world we see or perceive is not actually objectively seen, but it is in truth a construct of our own mind, and therefore is subjective. The world we perceive depends on our own upbringing, cultural boundaries, and memories—in

short, it is seen through the unique state of our own brain functions. There is more than one world; there are in fact 6 billion of them, all being seen through each individual human mind. If the world that surrounds us is so difficult to objectively perceive, how much more so is the inner world? Well, in fact, because this is a genetic or evolved universal archetype, it is a lot easier to understand. Add to this the hypothesis I have put forward for the collective superconscious quantum mind, and all inner realities are a reflection of the greater mind anyway (this would be the inner self, not the self that has been infected with influences locally—the ego).

Now that we understand a little more about consciousness we must move on to the scientists' issues with the mystical experience, and their attempts to reduce it down to biological, chemical, or genetic levels. As Gopi Krishna put it, "However brief it might be, the transcendental flight of the soul must be reflected in the cerebral matter in some way. Conversely, it can happen that as a result of a reaction caused in the brain by intense concentration, constant worship, prayer, extreme longing for the beatific vision or consuming love of God, continued for long periods of time, a process of transformation would start in the organ conducive to the extraordinary experiences of the mystical type."[4]

So, according to Krishna, we may consciously alter our material brain throughout generations to help us further our spiritual evolution. Through our yearning after spiritual fulfilment throughout millions of years, we may have in fact developed a biological, chemical, and electrical method of accessing a quantum dimension.

Gopi Krishna claimed to be one of those who have achieved full and true enlightenment, and wishes therefore to spread the word of this amazing part of human evolution. I have to agree with his statement in the respect that if this is a natural human reaction or effect, then it must be mirrored in the matter of our brain structure. Science therefore should be able to pick out these effects in the various elements, which make up our "mind," be they electromagnetic frequencies or chemical and biological actions.

There are many instances I could state whereby animals and plants have co-evolved together so that their own evolution, both now and in the past, has depended upon each other. This aid to evolution, between plant or parasite and animal, is perfectly natural, and is seen in thousands of studies. The pilot fish, for instance, depends upon the shark for scraps of food left in the wake of the larger predator's exploits. Many animals rely upon bacteriological agents for the digestion of food, and we as humans are now coming to this very same conclusion. It is not, therefore, a great step to say that in some way, the further evolution of humankind's mind has and will be aided by chemical and biological reactions. The difference with humans is that we are conscious (at least many of us are) of this fact, and so we can cause an effect upon our own evolution. This can be seen throughout the course of human history, whereby drugs from plants and animals have been employed to create altered states of consciousness.

These plants, and indeed even the venom of the snake, have then become sacred to people in thier religious teachings. Some of these are known today as the soma of the Hindus, the manna of the Hebrews, the peyote of the Shamans, and even to the extent that venom and blood eventually became the Eucharist of the Christians.

The truth is that the Shamans who led the process were finding ways to higher consciousness—to be closer to their gods. They all, without fail, claimed that these compounds aided their process and even brought them huge amounts of information that they would not otherwise be able to gain. This knowledge was passed on to the tribe, where required, through visual arts and in practical healing techniques. This in turn aided the evolution of the tribe and affected the course of human history. But, if we are to believe the purely scientific outlook to this process, all we shall see is that these drugs were nothing more than hallucinogens, and therefore any knowledge gained came purely from within the brain and whatever it had already learned in the course of its life. All the things seen through this process have therefore been nothing but an illusion created only within the brain. But this theory neglects the quantum side to existence—that all things are connected, that all is one, and that everything depends upon everything else, just the way the pilot fish depends upon the shark; so too may our mind depend upon the Universal Mind. This explains how the Shaman intrinsically would know the needs of the tribe and be able to find a suitable answer—*even if he himself did not know it.*

The drugs, however, are only part of the story of greater awareness for the mind.

People have striven to achieve this "extra" sense through other means, and this may be part of our own inbuilt evolutionary desires—in that we unconsciously know there is more, and strive for it in order to be the fittest of the species. These other methods are now ingrained elements of our world's religions. Meditation, prayer, fasting, and even dervish (spinning) are all processes developed by people to attain the heightened state of awareness or closeness to God, achieved partly by others through the use of drugs. These are all physical methods of entering a metaphysical realm; a biological and chemical way of people improving their own conscious state. There is much more to this process, as we shall learn.

The various psychological elements of the process described by many subjects in scientific laboratory testing are extremely interesting, and I felt the need to outline them as follows:

The transcendence of time and space

This is the feeling that time has either stood still or moved rather faster than normal. All references to where and when we are become blurred. In fact, what is described is the concept that all time and space are at one point; the edges between our perception of space and time become irrelevant as we are suddenly seeing reality in a different way. If human minds actually enter a quantum existence, then this would be completely true, and it is something we would expect. It is a reality—albeit a very different one from our ordinary experience of it. It is the emotion of a real experience.

Oneness

The feeling of all time and space being at one point is backed up by this other, unique feeling of unity. This loss of ego and experience of the self is exactly what the alchemists, occultists, and Gnostics speak of as necessary to obtain the true enlightenment. This surely is an indication of the true "knowledge" for which we are searching.

Sense of the divine and sacredness

Subjects feel they are at peace with existence and that they are in tune with the divine. Yet again, this is paralleled with the experiences described by our ancient philosophers.

Mood

Most subjects feel a positive mood, and their emotions express wonder and joy. They are elevated to such an extent that nothing in our reality can compare.

Knowledge

Subjects feel that they have gained insight into nature that they simply cannot express, but they believe this knowledge to be ultimate and authentic. The process gave them a strong sense of paradox, that they could not explain their own emotions or experience to others, and that their experiences were contradictory. Giving voice to the ineffable has always been the problem of the mystics, and I can personally vouch for the feeling of *knowing* that is expressed by these subjects. There are often moments of sheer illumination, which give one a sense of superconsciousness, however fleeting the feeling can be. I have too often felt

unable to express this feeling, that I have intense knowledge of why and how, and yet have been unable to explain this knowledge to others.

Persistence

The experience remained with them emotionally. They took their emotional experience with them into their own lives and it aided them, giving them a more balanced outlook.

Whichever way we look at these experiences—brought on by drugs, or even the physical activities of meditation, prayer, fasting, or dervish—we must conclude that this trance is a universal human phenomenon. Although all philosophers, Gnostics, religious exponents, and scientists explain the cause of the experience in different ways, it is our job here to come to a balance, to explain the process as it really is. I am neither a scientist nor a mystic; I am instead hoping to see these experiences from every perspective I possible can.

There can be no doubt that the various drugs bring on a process known to the mystics as enlightenment. There can equally be no doubt that these processes can also be brought on via physical and mental actions, creating neuron transmissions that affect our thoughts and release hormones. But all of this is simply reducing the process down to a scientifically physical, biological, and chemical action. The question is not how the experience is brought on; the question is, what truth is there to it? Is this process a truth of human evolution? And is this process being caused by the union of our inner selves with the collective superconscious state or Universal Mind? Are we in fact creating our own evolution in a quantum universe?

The scientist has the following politically correct get-out-clause: "Though the scientific method has its bounds, enlightenment for the mystic lies not in explanation, but in direct experience.... Irrespective of verification, mystical experiences remain the zenith of human endeavour into the hidden regions of the mind, opening doorways to the core of conscious experience itself."[5] The mystics concur with this statement, having no interest in the scientific realm; therefore we almost never find a balance, and a real debate is always seen as too dangerous.

However, we want to get to the bottom of this process, and I wish to see a balance struck between hard, rationalistic science and true human experience—if indeed that is possible. As Gopi Krishna wrote, "Religious belief and experience are usually regarded as beyond scientific explanation, yet neurologists at the University of California, San Diego, have located an area in the temporal lobe of the brain that appears to produce intense feelings of spiritual transcendence, combined with a sense of some mystical presence. Canadian neuroscientist Michael Persinger, of Laurentian University, has even managed to reproduce such feelings in otherwise unreligious people by stimulating this area." He then goes on to explain Persinger's findings, which were that there is a spike in a person's EEG at the time the subject claims to have been visited by God, showing a "slow-wave seizure" in the temporal lobe, as the rest of the brain shows no

Christ on the cross beneath the eclipsed sun,
Southwell Minster, England.

Here again, Krishna and Persinger demonstrate the belief that although the physical attributes of the experience can be seen scientifically, the understanding of the effect can still be seen as mystical. Where does the origin of this process truly lay? Is it God that gives us this element within our brains? Or is it our evolutionary connection with the Universal Mind, the collective superconscious state that is evolving us and with us? Or are we deluding ourselves?

Can this Universal Mind be perceived by the subjects scientists have tested? And if so, does this give us evidence for the quantum connection? Are people able to become conscious of the all-pervading presence of this superconscious state, just as the ancient Shamans, Gnostics, and others have expressed? As Ramachandran asks the questions:

change. Persinger reasons that the "spiritual dimension" is no less spiritual for being shown scientifically. As he says, "If God exists, it figures He must have created us with some biological mechanism with which to apprehend Him."[6]

If religious beliefs are merely the combined result of wishful thinking and a longing for immortality, how do you explain the flights of fancy of intense religious ecstasy experienced by patients with temporal lobe seizures, or their claim that God speaks directly to them? Many a patient has told me of a "divine light that illuminates all

things" or of an "ultimate truth that lies completely beyond the reach of ordinary minds".... Of course, they might simply be suffering from hallucinations and delusions of the kind that a schizophrenic might experience, but if that is the case, why do such hallucinations occur mainly when the temporal lobes are involved? Even more puzzling, why do they take this particular form? Why don't these patients hallucinate pigs or donkeys?[7]

The evidence shows that subjects do experience a great light or shining, just as the ancients have stated on numerous occasions, and which we know to be a part of the supposed enlightenment experience. It also shows a feeling of being connected to the divine, and a puzzling, archetypal effect whereby the experiences are universal—not different in each culture or ethnic background. They do not indeed see pigs or donkeys. This is either the result of a basic human genetic makeup or a connection via the quantum brain to a quantum state. The experience cannot be the result of humankind's search for eternal life, as each culture would have different results. This is, then, a result of human evolution, whether the simple biological, genetic, and universal process of evolution, or via a coevolved nature with the existence of another quantum dimension, which we are only now beginning to comprehend. This would explain the serpent image, which has been seen both as the double helix of DNA and as energy waves. Either way, the wavy line, physically manifested on this level of existence as the snake, is a universal image underlying the very basic levels of existence.

The fact remains that the enlightenment experience happens to humans around the world, and has been happening for a long time. The fact also remains that this experience has given rise to the very religions and beliefs to which we adhere today. This Otherworld, envisaged by the ancients and by mystics worldwide, has been physically manifested throughout time for all to see, and for modern science to research. These physical manifestations can be seen in structures such as the mandala and in texts such as the Bible, and we shall be looking at various forms of this manifestation in later chapters.

To also bring some evidence to the concept that the space between the planets and stars, electrons and nuclei, is nothing different from the Universal Mind or akashic records, we have to simply understand that via quantum entanglement, modern physicists have found that a subatomic particle such as an electron would somehow know what another electron was doing—no matter where the other (entangled) particle was. If scientists are prepared to say that the particle "knows" what its entangled particle is doing, then how much further is it to say that once conscious of this level of reality we too could "know" what the other particles entangled with ours are doing? We are conscious of our biological and chemical reality; why not then also our quantum level? These other particles to which we are entangled could be part of the Universal Mind, or even the activity in another valley, or another planet!

Now, when we come to this remarkable understanding that both modern science and ancient imaginative philosophy can truly be balanced in the way we have shown here, then we finally have the answers already given to us by the ancients—that we should not search for the divine in the clouds or even in the laboratory, but in balance with and within one's *self*. The balances that I and the ancients are talking about are constant; that is, they are balances at and within every level of life, both of the outer world and the inner world. They are balances within the very atom, as we have seen, and in the world around us, and in our everyday lives. Only through this understanding can we perceive the "knowledge" of the ancients. Only with balance both within our psyches and with the energies of the earth itself can we find the true Gateway locations and safely access the Otherworld.

Now it is time to move on and to see these secrets for what they are, and indeed *where* they are. Firstly we shall take a look at something I have personally found fascinating, and to my utter delight, entirely related to the story of the Gateway—round towers.

Chapter 5
Round Towers
and the Science of the Pyramids

n his paper "The Great Pyramid Texts," Clesson Harvey points out that in the pyramids of Saqqara there are more than 3,000 columns of texts from the 5th and 6th dynasties, which he believes hold the secret to the pyramids' use. These texts include incantations and magical formulae that were invoked in certain locations around the pyramid. In one of these pyramids, in the upper passage is an old megalithic glyph. Clesson's interpretation is that this glyph or phrase translates remarkably into "star door" and "tunnel opening gate."

In addition to the fact that glyphs are sadly lacking from most pyramids (the Great Pyramid is an example of this), this information is a startling discovery in relation to my theories. Indeed there were probably more hieroglyphs, which have since been destroyed, as when Herodotus was said to have visited Egypt in the 5th century BC, the outer casing of the Great Pyramid was *awash with hieroglyphs*.

Egyptologists claim that the "star" mentioned is mythological, and leave it at that. I will not, however, and will further state that this "tunnel" and "star door" is really the entrance to the Shamanic Otherworld—as "star" and "shining" are intimately linked in meaning, with a person having emerged from the trance experience triggered by Shamanic activity. The star symbol, incidentally, is the five-pointed pentacle we discussed in a previous chapter, and which relates to the head and the whole process of entering the Otherworld. Its symbol has remained with us, and has remained mysterious. Also, as expert navigator and author Crichton Miller pointed out to me, the pentacle is a perfect device for navigation via the moon and the sun— it therefore aids in the location of sacred earth energy locations.

I was already aware that the Egyptians called the area of Giza where the Great Pyramid is situated *Rostau*, meaning "Gateway to the Duat" or "Otherworld," and that it was this Rostau effect that could turn a man into a "god." This was a sacred location that simply must be on a place of earth energy convergence, as we have been discussing.

I was also aware of some of the metaphysical principles and scientific knowledge that had been encoded into the pyramids, but I wondered, how did the pyramid work in relation to the trance state or "altered consciousness"? And furthermore, were there any additional buildings or structures in the world constructed as a means to facilitate these experiences? And, if so, how?

First of all, perhaps we should look for any evidence of these mysterious structures having some metaphysical function we are unaware of that could be explained scientifically—maybe a link with human consciousness in some way. After having identified the experience, which has been

behind the religious impulse throughout history, it is now time to take an alternative look at the possible science behind these earth structures.

Pyramid Science

Back in the 1970s and '80s, a scientist named Joe Parr decided it was also time to take a look at the Great Pyramid, and pyramid shapes in general, and what he discovered is nothing short of amazing.

In his experiments, Joe set up a model of the Great Pyramid, aligned north–south and east–west, with flat coils placed on the north and south. A blown 1-microfarad capacitor was sparked across the gap using a battery, resistor, and chart recorder. This was done to simulate the electromagnetic energy of the earth passing over the pyramid— what are commonly known as earth energies; the same ones my friend Hamish Miller can detect with his dowsing rods, and which we have been discussing. The scientists registered the changes on a daily basis, recording the bizarre phenomenon of an energy bubble that surrounded the pyramid. Strangely, the energy actually stopped all kinds of radiation, and the bubble showed attenuation to beta emitters, ion sources, and magnetic sources when in the bubble. Feeding negative ions into the bubble actually intensified the energy.

The energy was also found to alter throughout the course of the year, and 13 years of experimentation gave good results. Most peculiar was the effect upon gravity, which is linked intrinsically to electromagnetic radiation. It appeared that the bubble

actually blocked out the force of gravity as well as electromagnetic energy, showing a 113,000-times increase in kinetic energy—leading the researchers to theorize that the pyramid actually *moved* in time and space—a place known to theoretical physicists as h-space or hyperspace. Incredibly, when negative ions were fed into the bubble, the pyramid was drawn to the moon—positive ions moved it away—an amazing correlation with the feminine, and therefore the spiritually "negative" aspect associated with lunar worship.

But what relevance could this have on my theory here?

Well, if, as it can sometimes misleadingly appear, all things point toward the Great Pyramid, then there has to be a good reason or two. My view, and a great many others, is that the Great Pyramid—the Shamanic "World Mountain"—was used as an entrance to the Shamanic Underworld or Duat. This seems to have been facilitated by incantations from the Pyramid Texts and Book of the Dead, as well as other techniques, which I will reveal.

The effect caused within the brain, which releases the hormones required for the trance-state, is basically electromagnetic, and is affected by all manner of ion activity. It therefore appears that the ancient serpent cult or Shining Ones were onto this in their own way, perceiving energy as the "serpent wave" and worshipping this invisible energy-god as a snake. Eventually, gathering sufficient knowledge of this serpent energy they erected buildings that conducted the energy into a controlling element. With the effect of the "plugs" in the air vents of the pyramid having a resonance also upon the electromagnetic energy, we can see how the pyramid could have been specifically honed and finely tuned to create the effect.

But, I thought, there must be more evidence of other ancient buildings with this peculiar inbuilt design—and there was. And so I moved my research sideways for a while, leaving the Great Pyramid for later.

Round Towers

One peculiar and often overlooked structure is the round tower. These circular structures are seen worldwide and number in the hundreds—and strangely they are linked to he serpent in almost every instance.

Tall, elegant, round structures, built by cultures as diverse as the Irish Celts and early Christians to the Hopi Indians and Egyptians—all of whom are linked with serpent worship.

In Ireland there are more than 65 round towers, many taller than 100 feet, and claimed by academics to be no more than 1,000 years old. However, as with most Christian buildings, they are generally built upon much more ancient religious ground, and indeed, many of them can be proven to be older than first believed. Some even have churches built onto them, as if to physically attach the church to the ancient serpent worship.

I have already shown in *Secrets of the Serpent* how St. Patrick kicked out the serpents from Ireland, and that these "serpents" were indeed an ancient serpent-worshiping cult—the whole story being symbolic of the Christian church taking power. Historian and writer Gradwell, in the 19th century pointed out that, "St Patrick and his followers almost invariably selected those sacred sites of paganism, and built their wooden churches under the shadow of the Round Towers, then as mysterious and inscrutable as they are to-day."[1]

Some claim these structures were fire temples dedicated to sun worship, and it is easy to see why, especially when we discover that sun worship is connected to serpent worship—the sun and the serpent both being inner realities. Others claim them to be watch towers that would relate nicely to the ancient Sumerian and Semite term for the serpent cult: *Watchers*. In fact, Hargrave Jennings, author of *Ophiolatraea*, relates them to the obelisk, that ancient phallic and serpent-derived pillar to the heavens. I already knew that pillars were variously used across cultures as markers for the Gateways to the Otherworld. I also discovered that these towers are also found close to rivers, streams, and holy wells, and this not only raises the question of earth energy caused by the water course, but also is very telling, as serpent deities were always associated with these watery places.

Water was indeed the subterranean home of the serpent race, and was the entrance to the Underworld or Otherworld—which is where the trance state was intending to take you. But it is this association with water that seems to be important to such structures in terms of earth-related electromagnetic energy. No wonder the River Styx was so important to the ancient Greeks and Romans.

There may indeed also be an important link between round towers and the Phoenicians, who had similar structures dedicated to their rain and water deity, Baal. There are thousands scattered across Sardinia, just north of the Phoenician city of Carthage, dating to at least 2,000 years before Christ.

But as author Ralph Ellis pointed out in his book *Jesus, Last of the Pharaohs*, the round towers are remarkably similar to the pillar, which was capped by the conical or pyramid-shaped ben ben stone. This pillar was said to have stood in the central courtyard of the temple at Heliopolis known as the Mansion of the Phoenix.

There are also those who believe that these round towers served as astronomical tools, similar to Stonehenge, and this may also be the case. The towers in Iran called radkan (*rhad* = "red snake," *kan/can* = "serpent") are thought to serve this purpose, and similar to the European towers of a much later date, they have conical caps.

In the Naga ("serpent") homeland of India, we have sacred buildings such as the stupa, and in China the pagoda—again, both forms are really based on the round tower.

In feng shui, we get a glimpse at the real use of the towers: the pagoda and indeed the stupa are thought to trap negative energy or chi (dragon/serpent energy), what we would call negative ions. Remember that these negative ions in Joe Parr's pyramid experiments were thought to cause antigravity and anti-electromagnetic effects.

The Chinese tale of Lady White Snake is popular all over the world, and ultimately comes from this electromagnetic energy.

It is the Lady White Snake or "lunar snake" that is trapped in the pagoda for a thousand years.

The Giant's Tower of Gozo, Malta, has also been related strongly by many historians to the towers of Ireland and Phoenicia. Early 20th century writer and historian Captain Oliver, when describing the Gozo Tower, said:

It may be conjectured, that these loculi [small holes] may have been intended to hold the small idols, whose trunks [headless], made of stone or clay, are not dissimilar to the conventional female figures of Hindoo [Hindu] representations, on the numerous large and small rudely shaped conical stones (possibly sacred symbols, analogous to the larger stone cones, on which female mammae are found engraved in the ruined nuragghi of Sardinia) which are found in those ruins. Somewhat similar small pyramidal cones, which by some have been supposed to represent the sun's rays, are to be seen in the hands of priests kneeling before the sacred serpent god in Egyptian paintings.[2]

More round towers can be found as far away as New Mexico, Colorado, Utah, Chichen Itza, and Africa. All are related to the serpent energy and serpent cult, and many have the same astronomical alignments. Indeed, the Hopi snake tribe actually refers to these towers as *snake houses*. The Hopi god of death and the Underworld is Masau'u, and he has to explain to the "snake mother" why her children cannot live in the house: "And Masau'u said, 'the snakes…should never again have a house, but should live under rocks and in holes in the ground.' But he also said the snake houses [round towers]…built for them should never again be destroyed."[3] Could this be an indication of the death of the snake cult? Could this be the Hopi version of the St. Patrick story? And if so, then it relates back to Ireland, where again there are hundreds of round towers connected with the serpent!

If it is the case that these round towers or snake houses are seen across the Atlantic with the same religious and cultural grounding, then it is also true to state that the Annakim, the Shining Ones of Semite history, are also related in some way. *Anak* means "long neck" or "necklaces." The Hopi have a similar word, *anaaq*, meaning "necklace" or "earring"—it is also an expression used when in pain from a snake-bite! Sumerian images of these Annakim show them to indeed have long necks. It would seem that the Hopi as well as the Mesopotamian and Egyptian traditions all came from the same source, and we will uncover more new evidence for this in the coming chapters.

But what about the science of the round towers? Is there anything that can be related to the energy within the pyramids? In the book *Ancient Mysteries, Modern Visions*, Professor Philip Callahan relays his research which amazingly shows that the round towers may have been designed as huge resonant systems for collecting and storing meter-long wavelengths of magnetic and electromagnetic energy. Sound fanciful? It did to me, so I dug deeper.

Obelisk, Rome. Could this be a connection device to the Otherworld?

The Great Callahan

During World War II, Philip Callahan, PhD, schooled as an entomologist, was stationed in Ireland as a radio technician. In his books *Paramagnetism: Rediscovering Nature's Secret, Natures Silent Music*, and *Ancient Mysteries, Modern Vision*s, Callahan goes a long way toward proving the ancient uses and benefits of what he terms *paramagnetism*.

In *Nature's Silent Music*, Callahan relates the way he believes that the ancient Hebrews, and indeed Egyptians, actually utilized the energy in rocks. He calls them "magical rocks," in that they were deemed "magical" by the ancients due to their innate electromagnetic energy, which he believes they tapped into.

The mythological and historical data would back up his theory. The ancients did see power residing in the stones and rocks in association with the earth and the surrounding universe. Using scientific methods, Callahan goes on to rate various rocks according to their measurements—with volcanic rock being more "magical." He claims that the ancients, including those of Celtic origin, understood the power of magnetic healing forces (which we are only rediscovering today), and relates this to the magnetic forces found within these stones.

It has long been theorized that stone circles and ancient monuments are to be found on "earth energy" lines, known currently as ley lines (even though Alfred Watkins, the discoverer of ley lines, did not intend their use in this way, seeing them as straight paths instead). Many have theorized that these standing stones are magnetic acupuncture points upon the

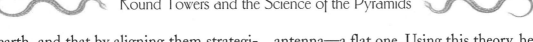

earth, and that by aligning them strategically, the ancients were building an energy pathway for some unknown reason.

Now we know the reason.

The power found within the rocks, according to Callahan, came from the millions of years of grinding and crushing of drifting tectonic platelets (moving earth), and that energy was trapped within the minerals that make up the various materials. Callahan calls the "positive and negative electromagnetic forces" found within the rocks *paramagnetism* and *diamagnetism*, respectively. He claims that these forces were known in ancient times, by the Chinese as yin and yang, and by the Irish as fairies and leprechauns—the powers within the earth. These are the male and female, positive and negative energies we have been discussing that require balancing upon the earth for us to utilize them.

Callahan's credentials are nothing short of heroic. It was Callahan who discovered the tachyon, which many had said, did not exist. The tachyon is a particle that actually moves faster than the speed of light— something we now know other particles to do via quantum entanglement. If humankind could utilize such a particle, we would actually be able to receive a message sent using the tachyon *before* it had been sent—thereby upsetting some fundamental laws of physics (see Chapter 13).

Callahan states that we must "treat rocks, stone, and even the soil as antenna collectors of magnetic energy waves." This statement relates to the round tower theory, of the structures being "earth antennas." He also points out that as fertile land is derived from volcanic activity, it too is an antenna—a flat one. Using this theory, he has gone on to show how practical applications can come from his research, by improving the growth in plants (organic antennas) by using the magnetism in the soil (through adding volcanic ash or even mineral magnetite). He even claims that by building small round towers in the garden we too can help the growth of our plants!

Basing the hypothesis of his work in insect antenna and the capacity to resonate electromagnetic waves, Callahan hypothesized that the tall round towers were made to be "earth antennas," and that similar buildings or structures around the globe could also have been built for the same reason.

He believed (before his time, I might add) that this energy would be *passed on to those meditating at the site*. It is my contention that this is true, and that it spurs on the trance-induced state and brings one closer to accessing the Otherworld— whatever one might believe that to be.

Of the towers tested in Ireland, Callahan found that the iron-rich rock they were made from indeed helped this effect along, though the towers made from other materials, such as limestone and granite, were still paramagnetic. Callahan goes on to show how the rubble within these towers, which has baffled people for decades, was truly there as a tuning implement—in much the same way I might say the "plugs" in the so-called air vents of the Great Pyramid are probably used for fine-tuning. It is my contention that further research should be carried out at all the round tower sites in Ireland and elsewhere, before the ravages of time destroy what could be a remarkable insight into the practices of the ancient serpent cult.

Now an image began to form in my mind of ancient and not-so-ancient sites located around the planet from various cultures, all with the unifying link of the serpentine energy field. I needed to look yet deeper into the science of electromagnetism and resonance. There had to be further explanations for the universally worshiped serpent. There had to be more science behind the Gateway into the Otherworld. And I found what I was looking for.

F-Sharp and Harmonic Alignment

Once I had looked at the electromagnetic effects of the pyramids and the round towers, I wondered about resonance and the sonic abilities of these structures. To my delight, this had already been deeply investigated by quite a few people, so there was much evidence to pull from.

One researcher, Boris Said, is quoted as having said:

Subsequent experiments carried out by Tom Danley in the King's Chamber of the Great Pyramid and in Chambers above the King's Chamber suggest that the pyramid was constructed with a sonic purpose. Danley identifies four resident frequencies, or notes, that are enhanced by the structure of the pyramid, and by the materials used in its construction. The notes form an F sharp chord, which according to ancient Egyptian texts was the harmonic of

our planet. Moreover, Danley's tests show that these frequencies are present in the King's Chamber even when no sounds are being produced. They are there in frequencies that range from 16 hertz down to a half hertz, well below the range of human hearing. According to Danley, these vibrations are caused by the wind blowing across the ends of the so-called air shafts—in the same way as sounds are created when one blows across the top of a bottle.[4]

In other research, scientists have found that F-sharp is actually the resonant chord of the Earth. To explain simply, everything in the universe vibrates, and these vibrations produce waves. At certain levels, our ears can sense these waves or vibrations, and we call that sound. Humankind eventually developed the ability to take these sounds and make music, by making waves at different pitches and volumes. These "notes" reveal to us the invisible vibrations of the world and universe around us. Just because we cannot hear the whole range of waves/vibrations does not mean that these infra- or ultrasound waves are not there—and these too have notes. So when we play an F-sharp on the piano, there are also many F-sharps at different pitches that we cannot hear, below and above our range. The Earth, made up of moving matter, creates a wave/vibration in space, which, if we could hear it, would be F-sharp.

The fact that the Egyptians knew this is startling. We may also note that as Callahan had previously pointed out the importance of certain stones in connection to electromagnetism, the stones of these "tuned" passages were made of granite—a

specific paramagnetic rock. Boris Said also points out that the coffer in the chamber itself is attuned to the frequencies of the pyramid. We should also note here that the vibrations were below those of the human ear, at 16 hertz or less—this will become very important later on.

In 1988, Dr. David Deamer, professor of chemistry and biochemistry at the University of California, made another chance discovery. Collaborating on a science-meets-art project, Dr. Deamer attempted to find the vibrational frequencies of four base DNA molecules. Cutting out all the technical science terms and bottom-lining the whole thing, it was basically found that the pitch that shows up the most frequently and "asserted itself as a tonic" was F-sharp—having been discovered three times in each base collection. It turned out that the frequencies in base DNA are harmonically ordered and perfectly in line with the frequency of the Earth—a secret we have only just discovered, and yet ancient peoples knew. It seems also that these particular frequencies turn out to be particularly pleasing to the ear, and indeed are thought to aid the healing process.

Now, did the ancients know of this correlation between harmonics, stones, the Earth, and even electromagnetism? Pythagorus gives us the answer from the 6th century before Christ. He described stones as "frozen music." His intuition apparently told him that the mathematics of frequency occurring in the planets, Earth, and other cycles, were in tune, and indeed told a story! At a basic level, our bodies understand this, and in the trance state, our minds do too. What the ancients did was

build structures that utilized the electromagnetic and harmonic effect, which work in unison with each other and us. They built in symbolism, power, and grandeur, but also the universal harmonic and paramagnetic power. They then ritualized the whole thing into great and magnificent stories and fables, and even developed religions accordingly—worldwide.

All of this wonderful balance came about simply because the universe is striving for order. Throughout billions of years the seemingly chaotic soup of the cosmos settled down into a wonderful equilibrium. Now, after millions of years of mankind attempting to understand this universal connectedness, we in the modern era have lost it. Instead, we have to rediscover it through hard rationalism and science—what we shall call our left brain. The question is, will we be able to experience it again, as our ancient ancestors once did? Only if we decide to use both sides of the brain in perfect balance will we fully begin to comprehend.

The Universal Frequency

According to scientists in the field of resonance, the fundamental aetheric (or Ryhsmonic) frequency of the universe is F-sharp, or 1.655×1043 Hz. As I have already shown, this is a key resonance. The same scientists tell us that "interaction" with this fundamental frequency under "resonance conditions" would result in the exchange of energy/information. But, more than this, tests appeared to indicate that subharmonic resonance with the frequency of 1.855 Hz (the Schumann frequency) actually resulted in the extraction of energy/information from the universe.[5] So interaction under the influence of F-sharp actually allows the transference of energy, not only between individuals, but also from the very universe itself. But where is this energy really coming from? And what influences are occurring?

Electromagnetic waves and particles, radio waves—or "energy" in short—are coming from every angle of the universe: from the sun, the stars, and even the moon. Much of this energy is millions, if not billions, of years old. It acts in ways that we are only just beginning to grasp—as was seen in the discovery of the neutrino. Throughout the course of millions of years, this constant interaction of energy particles/waves has plotted the course of human evolution. No wonder that ancient man believed his fate resided in the stars.

The question also now has to be asked, as radio waves carry information provided by the sender, do any of the waves transferring energy to us carry any kind of information that we are capable of receiving? The answer has to be yes. Of course the energy waves carry information: that of the universe from whence it came. The waves then impart this information genetically and psychologically into us. We have become balanced genetically with the resonance of the universe and should therefore be able to understand the information we are receiving—if not at a conscious level, then certainly at the "superconscious" level. This superconscious level is where we find the Otherworld, which is the place of knowledge to the ancients. This knowledge is from the very universe itself, and is profound to those who experience it, because

it is God to them. It is the universal bank of knowledge that is growing and expanding all the time and in every conceivable dimension.

The whole system—the Earth and its electromagnetic sphere, the universe and its dynamic energy, and us—all interplay in a harmony of operatic proportions. The cyclic nature of the universe as a whole has already been shown on numerous occasions to affect us as a species, as well as all of the other species living on the planet. Oysters open in harmony with the phases of the moon, regardless of their location. Humans are affected by 11.1-year cycles, causing upsurges in war and disharmony, following closely the solar flares of the sun. If this is not energy and information, being accepted and acted upon by the organic body, then what is it?

It is claimed that this huge amount of information is constantly bombarding the human biosphere, and that we react accordingly—as we should after millions of years of evolution with these affects causing reactions within us. Now, taking all of this information in for a moment, let's take a quick look at the human engine in relation to electromagnetic effects.

The electrical part of the human is the nervous system. It is this network of nerves that sends signals to and from the brain, and it is the brain that is the cognitive, functional part of the body. It is the brain that accesses the conscious, the subconscious, and even goes on to create the unconscious. According to Buddhist philosophies, nothing occurs in these realms without there being a cause, and we can see what that cause is. Consciousness had to have originated somewhere, and the nervous system

of the body is vertically arrayed to be in a perfect position (similar to the round towers) to act as antennae for the electromagnetism of the globe (and the universe). The body is the collector of the energy/information that the universe is sending, and sends the signals (or as we have seen, imparted energy) up to the brain via the vertically aligned nervous system—a perfect biomachine. This connection, because it utilizes the electrical energy of the body instead of the chemical connections, is instantaneous. The chemical connections are later altered according to the information being gathered.

Special methods used by the practitioners of trance states actually aid the receptive effect by reducing the wavelengths of the brain down to the alpha-theta hertz level, of which we shall learn more soon. For instance, the whole body is brought into rhythm with the universal frequency via breathing techniques utilized by most of the ancients. These meditation techniques can be seen in images of Cernunnos and the horned god, Buddha, and hundreds of other ancient deities seated in the lotus position. With each breath the electromagnetic field across the body is stimulated, modulating the transfer of signals continually up and down the spine to the brain—or so the theory suggests.

Certain drugs also affect this field. The use of drugs can cause a shift of phase in certain regions of the brain. Drugs may also shift the brain slightly out of phase with environmental wave energies. Some psychiatric drugs actually cause an individual who is normally out of phase to be more in phase with the environment. Therefore, it simply has to be the case that drugs temporarily shift phase within the brain to match or mismatch the wave/particle effects of the universe.

This interaction between the universe and humans is also affected strongly by gravity, which has been categorized as a wave/particle. This is seen on the larger scale also, for instance between the Earth and the sun. The changes in the magnetic field of the Earth of periods longer than decades are the result of changes of the Earth's core. The Earth's core is known now to change in correlation with the solar core—they therefore interact and influence each other, similar to entangled particles on the smallest level. If this is occurring on such a large scale with the force of gravity, then what effects are these forces having upon us?

These gravitational relationships between planets cause earthquakes, volcanic eruptions, and tsunamis. These seismic effects are similar to the effects caused in humans, with outbreaks of war, famine, disease, population migrations, and so on. But there are more subtle effects, caused by the constant stream of energy to and fro across the universe, and these cause smaller emotional traits within the conscious human being. Things such as the female association with the gravitational forces of the moon are an obvious example. It would seem from this information that "consciousness" is something that needs reappraising. We are conscious of our existence and the fact that we live, but we are not conscious of our greater role and place within a massive cosmic machine. Indeed, the "superconscious state" attained by the mystics, who claim to be in touch with the universe, and have done so for thousands of years, could easily be argued to be "true" consciousness.

This whole scenario is not just the domain of the researchers of the paranormal; instead it is being worked on by serious theoretical physicists.

Chapter 6
A Giant Leap for Humankind

I n the course of my extensive research, I have spent thousands and thousands of hours reading, traveling, and experiencing the wide variety of beliefs and cultures this world has to offer. But no books, ancient texts, or religious structures had prepared me for what I was now to uncover. What I will reveal here is of profound importance to humankind—both now and in the future. It is so profound that I needed to go through every element of quantum theory with a fine-tooth comb. The resulting headaches day after day were a testament to my hard labor—if I do say so myself (and I generally have to).

After consulting hundreds of books, dozens of scientists, and other interested parties, I will here try my absolute best to put across to the reader exactly what I discovered in as simple a format as possible. I feel that I need to begin this process by expanding the mind a little into areas that we would not normally wander. In order to help do this I decided to consult a paper that was presented to the United Nations in 1996 by Ingo Swann.

The paper was entitled "On-going Scientific Discovery of Sensory Receptors Which Account for Many Subtle Perceptions," and deals initially with the concept of modern Western science. Swann points out that our senses are limited to the five standard senses as taught in school. However, the whole purpose of the paper was to broaden this horizon and explain to the delegates that that was a false perception—there were in fact dozens of senses that science had discovered since the 1930s, and yet steadfastly refused to bring into balance with the psychic and religious understanding of these receptors.

Swann points out that for thousands of years the ancient Shaman, medicine man, or mystic, has believed in more than five human senses in relation to the earth and the universe around him, and that now *science* is the one catching up. This is something I have been pointing to extensively in this and other books, but in his paper Swann explains that there is now hard *scientific* evidence for the senses some would say are in the domain of para-science. Swann outlines five categories for these "new" senses as follows:

- Minute chemical receptors and sensors.
- Minute chemico-electro receptors and sensors.
- Neural-network exchanges of information in the bio-internal body substrates.
- Bio-electromagnetic information receptors and sensors.
- Bio-information transfer networks at the atomic, molecular, and neurological levels.

As Swann then points out, these can sound complex at first to the uninitiated, but taken simply they outline, even to the casual observer, that there are many more senses than the standard five we currently believe in. We have more senses than touch, smell, taste, sight, and sound. Our whole body is full of subtle sensors and "bio-information transfer networks"—which, simply put, means a method of dispersing the information around the body once received. We are a walking, talking, and communicating satellite dish that is far more complex and receptive than we ever imagined.

One of these categories in particular relates to our story here, and that is the existence within our bodies of minute physical and chemical bio-electromagnetic receptors that interact with the information-processing resources—spreading information around the body that the body is receiving. This information is constantly bombarding our bodies and being dispersed, but at what level is it being "understood"?

Well, the answer is simple: It is being understood at a conscious level. Take for instance the vomeronasal system (the nose), which picks up, at a bio-subliminal level, the minute chemical signals of another person. This system can easily detect pheromones and hormonal signals from another person and arouse, for instance, a sexual desire, which in turn emits a similar signal. We, as humans, are both aware of

this effect through becoming aroused and flushed, and yet unaware that we are immediately and effectively sending signals back.

This effect occurs on a chemical level, and the chemical is being dispatched via electromagnetic means, both internally and externally. I wondered whether there was any similar scientific evidence for external electromagnetic energy/information. Swann was already there with this one too, and goes on to explain that "scientists...have measured and begun to classify the brain's electrical activity outside of the scalp." I was amazed. Could there really be evidence of brain activity external to the brain? I read on and found that this has "led to discoveries that bio-electric activity extends... beyond the skin.... Now discovered bio-electromagnetic fields extending outside the scalp and outside the skin clearly equate to the 'auras' that many clairvoyants have specialised in 'seeing.'"

Preempting this discovery in 1977, Bob Becker in *Psychoenergetic Systems Vol. 2*, under a paper entitled "An Application of Direct Current Neural Systems to Psychic Phenomena," states, "The concept of a primitive electronic communication system in all living things can be a useful tool in understanding both 'normal' and 'paranormal' phenomena that have lacked a rational biological explanation. Indeed, it appears that human beings are tied to the universe in a web of electromagnetic energy."

So scientists themselves believe that the "universal" web of electromagnetic energy could explain many paranormal phenomena—that was a start at least.

Getting back to Swann's paper, he explains that the bottoms of our feet and hands have tiny receptors that can sense changes in magnetism. Of course, I have already stated on numerous occasions that I firmly believe that the ancients understood electromagnetism in their own way, and were not bound by the modern perceptions that this "power" or "energy" was weaker than the chemical "energy" of the bio-form—the two go hand-in-hand naturally. I have already stated that ancient structures were erected with electromagnetism in mind, and that feng shui and the serpent energy pathways of modern ley-line hunters are truly electromagnetic paths that people understood and had the receptors to be able to read. The fact that we have receptors in our hands and feet came as no surprise when I considered the methods used to discover these earth energies, which involve dowsing (standing on the ground and holding special rods as an antenna extension of the body to pick up the subtle energies), as we shall see in the next chapter.

But there is so much more.

Swann continues with a list of the senses and receptors, paraphrased as follows:

1. Receptors within the nasal system that are able to smell actual emotions, such as antagonism, sexual receptivity, and motives.
2. Ear sensors that can detect differences in pressure and electromagnetic frequencies.
3. Receptors on the skin detecting both balance and

imbalance of data external to the body itself.

4. Motion detection via skin receptors even when asleep.

5. Navigational abilities via the endocrine and neuropeptide systems.

6. Horizontal, vertical, and diagonal fluidic motion sensors as part of the whole body, including the hair.

7. Ability to recognize the temperament of other biological organisms via the skin.

8. Sound, heat, frequencies, and waves detected across great distances via a subliminal sensory system.

9. Ability to identify both positively and negatively charged particles at the atomic level.

10. Ability to convert mechanical, chemical, and electromagnetic energy into understandable nerve impulses.

11. Gravitational awareness sensors.

12. Senses within the brain able to modulate electrical information for biological storage in analog form.

13. Sensors in the retina able to pick up radiation, including X-rays, cosmic rays, infrared radiation, and ultraviolet light.

14. Sensors able to actually respond to external electrical fields.

15. Receptors in the skin able to perceive bonding and antagonism.

16. Nonverbal communication sensors (such as telepathy, now superseded or aided by the explanation of quantum entanglement).

17. Combined sensory system able to form meaning from more than 130 nonverbal gestures and 20 nonverbal messages.

18. Sensors that actually alert us to danger before it is directly seen or heard.

19. The ability to identify nonverbal emotional waves.

20. Anticipation and sensory cycle memory of light and dark, such as the sun and moon.

21. Sensors of solar and lunar cycles, solar flares, and lunar tidal flows (the ability to sense a coming storm).

22. The pineal gland as a nonvisual photoreceptor.

23. Ability to sense wave motions that are not visual.

24. Ability to sense oscillating patterns that are not visual.

25. Ability to sense magnetic fields.

26. Ability to sense infrared radiation.

27. Ability to sense electrical energy.
28. Ability to sense local and distant sources of heat.
29. Ability to sense geo-electromagnetic pulses and magnetic fields.
30. Ability to remote-sense almost anything at a distance (remote viewing, hearing, and tasting).
31. Whole-body receptors that can detect pheromones such as those of a sexual nature.

This amazing list of scientifically accepted receptors and sensors within (and without) the human body is quite remarkable, and links in with much of what the paranormal fraternity speaks of. We must always be cautious, though, as a substantial majority of these New Age mystical claims are simply false. We must also add now a growing scientific trend toward the idea of a sense of time, which is being shown to be more than simply a perception of the mind, but also a biological and evolutionary function—even so far as to the concept of an evolutionary internal device to enable mankind to predict the future.[1]

What we do have here is stark scientific reality, which appears to be verging on the world of the paranormal. In the world of the mystical etheric matter referred to in alchemy and Eastern mysticism as the "subtle matter," we have some explanation of what the ancients believed in. This etheric body was external to our own, and yet was our own. It is the aura spoken of by Swann, and is claimed to react to different frequencies of nature (because our energy is linked to that of our surroundings). In fact, where illness is present the frequency of the etheric body is said to change color. This has been shown in Kirlian photography, of which we will speak more soon.

The Nobel Prize-winning physicist David Bohm has actually presented some convincing scientific evidence for what he called the "implicate order" of the "holographic universe." This holographic universe is made up of this etheric body spoken of by Eastern mystics, and is something to which we shall return. Bohm believed that information was actually enfolded within the fabric of space and matter or energy. This actually agrees with Einstein's theory of $E=Mc^2$, whereby he proposed that energy was matter and vice versa.

In my researches, I found thousands of New Age practitioners of what is known as Vibrational Medicine, popularized a great deal by Dr. Richard Gerber in his book *Vibrational Medicine*. This "new" healing technique calls upon the ancient idea of the etheric body and the "subtle" vibrating energy that surrounds us, encapsulates us, and is indeed within us. This, surprisingly to many, actually relates to modern scientific discoveries as outlined in Swann's UN presentation—namely that we are receptors and sensors of this energy, and that it affects us in many ways. If we can indeed pick up this energy, then there is little wonder that it does make changes to our own bio-electromagnetic body—for good and bad.

The techniques used by these modern Vibrational Medicine practitioners were closely related to my research, so I decided to delve deeper.

Healthy Light

More than a thousand years ago Ja'far al-Sadiq, a Muslim scholar, teacher, and alchemist, stated, "There are some lights which, if thrown from a sick person to a healthy person, can possibly make that healthy person sick."

This was al-Sadiq's way of explaining Vibrational Medicine. Scientists today are admitting that it is theoretically possible for disease to occur at the cellular and bimolecular level, and it is this that affects the greater body. This insight, it is claimed, is based upon vibration or resonance which is termed in the world of the mystics and scientists alike as the life-force. These life-forces possess electromagnetic energy, which give them the vibration. It is this electromagnetism that al-Sadiq is talking about when he says "lights."

Now, according to many religions, the laying-on of hands to the head results in the healing process—which is now termed Vibrational Medicine. I had already seen that both the hands and feet were receptors and sensors of magnetism, but the hands are also strangely on the same frequency as the brain. In this respect I began to see how this subtle energy could have ramifications for the world's ancient religions. This laying-on of hands is normally part of a much wider ritual involving meditation or prayer, which has been found to turn negative frequencies into positive ones.

And this is interesting, especially because I had just read a paper by Dr. William H. Philpott entitled "The Value of Using Negative Magnetic Energy in Diabetes Mellitus," and which refers specifically to the use of magnetism in the healing of diabetes patients. To quote from the paper: "Specifically it is the energy of magnetism which makes biological responses possible.... It has been demonstrated conclusively that magnetism is two energies that have opposite biological effects when these energies are separated. It is the balance between these two energies that governs metabolism."

To Philpott, it is "critically important" that we come to an understanding of this magnetic phenomena, especially because, by using a negative magnetic field, he has controlled acid and inflammation.

Modern and ancient methods of healing involve certain tools, such as flowers, color and crystal therapy—and this is where I started to get excited, as it related entirely to my discovery.

As Dr. Philpott had discovered, magnetic energy can be a great healer. But with all due respect to the scientific community, this is something that the ancients across the world had *already* discovered—we just would not listen. So, I wondered, in what ways did the ancients, who seem to know things before we do, utilize magnetism or electromagnetism?

I contacted Kay Sturgis, who runs a healing and energy forum on the Internet called gridoflight.com, with a few questions. Firstly I asked about quartz crystal, for reasons that will become apparent. New Age healers claim that quartz crystal holds energy,

and therefore, they say, also information in a binary form. Was this true? I asked. *Yes, and more*, came the answer.

So, what about the New Age claim that this energy information can be tapped by psychics and scryers who are on the same resonance as the crystal? "Yes, and more," came the answer again.

Does the crystal hold energy that could be related to information? "Definitely."

Now it was getting strange. So I plucked up courage to ask, what kind of energy? "Anthropological, any consciously programmed information, records, etc."

Okay, I thought, one last question before they come to take me away. Would this information be as old as the crystal? "Yes, and there could be new programming as well."

Of course, Kay is on the "cutting edge" of New Age science, so I felt the need to consult some traditional experts in these particular fields.

Firstly I contacted Dr. Gebbie at the National Institute of Standards and Technology Laboratories in the United States, who was one of a small number of scientists willing to come anywhere near the subject matter. In the first instance I received a rather cryptic response to my questions about quartz crystal. "We cannot substantiate claims about quartz (or other) crystals that are made by others. The burden of proof for any extraordinary claims should, of course, fall on those who make them." Okay, so I took that as a "no comment" situation.

I asked further about the term *energy*, as it was increasingly being used in the same tone as *information*, and this was crucial to my thoughts. "Scientific terms such as *energy* may not mean the same thing when adopted by non-scientists." What was this? Another non-answer? "As a scientist, if someone put to me the proposition that crystals contain energy, my reaction would be sure, so what?" I felt as though I was hitting a nerve, having received quite a different reaction from a scientist—who is supposed to be open and objective—than from para-scientists (as I like to call them), who seem always eager to listen to new theories and relate their thoughts. Why would this be, I wondered, and assumed it was because science was today's religion, and must remain rigid.

So, I pushed again. "All matter contains energy, why should crystals be any different? I also know that within crystals (like all matter) there are negatively charged electrons and positively charged protons. Since a force of some sort keeps them apart, despite their natural tendencies to attract each other, I can attribute that to an internal energy (and one precisely described by quantum mechanics), as well."

So, eventually I had a little knowledge gained through hard effort. The force within the crystal is balanced by the energy—called a "force of some sort." I was amazed at the highly scientific explanations I got, and so moved on with my researches elsewhere.

I then bought a copy of *The Crystal Sun* by Robert Temple, which claimed to reveal an ancient and worldwide fascination with lenses. The book is well researched, and indeed it is a shame that archaeologists have ignored this erudite work, as I agree with Temple that the specimens he uncovered could indeed be lenses from antiquity.

Temple points out that "The ancient Greek Pythagoreans of the 5th century BC believed that the sun was a gigantic crystal ball larger than the earth, which gathered the ambient light of the surrounding cosmos and refracted it to earth, acting as a giant lens."

So, even if the sun is not really a giant crystal ball, the fact here is that in the 5th century BC, the Greek philosophers believed in and understood the use of crystal to *magnify* light. This in itself can prove that the ancients understood how crystals worked, and were therefore using them. Temple has uncovered hundreds of ancient lenses from around the world that are mislabeled in museum glass cases as "counters" or "pieces of glass." But, as Temple points out extensively, these "thunderstones" were an aid to meditative hallucinations and *a gateway to the enlightenment experience.*

The light from these crystals was indeed real, but it was more than that; it was also real on another level, in that crystals helped the adept generate an inner light, and this is the crux of my discovery here: Crystals across the world have been used by Shamans and others to induce or connect with the "Otherworld."

Temple also uncovered methods that the ancients have used to create these crystals: "I was able to demonstrate the existence and use of diamond-tip drills in Egypt, but they are so small they can easily be overlooked, just as the larger lenses always have been. I wanted to warn the diggers that those dirty little objects that might seem like tiny dark pebbles could be diamond drill tips. But alas, they still don't know."

I found this last statement startling—that there was ancient technology capable of cutting crystal similar to the technology utilized today. This in fact answered a problem I had discovered when investigating the crystal skulls of the world, and this is where the strange discovery I have been leading up to comes to the fore.

Crystal Skulls

In *The Mystery of the Crystal Skulls*, Chris Morton and Ceri Louise Thomas unravel the story of the crystal skull phenomena that mainstream science seems to ignore. The book is an excellent introduction into the world of crystal skulls, and should be a definite read for anyone interested in delving deeper.

At the beginning of the book we are introduced to what is known as the Mitchell-Hedges skull or "Skull of Doom." This is probably the most famous of all crystal skulls, and has been seen on numerous occasions on television and elsewhere. It is a clear quartz crystal skull, perfectly human in appearance, with two holes beneath it. It is made from one complete quartz crystal rock and has some peculiar properties. To quote from the book: "The prismatic qualities of the crystal are such that if the sun's rays are very strong and fall at a particular angle onto the back of the skull, they are focused and condensed and appear as a bright, sharp beam of light out of the skull's eyes, nose, and mouth." This statement rang a bell in my head—a distinctly irregular occurrence. The Shining Ones and serpent deities of the ancients

were all featured as having shining or bright eyes. Could this have been a coincidence?

In legend and myth these associations with bright eyes and even serpents eventually seems to have come through into Egypt as the uzait or uraeus snake, which adorned the brows of the pharaohs. The terms *uzait* or *uraeus* mean simply "the eye," and show the bright, swift, and powerful nature of the serpent energy. Similarly, in Europe, the infamous god Balder (Baldr) was said to be the most beautiful of gods. He was pure radiance and light—he shone. It was said that his snowy brow (the place where the Egyptian uraeus would be) "radiated beams of pure sunlight," which gladdened the hearts of men. Also, in Greece, Zeus, the greatest of gods, had shining eyes, which turned every way and dealt good fortune and bad—which turned out to be the heritage of the Mitchell-Hedges skull. In India, the son of Truth had shining eyes, as did both of the serpent-associated deities, Bacchus and Dionysus of the Romans and Greeks.

Back in Egypt again, we find that the father of all, Ptah, had shining eyes, as did Noah, and in Daniel we hear of "eyes as lamps of fire," just as in Revelation in which "his eyes were as a flame of fire." We find later on in folklore that many giants have shining or burning eyes, which relates perfectly, as I already knew these giants to be remnants of the Watchers from the Bible, who were the original Shining Ones.

So, in myth, legend, and fable, we can find all the relevant deities and characters with shining eyes. Could this similarity, across so many gods and right through to this crystal skull with its physical shining eyes, be a coincidence? I wanted to learn more, to see if there were further clues to the truth behind the crystal skulls, and if there was any relationship between the skull and the trance state of the shining experience.

The skull was said by the owner, Anna Mitchell-Hedges, to have come into her possession when she was on a dig with her father at Lubaantum in the 1920s and was therefore believed to be Mayan. There are many problems with the discovery though, and it has been claimed that the whole thing was a hoax. One of the other problems with the skull was that Hewlett-Packard (an independent company often called upon to perform tests because of its excellent laboratories) believed it would have taken 300 years to make the skull using conventional means. However, as with other skulls, it was tested by the British Museum, which found that it "must" be modern, as there were distinct diamond markings on the surface of the crystal. But, if Robert Temple is correct, and diamond drilling and shaping was possible in ancient times, then this whole area needs a serious new investigation.

In the myths of the Mayans, the Shaman, when coming to the end of his life, would need to pass on information to the next Shaman. In order to facilitate this, the aging Shaman would place his hand on the crystal skull and impart the energy-information into the skull—similar to the laying-on of hands. Next the new Shaman would follow suit, but this time "upload" the information directly through his hand into his brain. Strange, I thought, how the hand is on the same frequency as the brain.

In this way, the knowledge of the whole lineage of Shamans would be passed on via the skull, which itself is said to hold the knowledge of the universe, just as our para-scientist had suggested. All of this sounded too bizarre to be real, but I had already learned that the human body was highly capable of receiving huge amounts of information that we are not conscious of. And I had already learned that the universe sent out information all at the same time, everywhere. I also learned from Robert Temple that the ancients had understood about the magnification of energy—the same energy some believe to impart information. Could it be that this information is somehow held within the quartz crystal of this skull and others, and that it could somehow be extracted by a qualified adept? I needed to do more research, so I turned to the fringes of modern theoretical physics for answers.

Quantum Entanglement

Scientists in Beijing, the Hungarian Institute for Science, Stanford in the United States, and elsewhere, have been working on the quantum entanglement theory for some time. The Stanford Education Website (*plato.stanford.edu/entries/qt-entangle/*) gives us the following explanation of the theory: "Quantum entanglement is a physical resource, like energy, associated with the peculiar non-classical correlations that are possible between separated quantum systems. Entanglement can be measured, transformed, and purified. A pair of quantum systems in an entangled state can be used as a quantum information channel to perform computational and cryptographic tasks that are impossible for classical systems."

So, through quantum entanglement, which is "like energy," two separate systems can be measured, transformed, and even, similar to the ancient statements of mystics from across the world, be purified. It is a method of information exchange that is non-classical; that is, not as we generally understand.

In one scientific test, described by physicists Russel Targ and Hal Puthoff in their 1974 *Nature* article entitled "Information Transmission Under Conditions of Sensory Shielding," scientists put two people into separate rooms and connected them to a scientific apparatus, such as electrodes. One person is flashed 100 times with a bright light while the other person's reactions are being monitored. Amazingly, the initial results showed beyond doubt that the emotion of the flashing lights had transferred into the other chamber and into the mind of the second person.[2]

In 1965, two pairs of identical twins under observation were found to be quantum entangled too. As one twin closed his eyes the alpha waves in his brain were stimulated, and amazingly this same stimulation of the alpha waves was noted at exactly the same time in the opposite twin.[3] Scientists have said that the effect is brought about via quantum entanglement, and they are even now researching how this amazing particle effect can be used in communication devices and computers. It is a complex science, and it is something we shall return to in Chapter 13.

So, we know that, via the modern discovery of the perfectly scientific quantum entanglement theory, humans are capable of sending and receiving some form of information—human to human. Now with the added evidence of human sensors and receptors, crystal magnification, and the ordering of energy "information," it is starting to look perfectly possible. Added to this the evidence I discovered that crystals could actually hold energy and information, and that the resonant frequencies were similar to our own when in the trance state, I was slowly coming around, however nervously, to the idea that such information exchanging may indeed be possible.

The Mitchell-Hedges skull had been tested by the Hewlett-Packard company in the 1970s, and that test showed that the quartz of the skull was piezo-electric—the same kind of quartz used today in modern electronics and quantum computing. *Piezo* is a Greek word, which means "to squeeze," and *electrose* means simply "to get electricity from." Therefore, the term *piezo-electric* simply means that it will produce electric current if squeezed. This quality is due to the presence of silicon dioxide within the quartz crystal, which causes a negative and positive polarity, which, in the case of the Mitchell-Hedges skull, runs vertically like a battery, or indeed like our own spine. Applying electricity to such a substance actually makes it change shape. This made me ponder for some time the relevance of the two holes found beneath the skull, and whether these were some kind of battery antenna. Unfortunately, I got no further on this one.

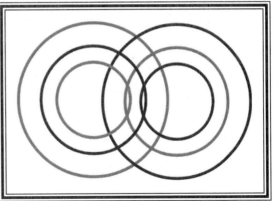

This is how a pair of entangled protons are depicted, like two merging water ringlets, or even the double circles that make up the Vesica Piscis.

Hewlett-Packard found that light entering the skull not only passes along the optical axis, but also rotates as it travels—like a serpent wrapped around a pole. This crystal skull was shown to hold an amazing electrical energy, but more than that, it actually controlled the oscillation at a constant frequency. Now, across the world, there are literally thousands if not millions of individuals who believe this skull to be a device to enter the Otherworld. A world occupied by the minds of the ancients, and therefore an ancient knowledge bank or a direct route to the infamous akashic records. Could this and other crystals be ancient computer-like storage devices, which utilize the natural electrical and magnetic energy within to store information that can be retrieved by the receptors that scientists are today admitting exist? Or even a route to revealing the source center we have been discussing? The chances seem to be stacking up in favor of either of these assumptions.

Another quote from Morton and Thomas's book is appropriate here:

...when we come into contact with a piezo-electric quartz crystal such as the crystal skull the electromagnetic energy waves we produce are received by the quartz. The crystal then starts oscillating and amplifying these signals and re-broadcasts them, in modified form, back out into the atmosphere, where they are picked up again by the cells of the body. In effect the quartz crystal modifies and amplifies our own electro-magnetic energy waves and relays them back to us. So, in the process, these waves of "energy information" become stronger and clearer. As we had just discovered, raw piezo-electric quartz is certainly renowned as a natural electronic oscillator, or resonator, or amplifier.

This oscillation or resonance is perfectly in tune with the frequencies of the human body, and indeed the earth, as I have discussed elsewhere in this book. It seems then that the knowledge of the ancients could very well be held within the ancient crystal artifacts of the globe, and all the time this knowledge is being ignored by modern science.

Science at least helps us to understand how this effect is possible. It seems that the now-infamous pineal gland is responsible for the receptive side of this amazing feat of nature, with its inbuilt magnetite (iron oxide). The pineal gland is responsible for location finding in birds, just as it is in humans. The magnetite in the gland picks up the subtle electromagnetic current of the earth, and gives the subconscious brain a location and bearing.

This links back to a peculiar practice archaeologists have discovered from Mesoamerica: purposeful shaping of human heads to affect a sloping brow by tying planks of wood to the head from birth. This has the effect of flattening out the pineal organ, making it even more receptive—similar to a satellite dish. No wonder that these strange-headed people from across the world were called Shining Ones and serpent deities—they were in fact in touch with the Otherworld or ancient knowledge system.

Today it is the psychic who claims to be able to connect to this ancient knowledge. I decided against going too in-depth here, as much in the realm of the psychic can be called circus trickery, and I could not entirely trust anyone's opinion on the subject. But what *is* amazing—and scientifically provable—is the fact that when an autopsy study was carried out on psychics and mystics, scientists discovered extra-large pineal organs!

There was simply no end of links and threads that I could have followed from this point. However, I decided that I would concentrate on one particular area, and found this yet again to be full of extraordinary wonders—the Great Pyramid.

The Great Pyramid

Right now, you are probably wondering how any of this can relate to the Great Pyramid in Giza. The truth is, I wondered the same thing, but as I researched the

whole aspect of the crystal issue, and the myths and history of the Great Pyramid, I was simply stunned by the links. I had already discovered that Giza was once known as "the gateway," and I was getting more excited by the minute as I unraveled the thread of this incredible ancient device.

Morton and Thomas had already pointed out in their book that the infamous Teotihuacan temple complex was built in the same layout as the Pyramid complex at Giza—the Orion correlation theory, in which two pyramids are in line with each other, next to a third slightly out of this line, just like Orion's Belt in the sky. Why exactly this should be seen in Egypt and South America nobody knows, but I am of the opinion and have stated that the ancient priesthood known as the Shining Ones were responsible for many of the similarities seen around the world. These same Shining Ones were the adepts of the trance, and it would be these same people who developed the use of crystals as an aid to gaining deeper knowledge through the bio-electromagnetic energy information system.

The Aztecs and Mayans, among others, believed strongly that the priests held their secrets "within the mountains," meaning pyramids, and of course the Otherworld womb, which is nothing other than the Otherworld itself. And so I decided that there simply must be something here worth investigating—as these were the very locations I was finding to be the Gateways to the Otherworld.

I noted how the word *pyramid* could actually mean "fire in the middle," or "fire mountain." This would be an allusion to the fire of trance that I believe was possible in the pyramid. In fact, what I was discovering was that the pyramid was a superconductor of electromagnetic energy, which synchronized with our human resonance and aided the oncoming of the trance state—it boosted the internal enlightenment. But what was different now was that it began to appear that the pyramid could also be a gateway to ancient information, held possibly in or found via the quartz crystal.

What brought on this strange idea, I hear you all ask? Above the King's Chamber in the Great Pyramid is a layer of granite blocks, brought hundreds of miles to this particular site. It is important to realize now that the majority of the pyramid is limestone.

Limestone is composed of calcium and magnesium carbonate. Calcium carbonate is electromagnetically anisotropic; in other words, it is an excellent receiver of electromagnetic waves. Strangely, it also becomes luminescent when rubbed, giving rise to the word *limelight*. The majority of granite is made up of quartz, which we have found to be piezo-electric, and is an excellent converter of electromagnetic waves. Basically, because of the placement of large granite blocks above the King's Chamber, I conjectured that the chamber was in fact a massive crystal-skull-type receiver, which could transmit information, given sufficient energy resources—such as loud noises.

This was just too much. The Great Pyramid as a crystal skull that could theoretically receive information? From where? I was obviously losing my mind. And yet, it is an established fact that pyramids and

temples in South America were fashioned to enable the carrying of sound waves. For instance, at Tulum in the Yucatan the temple gives a crystal-clear whistle or howl when the wind blows through it—a sound that is magnified. At Tikal the Mayan temple pyramid allows a clear projection of sound, as a speaker at the top of the pyramid can be heard for great distances. The same is true at various other temples. These sounds are waves, and structures have been created by these ancient people to carry these waves across long distances. Adding to that, these sound waves were more than just mere noise, but special, ritualized, and deeply religious sounds being carried across the expanse. Could it not be possible that they could have also created a device such as the Great (and notably central) Pyramid in Egypt to be a massive communication device of ritualized, internally esoteric, and religious information from the Otherworld? There will be more on this in Chapter 12.

There were yet more strange coincidences that I found regarding quartz and the pyramid. Quartz grows in a particular geometric pattern, as do all crystals. In this instance though, quartz grows in the form of a triangle or pyramid with an angle of 51.43°—*the same as the outer walls of the Great Pyramid!* Could this too be a coincidence? Or were the ancients matching the angles of this great communicating crystal? Amazingly, this very angle is a natural angle that can be created with the use of a circle and a line, as author Crichton Miller told me over lunch one day. This was the method used by architects of sacred geometrical buildings to square the circle, and it produced an almost 52° angle. I thought to myself, as I drank my orange juice, that this works beautifully on every level, and is mathematically perfect—direct from nature. Humans, it seems, discovered intuitively these wondrous natural mathematical phenomena, and made them real and physical. Surely, I thought to myself, if there were going to be any physical construction that would aid the quantum communication that we in the modern age have neglected, then it would have a magnificent mathematical pattern.

Quartz

Now I decided it was time to have a serious look at quartz, especially as it was cropping up so often in my research.

Quartz crystal begins its life deep within the earth from hot vapor, which is a supersaturated solution of silicon dioxide. As it cools, a unit cell of quartz forms around a nucleating site (seed) in the same way that an oyster forms. It is a matrix created around a seed point. The forming atoms and bonding are laid down where there is the most energy—the molecules adhering to the base silicon matrix. Made up as a tetrahedron-shaped molecule, it is now composed of four atoms of oxygen with one silicon atom suspended within. This primary cell unit now attracts other silicon dioxide molecules, and in time, trillions of these cells link together in a *spiraling motion*, layer upon layer until the crystal is made.

The crystal is a known quantum converter that is able to transmit energy in a magnified state, and this energy can easily be absorbed or received by biological matter—such as the human body.

So, in conclusion, the crystal is formed via a serpentine spiraling motion, and is a known quantum converter, transmitting energy-information at a magnified rate. Simply amazing.

So that was a little standard science behind quartz, and it was very revealing, but was there any more scientific information that related to my study? I asked around and was quickly put onto an article that appeared in *Nature* magazine in January 2002 by Philip Ball, entitled "Solid Stops Light." In this article, although not actually about quartz crystal, Ball shows how scientists had managed to bring light to a complete standstill inside a crystal. He said, "the trick could be used to store information in a quantum computer," and I thought immediately—yes, but a few thousand years later than the ancients seem to have done.

Quartz crystal is similar to that used by these scientists. It is made up of a latticework of silicon and oxygen atoms, which surround a relatively open space. It is this open space that can be compressed (squeezed) and expanded with certain stimuli. This same stimulus also makes the crystal vibrate, or "sing." These vibrations make waves, which human receptors pick up and convert back to binary information. This means that vibratory information or energy of different frequencies can be stored (as did the light that came to a standstill) inside the empty space. These crystals do much more though—they also amplify the energy the way temples magnify sound. By moving them, applying pressure or other stimuli (such as touch), these crystals can be forced to offer up their information energy (or possibly that of the holographic universe to which we have shown all things are connected, including the wave-particles within the crystal).

Marcel Vogel, a scientist working on computer chips, noticed that, while observing certain liquid crystals through a high-powered microscope, when he projected certain thoughts into the liquid, just before it turned to solid it would shape itself into the approximate *shape of his visualized thoughts!* Indeed, he has even stated his belief that these quartz chips can be programmed by the mind alone—as in fact, thoughts are simple energy waves in themselves. If these crystals could read the mind of a scientist in such a way, surely they can also read the mind of one who was an adept, and who had a large or malformed pineal organ, such as those "serpent" people of South America, Malta, and elsewhere. The difficulty for ordinary people, we are told, is that we cannot focus sufficiently well or long enough. Western metaphysical beliefs actually state that when the thalamus gland is stimulated, the subconscious seems to yield more information, and according to many psychics, it is with the aid of the crystal—or indeed the magnifying effect of the pyramid, which makes it possible for this energy information to be picked up by ordinary people. I doubt this, however, and am still firmly of the opinion that if this information was being picked up, then these tools—the pyramid and the crystal— were there simply for the adepts who had already trained extensively for the process. At least that is what history tells us. This history relates to us that crystals are to be found in the correct context in alchemy, Witchcraft, and general magic, as well as being discovered at various prehistoric sites around the world in ritualistic locations or contexts.

Kirlian Photography

Kirlian photography measures electromagnetic energy emitted by a given body, and through it, alternative medical practitioners are able to "see" negative points in the body that need healing. These negatives come up as different colors on the photograph, and the practitioner can then use crystals or other tools to balance out the energy—at least that's the claim. It has, goes the claim, been an extremely effective tool in the medical armory, even though orthodox medicine derides its use. Some doctors even within the orthodox world, however, do sign up to its methods, while other practitioners are simply enthusiastic individuals who recognize its importance.

One day, when using video Kirlian photography on a female patient who was holding a crystal, Harry Oldfield, a teacher in Middlesex, England, later noticed a white serpent shape emerging from the crystal. Although Oldfield insists on calling this peculiar phenomena, of which he has many images now, an *entity*, it may be that this is purely the serpentine energy wave of electromagnetism, seen here visually, just as the Shamans of the world claim to be able to see it. Another interesting effect of holding a crystal while using Kirlian photography is that the "subtle energy field" of the body is *doubled*.

The power of quartz is not entirely understood even now, but there are many that are championing its cause. One of these is Dr. Richard Gerber, who has written an international best-seller on the subject of healing called *Vibrational Medicine*. In it, he says, "When one uses quartz crystal to heal the body, energy transference occurs partly because of a resonance effect between the quartz crystal and those cellular crystal systems with quartz-like properties." Again, it is the frequency synchronicity that is required for healing to come about, and I would suggest the same thing in relation to "transference of information." But is this believed by anybody in the scientific community, as I tried to discover at the beginning of this chapter?

Gary E.R. Schwartz, PhD, and professor of psychology at the University of Arizona, has said, "Do [crystals], as quantum physics tells us, vibrate and resonate with the info-energy around them? If we envision them to be dynamical systems, the possibility arises that they do."[4]

Another interesting statement comes from the author Dr. Kahili King: "Where attention goes, energy flows," which I found to be rather telling in this respect.[5]

Marcel Vogel, whom I mentioned earlier, also found that crystals affected the molecular structure of water. If we ponder further we find that more than 70 percent of our own body is made up of water, and so crystals could indeed have an even more profound effect upon our body than previously thought. If we also take into consideration that some believe the coffer in the Great Pyramid was a flotation tank, or that the chambers above created by the granite

blocks contained water, then we can see how an extra magnification effect may have been taking place. It seems the beauty of the crystal is in its innate regulatory effects and ability to hold information in order. This order is thought to aid the balancing of the human "subtle energy," collecting the energy and magnifying it back in a *balanced state*.

In fact, the earth is thought to be made up of 40 percent quartz crystal, and may be an aid to the thermodynamic balance we sustain on the macro scale. In line with this thought, my mind turned back to the Great Pyramid and the fact that it has all of these fundamental constituent parts. What claims had been made for its use, I wondered. And which of them could now be possibly true in light of this collection of evidence?

Delving deeper into the shape of the pyramid, I scoured the Internet searching for wild and weird opinions, and came up with the following list:

- *Pyramids aid concentration.* Well, this could be simply the effect of sitting quietly inside a pyramid, or it could be the balancing effect of the crystal and the electromagnetic field created by the shape.

- *Pyramids heighten the charge of psychic energy.* This again could be purely in the mind, or it could be true.

- *Pyramids sharpen razors and blunt instruments.* This, amazingly, has been proven scientifically, and is an effect caused by the electromagnetic field—surely then this must have an effect upon us.

- *Pyramids purify water.* Again, scientific testing has shown this to be true, and is again down to the electromagnetic effect. If so, then as beings made up of 70 percent water, we must ask the question—are we purified too? Is this the "pure place" spoken of in ancient Sumerian literature?

- *Pyramids mummify dead animals and humans.* Again scientifically proven—in grade school classrooms, no less, where teachers demonstrate the way the shape of a pyramid forces "damp air" out to "mummify" fruit.

- *Pyramids help keep milk fresh without the use of a refrigerator.* Amazing result—in fact some milk manufacturers in France are even putting milk in pyramid containers because of this effect.

- *Pyramids increase the growth rate of plants.* Because of the electromagnetic qualities of pyramids, this works the same way that electromagnetically charged rocks have been proven to aid the healthy and speedy growth of plants.

❧ *Pyramids promote the healing of cuts and bruises.* Again, scientifically proven, and similar to the milk and plant growth, is due to boosted and balanced electromagnetic energy.

There certainly was more to all of this than first met the eye. But then I remembered something I had learned before. There is an ancient Hindu structural design dating back to 3000 BC, supposedly before the building of the Great Pyramid, called the Sri Yantra. This amazing image is both 2-dimensional and 3-dimensional, and can be a drawn mandala, or a building. It incorporates just about every geometric pattern possible, but most amazing is the fact that the base angle of the Sri Yantra is 51.5032°—virtually the same as the Great Pyramid and the triangular structure of the quartz crystal.

The idea of the Sri Yantra is to balance and clear the negative energy that is in us and around us, whether we meditate upon the form or actually stand within it. The term simply means "wealth bringer," and is a reference to the fact that in China and India it was used by the elite to bring good luck and prosperity, and is also linked to the goddess Laxmi, who is also the goddess of wealth. Today, Sri Yantras are reproduced in quartz crystal, as it is believed that this doubles the power of the shape and the crystal—obviosly nobody has yet scientifically tested the results.

I had learned a lot, and had my own mind expanded in the course of this research—to a point that I hadn't thought possible. The research answered many questions, and raised even more. Was it really possible for the mind to communicate with the tools of the crystal and the pyramid? What else did the ancients really know? And how did they discover the secrets? Some questions I believe may never be answered, but one thing is certain: The ancients understood the subtle energy of electromagnetism and its effects upon the human body. They understood that they could use these natural tools to communicate information and to heal the sick. They understood and were closer to nature than we can possibly imagine. We should therefore give them the respect their ancient knowledge deserves, and not close our orthodox eyes to the possibilities that are now open to us.

Chapter 7
Ancient Scientists

n my search for the ancient Gateways I came across numerous groups, cults, and religions. In ancient Sumeria I came across the Egregor, or Watchers, who are thought to be the angels of the Lord from the Bible. Enoch wrote about them, and theoretically *for them*, in the book of Enoch, which was later to be suppressed by the zealous Christian authorities.

In the Bible and elsewhere these enigmatic characters have been called giants or men of renown. I already knew that I would find stories of giants around the world in myth and folklore, and I felt that I didn't need to repeat the whole history here again. It was the Shining Ones, or serpent worshipers, who had literally spread themselves across the world, split apart by modern interpretations and hidden from our eyes as Shamans, priests, witch doctors, and medicine men. I believed that if I could find the giants of old, then I would find the remnants of the Watchers, and they would guide me to the Gateways they built.

Much of the biblical writing concerning these giants speaks of antediluvian times—the time before the great deluge. I read from these same tales from

Christ in glory emerging from a Vesica Piscis; from the Otherworld,
in Southwell Minster, England.

Mesopotamia and the Book of Enoch that they were the result of a war in heaven caused by a union between the Watchers, or giants, and the women of earth. It seems that these Watchers or Shining Ones survived the flood and went on to spawn civilization as we know it today. Whether this was a real flood or some esoteric language describing the survival of the initiation into the mysteries did not matter at this point.

I now wondered how these ancient stories of Watchers and giants had spread into Egypt, and I found initially that the Ta Neter, the land where the gods were said to have come from, meant also "Land of the Watchers," so they had come from

the same place. The gods in Egypt, it seems, were called Ntr, or Watchers, and this included the great father Ptah, whose name I then found actually meant "he who fashioned things by carving and opening up." This links Ptah to the "builders" side of the Watcher elite, the same as those who "went North," according to Enoch, "in order to measure." This is also the same as the Mesoamerican Votan, who is fabled to have built the first city, and was indeed seen as a serpent. Votan is recorded in the *Legend of Votan* as being a guardian or *watcher* of the race of Can—the serpents. Here though, Ptah is "opening up," and this is an indication of the earth or rock being opened—making caves. This would become extremely important in my search for the Gateways to the Otherworld.

Another term the Egyptians gave to the Watchers was Urshu, and they were said to be the intermediaries of the gods—just as they were in Sumeria. This is an indication of the ability to talk to the spirits on the other side.

The Egyptian Book of the Dead asked, "Who are these Watchers? They are Anubis and Horus in the form of Horus the sightless.... Matchet, who is among them in the House of Osiris. He shooteth forth rays of light from his eye, being himself invisible; and he goeth round about heaven robed in flames which come from his mouth...."[1]

Amazingly, this light coming from the eyes and mouth is the same as that of the original serpent Shining Ones of Sumeria, and the giant Cyclops, among others. It is also the same as that of the crystal skull, and furthermore, skulls are symbols of caves—and vice versa. The fact that Matchet was

"invisible" could also relate perfectly to a *clear* crystal skull. I also found that the Egyptians said that the Watchers had come from Ta-Ur or Ur, and we have already noted how Abraham had learned his trade in Ur, and is intimately connected to the tale of the Shining Ones and Horus. It seems from even a short biblical and Middle Eastern study that various tribes or nations had indeed emerged from these early Watchers, and they were linked to the shining enlightenment, caves, and building.

In Europe there are literally hundreds of tales of giants, and most are similar to each other—showing a common origin. In Ireland, for instance, and elsewhere, we have the giants purportedly building the Giant's Causeway out to sea and to their underwater or *cave* realms—both indications of the Gateway.

In England, some myths have giants as the descendants of the 33 daughters of the emperor Diocletian (who was a great builder) who murdered their husbands and were set adrift in a ship that eventually reached England. I had to laugh at the obvious Masonic allusions within this tale—with 33 degrees in the Craft, murdered husbands, and Diocletian being a "great builder"—all possibly predating the Masonic texts, but certainly influencing them or derived from the same root source. Was this the influence of the "giants" of old acting upon modern secret societies?

Across Scotland there were various groups of giants, one of them the Formorians, who lived in the highlands and have a name similar to the Fomorians of Ireland—where we found the round towers. Indeed, it is believed by some that the Formorians and Fomorians are the same group of people, who escaped Ireland for Scotland—bringing their tales of giants with them.

The Fomorians were a race of fabled giants who occupied Ireland in ancient times (the dates are unspecific, as we are talking about myth). They were not the first people there, however, and had to do battle with the native inhabitants—the Partholons—to claim the land. Following the Fomorians came the Nemeds, who were easily beaten and enslaved by the Fomorians.

Next came the Firbolg, who were more successful and actually subdued the Fomorians, going on to eventually live peacefully with them. However, the peace was shattered when along came the Tuatha De Danaan, the people of the goddess Danu, or Shining Ones (related to An or Anu, the original father god of Sumeria). They for some reason chose to pick a fight with the Firbolg, dealing out land and privileges to the Fomorians. The Tuatha De Danaan even intermarried with the Fomoriansin a tale similar to the fallen Watchers of Sumeria.

There can be only one reason that this later wave of Shining Ones, under the title Tuatha De Danaan, were more lenient on the Fomorians than the Firbolg, and that is that they already knew each other as Watchers and gods of ancient Sumerian myth—it is possible that the Firbolg were even fallen Watchers.

In Basque mythology, the giants were responsible for the making of dolmens and menhirs—the burial mounds of Neolithic peoples across Europe—and this was one particular area that I decided needed further investigation: the role of the Watchers in the stone monuments of Europe. It is a common folktale across the whole of Europe that these ancient stone monuments were built by giants or *fairies*—a term also related in etymology to "shining." I found the most amazing to be those surrounding Stonehenge in England.

Stonehenge

The earliest recorded legendary history of Stonehenge comes from Geoffrey of Monmouth's *History of the Kings of Britain* (1136). We cannot, as some scholars have pointed out, take this text as a literal historical document any more than we can take the myths of Arthur, but we can read the symbolic element that Geoffrey included.

The story goes that Aurelius Ambrosius, king of the Britons, wanted a monument built to commemorate the slaying of 460 British nobles by the troops of Hengist the Saxon. Aurelius summoned the magician or Druid, Merlin, who gave the following advice:

If you want to grace the burial place of these men with a work that shall endure for ever, send for the Giant's Dance that is on Killare, a mountain in Ireland. For a structure of stones is there that none of this age could erect, unless he combined great skill and artistry. For the stones are big, nor is there a stone anywhere of more virtue; and, so they be set up, there shall they stand for ever. Giants of old did carry them from the farthest ends of Africa, and did set them up in Ireland when they lived there.

Firstly, many have claimed "Killare" to be Kildaire, or other such places. This does not entirely matter—spelling in the 12th century was not any better than it is today. What is of great interest, however, is the idea that the stones came from Ireland, even though it is now known that they came from Prescelly in Wales. Ireland has been the home of so much that revolves around the story of the Shining Ones, from snakes to giants. A lot of this is due to the untouched nature of its traditions and folklores, whereas a place such as England has adapted, evolved, and been manipulated and cajoled by every invader who has darkened its shores.

Secondly, if Ireland was chosen for its seeming mystery and connection to the ancients, then what is most interesting is the idea that the stones originated in Africa and that they were brought to Ireland by giants. Africa is the home of ancient Sumeria and the Shining Ones—and has thousands of stone circles and monuments, many said to have been built by the age-old giants. The giants are the Watchers who brought the great knowledge of building and measurements with them. In a Welsh version of Geoffrey's tale we find that this elusive Killare is called Mount Kilara, and the circle is the Giant's Circle.

There are similar tales across the world, in which giants are associated with megalithic monuments. One of the oldest is Ggantija on Malta, which means, "belonging

Mary crushes the chaotic serpent underfoot, in Rome.

to giants," or "tower of giants." Indeed, legend states that Malta was once inhabited by serpents, as was Ireland, which links it to the serpentine Shining Ones and many towers.

Christopher Knight and Robert Lomas point out in *Uriel's Machine* that the Watchers used the network of megalithic monuments as a kind of worldwide calendar. In Andrew Collins's work *From the Ashes of Angels*, and again in *Gods of Eden*, he points out much the same thing, with an awful lot of background work. Christian O'Brien also delves deeply into the subject in *The Megathlithic Odyssey*, and I would say that a good read of all these books would serve the serious researcher well.

The shining elite spread their worship across the planet, from Sumeria and Mesopotamia to Europe and America, and left behind symbolic religious language that has baffled historians ever since. The truth is that for thousands of years the Shining Ones have worshiped the light within themselves and the sun in the sky as if it were God, and have spread this idea of illumination wherever they went.

And wherever they went, they somehow managed to find specific locations to build their great monuments, which had various kinds of geomagnetic or telluric energy. Science is now, ever so slowly, coming around to the conclusion that ancient man may very well have located his structures on special "energy" centers.

Thousands of sites have been tested and shown by hundreds of disparate researchers to actually have peculiar electromagnetic radiation, to have been built on top of underground streams that alter the energy flow of the Earth's magnetic energy, to have been founded on areas of tectonic plate movement, to be on top of underground caves, and much more.

In *Twelve-Tribe Nations and the Science of Enchanting the Landscape*, authors John Michell and Christine Rhone point out:

The first requirement of a ruling priesthood is to locate and occupy the naturally powerful centres of spiritual energy in the landscape. This involves the use of geomancy, meaning divination through the earth or earth magic. Through geomancy are discovered the most effective sites

and designs for temples in relation to the spiritual energy field of the country as a whole. The many sciences, which contribute to geomancy, include astronomy and geology, for temples should be sited at natural meeting-places between the powers of heaven and earth. This principle is now recognised by archaeologists, who have discovered in recent years that temples and old stone monuments in all countries are related to their surroundings in two ways, astronomically and geologically.

To add to this I would say that man also included a sacred geometry for the buildings in question—a sacred pattern and structure, a sacred building material (mainly granite, which includes quartz), which drew on the energies they had located. These centers were called omphalos.

The superstition of the omphalos was as widespread as the serpent belief systems from India to Greece. It is a boss or orb with spiral lines of energy or waves thought to represent coiled serpents. There are similar markings on ancient stone monuments across the world—especially at Newgrange in Ireland. Roman author Quintus Curtius also pointed out that in Africa there were such stones with spiral lines drawn, said to be a symbol of the serpent deity.

To the Etruscans the omphalos was seen as a route to the Underworld. It was placed in a trench called a mundus, and the first fruits were offered into the trench, which was then covered by a huge stone. The entire city was centered on this spot, with all roads leading to and from it. It was a very special location in an age when the sacred was paramount.

Probably the most famous omphalos is the one now in the museum at Delphi. In Greek history the Delphic Oracle was called Pytho or Pythia (python/snake, and she was active for more than 1,000 years, getting involved in anything from mundane day-to-day prophecies to matters of state. Nobody really has any idea how the oracle managed to do her business. Some have suggested that volcanic vents issued hallucinogenic drugs up into the chamber, and some say that sacred mushrooms were used. One strange vase may give us the clue: A fourth-century Vulci cup shows King Aigeus before Pythia, who holds a bowl and stares intently into it. This is no vented drug or mushroom, this is the sacred cup of the Agathodaemon in another form—the prophetic snake yet again.

The snake has, throughout history, been associated with powers of "future sight"—known to us today as precognition. Around the decoration of this cup are the familiar spirals of the snake, and Pythia herself is seated upon the tripod, sacred to the sight. Another indication that the serpent is associated strongly with prophecy is the stark fact that the words for "divination" in Hebrew, Arabic, and Greek all mean "serpent" also. This alone indicates that Hebrew, Arabic, and Greek are following the same beliefs, throughout a vast period of time.

When speaking of the great Christian buildings, however, which overlaid the pre-existing Pagan structures such as stone circles, author Nigel Pennick in *Sacred Geometry: Symbolism and Purpose in Religious Structures*, points out the reason for the location of the center point:

It is based upon the central omphalos, the point at the crossing over of the main tower and spire would stand. This very centre, the overlapping point of the three squares representing the fusion of the trinity, often marked a powerful geomantic center. This is discernible by dowsers in the form of a powerful blind spring with its associated spirals. Such a geomantic omphalos exists at Salisbury Cathedral, which has the tallest spire in England and marks the spot on a ley line from Stonehenge to Frankenbury.

Pennick points out that Louis Charpentier made a suggestion that it was possible for the ancient standing stones to be absorbing cosmic and telluric energy, used by our ancestors as instruments of vibration. If these stones were instruments, then, he claimed, they could accumulate and even amplify the vibrations something similar to a drum. The Christians later took this a step further and developed stone walls and vaulted cathedrals. Pennick states that if the geometry of the stone circles was actually dependent on the wavelength of the earth energies, then it follows that the geometry of a vast building or structure would actually act as a channel, resonating with the trapped energies within. Legends of dragon-slaying surrounding many of these sites could therefore be tales of fixing the serpent or dragon energy in these specific locations, which almost always have tales of great solar heroes doing battle with dragons. Pennick believes that this is an indication that the earth energy is

Mary, in perfect balance, and emerging from the portal of the Vesica
Piscis in Kykoss Monastery, Cyprus.

being anchored in specific locations for use by our ancient priesthoods.

Pennick also states that cathedrals and churches were built using the natural geometrical patterns and ratios of the Earth, and were therefore perfect conductors. The wavelengths of telluric earth energy are fixed by occult methods and enshrined forever in unchangeable sacred measures. He points out that even the Benedictines used these forces as a means of enhancing physical sounds, such as Gregorian chant. Such uses aided the process of attaining a higher consciousness.

So, the information and knowledge developed by the ancients did not end when Christianity erupted upon the world—it continued. It continued for a purpose, to

bring on altered states of consciousness, to contact the deity. No wonder that the cathedrals of the globe have images of the Vesica Piscis, which is the Christian symbol of the Gateway. They were opening up the path to heaven.

In *Myths and Legends of the Celtic Race*, author and historian T.W. Rolleston pointed out that, "Very soon after the conversion of Ireland to Christianity, we find the country covered with monasteries, whose complete organisation seems to indicate that they were really Druidic colleges transformed en masse." So Christianity overlaid the preexisting Pagan sites, and in fact fit in so well that we are left to wonder whether there really was any difference between them. This is why burial mounds and remnants of megalithic structures are found in ancient churchyards across Europe.

Barry Dunford, in *The Holy Land of Scotland: Jesus in Scotland and the Gospel of the Grail*, states:

The megalithic tradition in the British Isles can apparently be traced back to at least 3000 BC, if not earlier. This tradition seems to have been based on a very sophisticated philosophy of sacred science such as was taught centuries later by the Pythagorean School. This ancient sacred science revolved around an awareness of the microcosmic energy systems of the earth being interconnected to a vast macrocosmic stellar matrix encompassing the heavenly firmament. This is clearly portrayed by the geomantic and astrological alignments of numerous megalithic stone circles and other ancient sites throughout the world.

We also get another insight into the astronomical alignments of these ancient Gateways from an early 19th-century book by the Reverend Edward Davies entitled *The Mythology and Rites of the British Druids*. When speaking of Stonehenge, Davies says:

...In the first place it is circular, as it is there proved, all ancient temples to the Sun and Vesta were. In the second place, the Adytum or Sanctum Sanctorum, is of an oval form, representing the Mundane Egg, after the manner that all those adyta, in which the sacred fire perpetually blazed, were constantly fabricated. In the third place the situation is fixed astronomically, as we shall make fully evident when we come to speak of Avebury: the grand entrances, both of this temple, and that superb monument of antiquity, being placed exactly North-east, as all the gates or portals of the ancient caverns, and cavern temples were; especially those dedicated to Mithra, that is, the Sun.

So, the circle was symbolic of the sun, which is manifested in the sky as the golden orb—the "as above, so below." Also, the circle has come down to us in our numerals as nothing, zero, void. It is also none, related to the word *nun*, which to the Egyptians was the cosmic ocean—the Waters of Nun. These waters were the Gateway (as water is often seen as such), and any who passed between must therefore have been "fish." This explains why many ancient deities were seen as fish or serpentine spirits, such as Jesus, who was the Hebrew *nun*, which means "fish," and

Vishnu (*fish*nu). We now have a clear explanation as to why "walking on water" was so important, because this revealed the true adept that could walk between the worlds without fear.

This oval is the Mundane Egg from which new life is born, and is a symbol of the Ru or Gateway seen in the Christian Vesica Piscis. This almond shape is the same as that from which Jesus and Mary emerge; and the orientation of sun temples is northeast—along the energy lines.

But there is more to the symbol of the circle than just the mere sun, which would make sense if the sun spoken of in ancient texts were really an inner sun also. In the *History of Initiation* (1841), the Reverend George Oliver says:

The places of initiation and worship were generally either circular, because a circle was a significant emblem of the universe, governed and preserved by an omnipresent deity, who is described in the writings of Hermes Trismegistus, as a circle whose centre is everywhere, and whose circumference is nowhere; and pointed out the unity of the godhead; a doctrine distinctly asserted by the druids; or oval, in allusion to the Mundane Egg; though the instances of this form are of rare occurrence, the adytum being more frequently oviform than the temple; or serpentine, because the serpent was the symbol of the deity, who was no other than the diluvian patriarch Noah, consecrated by the druids under the name of Hu; and the common emblem of a serpent entwining himself over an egg, was intended to represent Hu preserved in the ark; or

winged, to figure the motion of the divine spirit; or cruciform, because a cross was the symbol of regeneration and life.

So, not only is the circle more than the sun, it is also the universe whose circumference is "nowhere" and yet "everywhere." It is linked here by Oliver as being for the deity of the serpent, who is Noah in the ark, just as Aaron's rod is in the Ark of the Covenant, and is the rod that turns into a serpent. The two stories of the ark, both the boat and the one in the tabernacle, are the same, and both point toward the union of the opposite energies and the link between man and the earth (which, when out of phase, causes big problems—such as the flood). This is why the Ark of the Covenant is a deal between us and the deity of the Otherworld. The tabernacle, which held the sacred Ark, was a mobile device, connecting man to the Otherworld.

Paul Devereux, in his book *Places of Power: Measuring the Secret Energy of Ancient Sites*, tells us more:

The ancient sites of power were sometimes found and sometimes deliberately constructed to mimic or enhance what could be found in nature. In either case, the forces of the natural world were used. And they were used for a variety of purposes, such as the promotion of fertility and for healing. But the overriding purpose was the need to have gateways through which contact with the spirit could be achieved. In the ancient world there were certain people who knew how to work with the physical world in order to create access to the spiritual.

The Masons of Lichfield build their superstructure Gateway,
in Lichfield Cathedral, England.

I had to ask the question: How on earth did ancient man, without being able to resort to modern electronic technology, discover these holy locations? There can be only one answer. But within that answer lies a great many problems, as I was about to discover.

Dowsing

There had to be a tool utilized to discover these electromagnetic signatures, which were used by these "giants" who seemed to have been the planning agents of the ancient world. I pointed out in a previous chapter how thousands of images of ancient deities were seen holding serpents: the Minoan snake goddess, who holds aloft two squirming snakes in either hand; the Long Man of Wilmington; thousands of images of Hathor from ancient Egypt, and many more. There are also long winding wands of a serpentine nature discovered across the world on many sites, which are always classified as "religious implements"—a phrase often used for "we don't know."

In the relationship I am now stating between the access to the Otherworld and that of the religious trance experience—the shining—these artifacts and images must simply be pointing toward the diviners or dowsing rod. These are the rods that Enoch mentions, which have baffled historians for centuries—these serpents of the Minoan goddess are symbolic representations of the electromagnetic wave that the ancients perceived as serpent energy. I know they perceived sound as a serpent wave, as sound creates a wave in sand, and sand has been found in the stone bowls at Knowth where the shapes created were mimicked on the rock art surrounding the whole area as waves, spirals, and snakes. I also know that sound—termed often as *wind* or *logos*—was seen as the physically heard element of the presence in this world of the spirits from the Otherworld ("and the word was manifest"). It is now only a minor step to understand that this electromagnetic energy, which was a catalyst to the Otherworld experience, was seen as the spirit of the great serpent. It was also the creative "spark" seen by Kabbalists as bringing life to Adam, when God united with "Edem" or earth, thus giving the golem of Adam life (hence the "Let us make man" statement in Genesis 1:26). In this way, the energy to which we need to reattach in order to see the Otherworld is the same energy that gave us life in the first place.

The great serpent spirit was in fact also seen as light. It was the light of the Ophites' (serpent worshipers or Christian Gnostics) Sophia.

In a correspondence from a Major Menzies, who lived during the early 20th century, we can see how and where this "light" serpent is to be found.[2] The story goes that during the First World War, British Army Engineer and surveyor Major Menzies was interested in Chinese geomancy, and so made an effort to learn the art of feng shui (similar to our ley lines). He learned quickly how to use the Chinese geomancers' compass in relation to his British Army version, and actually discovered how to track down the earth energies. When he finally returned to England he carried on researching, and in the 1940s he came to Stanton Drew near Bristol. These various stone monuments date from at least 3000 BC and are thought to be associated with solar worship. In the text from George Sandwith, to whom Menzies related the story, we find this incredible experience:

Although the weather was dull there was no sign of a storm. Just at that moment when I was rechecking my bearing on one of the stones in that group, it was as if a powerful flash of lightning hit the stone, so the whole group was flood-lit, making them glow like molten gold in a furnace. Rooted to the spot—unable to move—I became profoundly awe-struck, as dazzling radiations from above, caused the whole group of stones to pulsate with energy in a way that was terrifying. Before my eyes, it seemed the stones were enveloped in a moving pillar of fire—radiating light without heat—writhing upwards towards the heavens: on the other hand it was descending in a vivid spiral effect of various shades of colour—earthward. In fact, the moving, flaring lights gyrating around the stones had joined the heavens with the earth.

What we have here are the same descriptions found in the Bible—descriptions that in fact depict the image of God as a pillar of fire. Descriptions similar to those of the Zoroastrian or Persian fire worshipers, who traveled from one sacred site to the next, worshiping the sacred fire and the altein (*al*="stone" and *teine*="fire") stones of Scotland and elsewhere.[3] So, this whole resonant, electromagnetic world of energies not only explains a "mental" effect that gives rise to the spiritual, but also manifests a physical effect, again giving rise to the concept of god in the mind of ancient man. This was where heaven indeed touched earth.

In *Phoenician Ireland*, Dr. J.L. Villanueva tells us more:

That the ancient Irish were worshippers of fire is a point upon which the antiquarians of the country are unanimous. The town of Uregare, in the barony of Coshma, and county Limerick, is obviously compounded of ur-egar, meaning, a shrine dedicated to fire; or else, of ur-egur, an altar consecrated to the same. Urglin, too, the name of a village in the barony of Catherlough, county Carlow, is made up of the words ur-glin, a manifestation or revelation of fire; or ur-galgin, fire in a round head of stone; for glin, in the Syriac, means heap of stones, as well as it did a manifestation; and galglin, rotundities or roundnesses. St. Jerome makes mention of this fire worship amongst the Chaldeans. The same is asserted by the ancients of the Medes, from whom this superstition was transferred to the Syrians, and from them again to other nations inhabiting Asia. In 1820 Henry de Loundres, archbishop of Dublin, put out this fire, called "inextinguishable,"—which had been preserved, though a remnant of the pagan idolatry of Baal—from the earliest times, by the nuns of St. Bridgid of Kildare. It was re-lighted, and continued to burn until the total suppression of monasteries; the ruins of the fire-house and nunnery still remain.

In the same text, we also learn that the Phoenicians termed their fire *cammia*, meaning "hidden." One thing is sure, if the ancients were truly worshiping the fire as the sun, then they would not associate the word *hidden* with it. This was the inner and therefore hidden sun, and now we know why it was also crossed and confused (by modern historians) as the serpent.

It makes perfect sense then to try and track down these serpent currents, these places of the serpent deity, with a serpent rod; and we see with the use of the Minoan snake goddess and her double serpents, the existence of archaeological evidence to back this up. But there are also textual evidences of similar tools, such as the great Rod of Aaron, which turned into a serpent as it struck the earth.

Therefore, by using the Rod of Aaron (caduceus staff, or wand of Merlin) to divine this great serpent spirit in the ground, the ancients were placing their markers or stone monuments on the entry points to the Otherworld of the serpent.

It is an amazing fact that this ancient dowsing practice is still alive today, and still misunderstood and victimized, just as it was

in the Bible and in later Christianity. In the 21st century, this practice is still relatively unknown for what it truly was. I myself had never tried it until meeting author Hamish Miller, who just happened to be a blacksmith. He made me a pair of dowsing rods with images of serpents, and I eagerly awaited their arrival. Then early one morning the postman brought a peculiarly shaped package, and I ripped it apart. Immediately I intuitively knew how to hold them, which shocked me. But the biggest shock came when the rods started moving, and I knew I was not the one consciously doing so. Even my children used them and found them to work!

An omphalos from Lagos, Portugal— the navel or center of the universe.

Modern dowsing techniques then seemed to be the answer to the question of how ancient man discovered the electromagnetic energies. But what I really wanted was scientific proof that dowsing worked and that these locations were really on energy sites.

It seemed to me initially that there was a lot of skepticism on the subject. But as I pressed on I discovered that this skepticism emerged from the various uses the process had been put to. For instance, some dowsers claim to be able to find energy through maps, and this has no scientific basis whatsoever. This, and other peculiar uses, seemed to have driven the practice into the world of the paranormal. Nevertheless there is a vast amount of scientific research that has been carried out on normal dowsing.

The history of dowsing is a long one, and not something I need to delve into too deeply. It has been around for an awfully long time, and many claim to have evidence of its use as far back as Egypt and Sumeria—which would relate well, and I agree with itentirely.

Commonly, the term *dowsing* is used to describe the practice of discovering underground water sources or lakes. There have been many reports on how it was believed the ancients used dowsing to build their sacred monuments. In the 1930s Captain Boothby wrote an article entitled "The Religion of the Stone Age," in which he described how water fissures and springs ran directly under tumuli (ancient graves) and other archaeological sites. Boothby believed that the layout of these ancient monuments depended upon underground water features. Many dowsers have since

shown Boothby to be correct—as far as dowsing is concerned. In 1939 another dowser and archaeologist, Reginald Alexander Smith, gave a lecture to the British Society of Dowsers on the matter, pointing out that in France it had been discovered that erect standing stones were situated upon intersections of underground streams. This is, I believe, the crossing of the opposite energies we have previously discussed, such as the crossing of the serpent on the caduceus. Smith also pointed out that tilted stones were specifically tilted toward these intersections, and that dolmens and other such features were in the corners or "waves" of the meandering stream.

Dowsing has also been used extensively for all manner of applications, such as determining the sex of an unborn child. This sounds completely mad, but as I was to discover, scientists had actually discovered that the sexes reacted differently to certain dowsing experiments and gave off different electromagnetic results.

The purpose for me was to discover whether dowsing really worked, and could therefore be a method of uncovering the subtle electromagnetic energies of the globe—and in fact even areas of extraterrestrial energy coalitions.

There seem to be certain main tools used. The Y-rod, the L-rod, the U-rod (all named for the letters their shapes represent), and a pendulum. I was also of the belief that a T-shaped rod was once used in the past. This would relate to the Tau cross, which itself was a symbol of "hidden treasure." However, what does make the shape of a T is almost esoteric in itself.

Most dowsers use two L-rods and sometimes these are held together in such a way that the two Ls form a T. It's a kind of bringing the opposites together in union! I did find that T-rods were used in the past, and they eventually morphed into the Y-rod. In the experiments I checked out the L-rod seemed to be more effective.

Hundreds of institutions and companies around the globe still utilize the dowser in their search for water, oil, and other hidden treasures. The U.S. Army Corps of Engineers has even hired dowsers for these very purposes, as did the U.S. Marine Corps, who used them during the Vietnam War. Even archaeologists are using dowsing rods to survey land quickly prior to excavation.[4]

There have been a few explanations for how the practice works: ESP (extrasensory perception), for instance, or even simple observation, whereby the dowser observes differences in the texture and color of the ground. The majority that I discovered however seem to veer toward the physiological reaction to radiation, such as electromagnetism.

In one experiment, William F. Barrett, professor of physics at the Royal College of Science in Dublin, hid a coin in a room full of 45 chairs, all in the absence of dowsers. A dowser was then asked in to find the coin. Five successive attempts were made by different dowers, and each time the coin was found on the first attempt. The mathematical probability of the chance occurrence of this was 80 million to 1. Basically, it was impossible to discover the coins first time every time by pure chance.

In 1939, J.C. Maby and T. Bedford Franklin in their book *The Physics of the Divining Rod* concluded that ordinary dowsing sprang from a special physiological faculty in humans, and this belief has been stated time and time again.

Professor of physics at the Ecole Normale in Paris, Yves Rocard studied the relationship between electromagnetism and dowsing, and revealed his discoveries in *Le Signal du Sourcier* back in the 1960s. What Rocard discovered and clarified were the minute levels of electromagnetic radiation that humans could actually pick up. These findings, along with those of others such as Dr. Zaboj V. Harvalik, show that the subtle electromagnetic radiation that is prevalent across the earth is easily, but probably unconsciously, received by the human body. By the use of rods, or "wands," as the ancients would have seen them, the human receptive machine transforms these signals into muscular movements, completely inadvertently and unconsciously. These are no different from the antennae of the round towers we saw in a previous chapter—in fact, it seems that these wands act as antennae on the human body.

Imagine this effect then, if the dowser was actually in a trance state, as we have been discussing. Imagine that this trance is a place lit by the electromagnetic universe, and that this Shamanic divination was tapping into another realm of vision—the dowser would become conscious of the visual element of the slithering energy snake. It is highly possible, given all that we have learned so far, for the ancient Shining One to have been more in tune with this resonance than we can possibly imagine, and to have visualized the world around him as full of serpent spirits, which throughout the course of thousands of years were classified into a whole pantheon of anthropomorphic gods.

This is the wonder of the Gateway to the Otherworld. It is an incredible world on our very doorsteps, which has been marginalized by the false rationalization of modern man. We have thrown the baby, and all of his brothers and sisters, out with the bath water.

❦❦❦

So, now I had the science of electromagnetism, the method of locating areas on the earth, which were aids to the mental electromagnetic process, and I also had our historical Shaman guide to help us find the Gateways of ancient man. It was now time to delve into the mind.

Chapter 8
Memory Man:
The Science of Enlightenment

It was a beautiful, sunny August morning. The sky was clear and blue, and with trepidation I set out at 5 a.m. to take the road south to meet up with a friend in London. Then it all turned bad. After only an hour the roads became congested. Accident after accident seemed to be happening on the busy motorway, slowing me down to a crawl. It was as though the whole motorized world was against me.

We had planned to meet up in a pub car park, and I knew that my friend would be waiting. To make matters worse, my mobile phone was not working, and I was dying to go to the toilet. Eventually, after battling through the wreckage-strewn motorway and utilizing a tree somewhere south of Watford, we met up an hour and a half late, just as clouds had moved in and it started to rain.

We were heading for the home of Dominic O'Brien, the world's eight-time memory champion and mind expert. O'Brien was pioneering a new method of balancing brain wave patterns in partnership with Henry Hopking, a speed-reading and creative-thinking expert and champion.

Dominic O'Brien, eight-time world memory champion and brain expert, who is pioneering the bineural beat technology for healing.

A week earlier, I had heard a radio program featuring O'Brien and his new research, which was now drawing the attention of academia, and decided to get in touch. Something about the research grabbed my attention, in relation to techniques I knew had been extremely old. I was of the opinion that Shamans also utilized the balancing of brain waves, but did it in a different way. Essentially, the Shamans of the past balanced the waves using entrainment, a process whereby the wave patterns in our brain match or copy externally produced wave patterns. Our brain waves can be entrained by such things as the banging of drums and the flickering of lights. Shamans used these techniques to entrain the brain to certain levels, which I will discuss later on.

Eventually we arrived at O'Brien's home in the heart of the beautiful West Sussex countryside, and over a few cups of coffee discussed his research and saw the amazing video evidence of his work. He had been using his "Brainwave Conditioning System" to cure all kinds of problems, from dyslexia to blepharospasm, a form of dystonia, which affects the eyelids. Spasms or clamping of the eyelids can render a person virtually blind, and stress or trauma can trigger the disease.

There is no known cure, and the orthodox medical world has had severe difficulty in dealing with it. One man whom O'Brien showed us had an issue such that his eyes would not blink. Instead the lids of his eyes, once closed, would stay closed. The man would have to physically open

them with his fingers. After having gone to various physicians to no avail, he tried the Brainwave Conditioning System and was 90 percent cured, as O'Brien's video footage proved. Another local woman had the same problem following an accident, and over lunch at the local pub we met her in person and heard her own story—direct from the horse's mouth, as it were. Following a car accident, she had suffered from blepharospasm and could not find any cure. She had heard of this local "memory man" and his work, and asked him to try it out on her. After only six sessions she was virtually cured, and proved the fact to us by blinking her eyes quite normally.

Blunt as ever, I asked her the straightforward question: "Do you own any shares in O'Brien's work?" The answer was a laugh and an equally direct no. She claimed that she would shout about the new process from the highest hilltop, and was indebted to O'Brien for what he had done, and I believed her completely. There was no sham going on here; there was instead serious science behind what O'Brien and Hopking were doing, and it was proving to be beneficial.

In other cases that we discussed, the pair were working on people, especially children, with dyslexia. Amazingly, following a few sessions they too were coming home from school with improved results—and probing questions from teachers who were noting the incredible results. In most cases the parents were specifically not informing the teachers or doctors of the sessions with O'Brien, in order to judge the response in isolation. One 12-year-old boy reported serious improvement after just one

session. There was indeed more to all of this than a placebo or psychological effect.

O'Brien and Hopking were also using the process on people who had no health problems and were just attempting to improve their mental capabilities. In all cases people were reporting improvements in energy, mental capacity, and lucidity, such that colors and objects around them were suddenly more colorful, bright, and sharp.

According to O'Brien, "This in time could lead to the key for world peace." The reason was simple. In all cases the people undergoing these experiments were relating a balancing effect in themselves—just as their brain waves were being balanced. O'Brien claims that the process "enhances the spiritual and artistic side of human nature." Not surprisingly, then, I was to find that the history of the process was to be discovered in some of the more "peaceful" religious works of humankind's past.

For my part, I believed that what was occurring was an oscillation between the hemispheres of the brain. The left and right brain, being brought into balance, were then able to communicate with each other more rapidly and lucidly—opening up avenues of communication that the ancients understood as "union." There are instances from ancient sources and various religious practices around the globe such that physical techniques were employed to enable this process, and which, it seems, science is now beginning to understand. For instance, the steady drum beat of the Shaman struck four-and-a-half times per second is known to entrain the brain's frequency to theta levels, which, as we shall see, are incredibly important in transforming the mental state into the trance state or Otherworld. The constant, rhythmic drone of the Tibetan Buddhists has the same effect on those participating and those listening. There are also frequencies that occur in nature that also entrain a relaxed state, such as the crashing of waves on the shore, the wind in the trees, and the trickle of water. Even the U.S. government experimented with beating-drum techniques when it was attempting remote viewing in the Stargate program.

There are also various breathing techniques that aid the process. Holding down the left nostril and breathing through the right, and then doing the opposite, in equal amounts, actually effects and entrains each side of the brain, until they become in balance. As the author of *The Brain Book*, Peter Russell, points out:

Probably the most detailed left–right symbolism is found in the Tantric writings of northern India. These are fascinating in that although they were written many hundreds of years ago, they foreshadow much of what we are now discovering about the left and right hemispheres of the brain.

They maintain that the breath rarely flows through both nostrils equally, for a while it flows predominately through the left and then for a while through the right, the changeover taking place every twenty minutes or so in the healthy person.

When the sun breath is flowing—that is, when the right nostril is dominant—one is advised to undertake the actions involving speech and instruction, as well as combat and physical exertion. These correspond to the linguistic functions associated with the left hemisphere, and the "active," competitive mode. When, on the other hand, the moon breath is dominant, one is advised to engage in painting, composing, listening to music, and other creative and artistic activities—that is, with functions associated more with the right hemisphere.

The Tantrists also claim that when a person gains enlightenment, that is to say, when he is fully aware both inwardly and outwardly, the breath is found flowing equally in both nostrils. This presumably reflects the fact that such a person would be using both hemispheres of the brain in balance, rather than temporarily suppressing one in order to make full use of the other.

Well, I decided to have a go on O'Brien's machine, to test out the system for myself, and to see the process firsthand.

First, O'Brien attached electrodes to my head and ears in order to make an assessment using an electroencephalogram (EEG). The brain waves are then viewed on a computer screen nearby, showing left and right brain waves separately. It is then possible to see which brain waves are out of balance. It is this imbalance that O'Brien and Hopking claim "hinders the performance of the individual."

Once the assessment of my brain waves had been made, O'Brien placed a pair of black science-fiction-type glasses on my head. These consist of seemingly ordinary glasses, without the glass. Instead they have

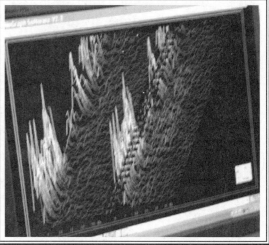

The author's brainwave patterns, showing balance.

The author's brainwave patterns peaking or highly energetic.

a series of LED lights, which flash according to the computer program and the desired entrainment. Next, he put on me a pair of headphones, which emitted a sound or bleep in unison with the lights from the glasses.

According to O'Brien, I had a very well-balanced brain anyway, and he did not expect great improvement—as the people who normally came to him were out of balance. However, following the readings, O'Brien noted that although I had a "Ferrari brain," there were a few tweaks that he could make to help the weaker side match up with the stronger side. And this is how he sees the process: Instead of reducing the strong side of the brain to the weaker side, thus reducing the whole brain down to the weakest part, he improves or entrains the weakest side to match the strongest.

I was now told to relax and was guided through the process by O'Brien, who then started the computer program. Lights flashed and bleeps sounded as the program attempted to entrain my brain. After a 20-minute session of the most psychedelic 1960s sci-fi experience I have ever had, I was unplugged, and we all went out into the now-sunny back garden to see if I was any more lucid. At that stage I reported feeling no different at all. However, O'Brien said that it may take a couple of days for me to notice any difference—and I did.

Normally I suffer from headaches every couple of days. I figured it was from having to write and research books, run a business, travel extensively lecturing, take care of two noisy kids, and endure long hours and British traffic. It had become a perfectly normal and acceptable way of life. However, one week after the process I had not had any headaches, and I also reported feeling extremely lucid and alert—coming to all sorts of discoveries from information I had previously locked away in my mind.

A few days later I flew to Cyprus for more research. The journey took nearly a

The author undergoing a bineural beat technology experiment to balance out brainwave activity.

crickets or fireflies eventually end up in harmony.

The brain is an amazing organ—a computer to beat all computers. Within this incredible machine there is a tempest of electrical, chemical, magnetic, and biological activity. All of this activity seems chaotic, and yet it is the one thing that allows us to perceive order and to order our own lives. However, scientists have for decades been breaking down this seeming chaos into definitive elements; left and right hemispheres having been assessed as having alternatively logical and rationalistic or artistic and spiritual tendencies. The thalamus, pineal, and other "organs" were broken down into constituent parts of the whole. Even the cerebral cortex or "old brain" was classified and given a role. In this way the picture of what the brain does is becoming clearer—at least to modern science.

I have found, in research for this and other books, that ancient people did very much the same, and understood that the brain was made up of these constituent parts. They developed names and symbols for them and knew what each part represented—in their world. I am also of the opinion, and with good reason, that ancient people understood the extremely low frequency wave activity held within their own brains, and even built great monuments accordingly, as we shall see. So, what has modern science found about these waves, and how does this relate to the Otherworldly experience of so many millions of ancients?

There are different brainwaves acting in our minds all at the same time, and all of them at extremely low frequency, or ELF.

day, through one delay after another. It was a stressful time and I had eaten little—in-flight meals are not what they used to be. A few days later, in the 110-degree heat of the midday sun on an archaeological dig at a Roman villa I was still perky and without headache. Normally, all of this would have brought on the usual pain, but for some reason it did not. It was weeks later that I reported my first headache, and even then it was weak and only followed by another weeks later. Since that first meeting my headaches have seriously fallen away.

What explains this healing ability?

The special headset and earphones used by O'Brien and Hopking, audio-visually entrain brain waves to certain frequencies. The waves in our brain then follow the regular patterns being emitted by the devices, and we become "in tune" with them. It's a kind of synchronicity, and works in a perfectly natural fashion, much the way

They are categorized in Hertz or pulses per second. Researchers and scientists across the globe are divided as to the exact frequencies of the five main categories, because they seem to fluctuate according to the experiments conducted. However, we can roughly break them down into the following categories:

Beta	15–30 Hz
SMR	12–14 Hz
Alpha	7–11 Hz
Theta	4–6 Hz
Delta	1–3 Hz

Now I need to explain the effects of these brain wave categories upon the mind.

Beta frequency is for high mental activity, and is associated with decision-making, logic, and problem-solving. Sometimes beta waves are also referenced as expanding into the high hundreds of Hertz, showing high levels of brain activity and alertness. There are chemicals that can be taken to induce beta activity, such as alcohol and caffeine, but I don't advise that you increase the amounts you take already, as excessive amounts of alcohol induces *delta*—sleep.

SMR, as described by O'Brien's "Peak Performance Training" pamphlet, is "the ideal level for heightened concentration, memory, and being 'in the zone.'"

Alpha is for the alert state of mind, allowing total focus and concentration. This frequency is best for reading, listening, and "optimal sporting performance," according to O'Brien. This frequency is also associated with ESP and other paranormal activity—but in association with theta.

Theta is the best state of mind for memorizing and recalling information, as well as creativity and the development of high IQ. People often experience rapid eye movement dreams or hallucinations when in theta. This state makes the central nervous system reduce the sensory input from the overall nervous grid, allowing mental lucidity and increased functioning power. This frequency is closest to the Schumann Resonance, of which I shall discuss more later in the book.

Delta is deep physical relaxation, and is often used for pain relief and to help relax stressful people.

The specific areas of interest to me were alpha and theta, and as I was to discover, more likely somewhere in between.

Einstein is said to have discovered the theory of relativity when in alpha-theta, and Watson and Crick are likewise said to have visualized the serpentine double helix of DNA while in that state. Most of us only ever experience this state as we are falling into sleep and see the images of a dream beginning before we lose consciousness of it. It is frustratingly at this moment that we have some of our most amazing ideas, theories, and inventions. When we wake up, we have generally forgotten exactly what it was we thought of, but know intuitively that it was profound. Imagine then being able to hold this information, play with it, and develop it further—we would be more creative and intelligent, we would seem as gods, like Einstein, Watson, and Crick. But it isn't another world; it is simply a gateway to the unconscious self.

In a paper by Erik Hoffman, Jan M. Keppel Hesselink, and Yatra-W.M. da Silveira Barbosa, entitled "Effects of Psychedelic, Tropical Tea, Ayahuasca on the

Electroencephalographic (EEG) Activity of the Human Brain During a Shamanistic Ritual," the researchers of this catchy-titled little paper discovered some remarkable links to the enlightenment trance state: "EEG data from twelve volunteers...were recorded...before and after a Shamanistic ritual in which the psychoactive tea, Ayahuasca, was consumed. Following three doses...the subjects showed...increases of both EEG alpha (8–13 Hz) and theta (4–8 Hz) mean amplitudes.... We suggest that these findings...reflect an altered state of consciousness." The paper goes on to state that the subjects were more aware of their subconscious mind than even when in a meditative state, promoting Ayahuasca as a potential aid to psychotherapy.

This was extremely interesting to me, as it showed that the drugs used by the ancient Shamans (in the Amazon) were enticing the brain waves down to alpha and theta levels, and therefore bringing on "altered states of consciousness." These states become nothing more than entrances to the Otherworld (unconscious) via the unique training methods of the Shamans.

Furthermore, Ayahuasca is a tea extracted from plants in the Amazonian rain forest. This drug seems to have been brewed for as long as people have inhabited the Amazon, and has an acting agent called dimethyltryptamine, or DMT, which is structurally similar to serotonin.

This similarity to serotonin raises the issue that there is more than a simple brain wave reaction, which causes the entrance to be opened. The whole cause is biological, chemical, and electromagnetic; it is a case of holistic convergence that causes the effect. This is something that the ancients, as I believe, understood, and I know this because they utilized sound (drum beats), light (fire), and drugs. I was also aware of the modern medical practice of light therapy, which releases serotonin. Light is seen by the eyes and absorbed by the body as waves (and particles), and processed by the hypothalamus—which links the nervous system to the hormonal system. When hormones are exposed to light they undergo changes and have various effects upon the body and mind. People who are subjected to long periods of darkness, for instance, suffer from vitamin deficiency and hormonal disorders, leading to depression and health issues. This is an imbalance between light and dark, and is corrected by modern science with drugs.

The charm of O'Brien and Hopking's machine is that healing effects are created without any risk of attachment to a drug. I asked O'Brien specifically whether there was any noted dependence upon his process, and to date he had not noted any. The beauty of this small scientific experiment is that it highlighted for me the true science behind the trance states spoken of endlessly by the ancients.

The authors of the Ayahuasca paper speculated that the subjects' theta waves were so high during the ritual because they were "drowsy," pointing out that theta waves usually increase during light sleep, while alpha waves, indicative of conscious attention, decrease. However, both theta and alpha waves increased during the experimental ritual, so the subjects could not have been particularly sleepy.

The Ayahuasca tea is believed by the Amazonian people to give the individual access to the unconscious mind. It allows them to step through their consciousness to see, and even, through training, to control, that unconscious mind. It is, in essence, a key to the doorway of the Otherworld. Adding in to this the element discovered by O'Brien and Hopking, that people in alpha-theta experience lucidity and even see auras, which are electromagnetic signatures of the bodies around them, then we have a true scientific grounding for the process of trance and so-called Otherworldly travel.

In the Ayahuasca paper, the authors explained that the trance state brought about by the tea is similar to other "altered states of heightened unconscious activity," such as hypnosis and meditation. They postulated that the tea expands this meditative state, and allows the person to stay awake and conscious through it, and may indeed aid the meditative process. If the influence of the theta waves, as the science seems to support, increases the access to these unconscious and subconscious memories, then it is these specific waves that open the doorway and allow the alpha waves to concentrate upon them. With years of training, the Shaman would already have built up a huge reservoir of imagery, which he could call upon. This imagery would include nature spirits such as the spirit of the tree, of the bird, and of other animals—anything remaining would simply be summoned by the imagination. Once inside the Otherworld mind-state, the Shaman would be enlivened to the energy signatures (auras) or electromagnetic frequency levels of the natural world around him, and would

be able to draw upon that reservoir of imagery to associate with the signatures he was seeing. The question now arises, could the Shaman then control and call upon these energy signatures or "nature spirits," as he or she has claimed for thousands of years? This is a question I would be returning to.

O'Brien and Hopking's work does not exist in isolation. There are others in the world that are coming to the idea that balancing out the waves within the brain is a good thing. Hemi-Sync, in the United States, is a trademarked product of the Monroe Institute, and works in much the same way. Using similar audio binaural beats, relaxation techniques, and "guided imagery," the Hemi-Sync process is extremely similar to, but faster than, the methods used by the Shamans of the globe. The scientists at the Monroe Institute, similar to O'Brien and Hopking's research, claim on their Website (*www.healingproducts.com/montroe.htm*) that:

Hemi-Sync influences brainwave patterns and appears to transform states of consciousness.... [It] encourages coherent brain-wave activity through synchronisation of the left and right hemispheres of the brain. Different frequency sound waves are transmitted to each ear through a set of headphones and these waves entrain the frequencies of each hemisphere to reach a point where both are harmonised and synchronised so as to create a centred state of consciousness. In effect, the Hemi-Sync process had really been designed to lead one's consciousness into a Hypnagogic State—i.e., the borderline state between waking and sleeping consciousness.

So here we have a scientific method and a scientifically explainable process, which leads the brain through the balancing and controlling aspect of the alpha-theta waves to enable the mind to enter the trance state.

According to psychophysiologist, author, speaker, and doctor Eugene Peniston, "the theta rhythm state is...a dominance for 4–7 Hertz brainwaves. Transient elevation of theta occur during Zen meditation or while entering the early stages of sleep and are...associated with vivid visualization, imagery and dream-like states. The origin of theta waves is predominantly the hippocampus, although theta activity can be recorded throughout the cortex and cerebellum."[1]

So, here we have scientists telling us that Zen meditation can enable the elevation of theta waves, and Peniston also points out that alpha-theta waves also enable the trance state. Interestingly they are also pointing out the origin of the theta frequency as being in the hippocampus, which explains how certain drugs can chemically induce the state, although there is debate on this.

Now, if we can access this state, and we have already questioned whether we can control this state, then can we also use this process to explain many other paranormal processes?

Dr. Michael Persinger, a well-known neuroscientist (professor of psychology and head of the Neuroscience Research Group

at Laurentian University, Ontario, Canada), has done some work in this area. The question was asked, are we predisposed to a belief in God? To answer this, having the electromagnetic element of the brain in mind, Dr. Persinger designed a helmet that produced a very weak (ELF) rotating magnetic field between 10 nanotesla and one microtesla (we shall discuss Nikola Tesla in a later chapter). This helmet was placed over the temporal lobes of the subjects, who are themselves placed into a controlled environment (such as a closed, quiet room), and blindfolded. There is therefore no risk of any suggestive elements creeping into the experiment. The subjects were told nothing about the experiment other than that it was for relaxation. They were also not told when the field was turned on and when it was turned off.

What the Persinger found was quite amazing, and has been replicated by various scientists around the world in several ways. Persinger found that more than 80 percent of subjects reported paranormal experiences: ideas of a sensed presence, such as a ghost or supernatural being, or the feeling that someone was in the room with them. Religious subjects generally reported this effect as God, and atheists tried to explain it as a trick of the mind, as when taking drugs. Either way, the electromagnetic effect was to induce "feelings and emotions" of a presence. Of the other experiments conducted, one using subsonic (infrasound) waves played to an audience in a theater in Salford, England, had the effect of causing many in the audience to feel a presence near them.[2] The conclusion to be drawn from this is that external influences (such as frequencies) can bring

on the supposed Otherworldy activity spoken of by mystics. It is not only an internal meditative process, which is spoken of purely as a method of balancing oneself out before attuning to the energy at a special location where the external influence can be found.

Following my trip to see Dominic O'Brien, he decided, along with Henry Hopking, to test what they tentatively called The Holy Grail Frequency (alternating frequencies of alpha and theta of 7.83 Hz), which I recommended, on various subjects. The resultant effects caused were exactly what I predicted, with feelings of a presence and all manner of "spiritual" experiences: One subject claimed to be in "another place," a scene of flowers and cows. This amazing "other place" is the Otherworld of which we have been speaking. Other subjects perceived it as a psychedelic light show, or just slipped off to sleep. Either way, as O'Brien said, "early indications are that this is a great healing frequency" (this particular frequency will become more important in the next chapter). O'Brien was in fact creating a location point—producing external influences, quite similar to the ancient sites we have been discussing.

To add to this "wave" field theory, I must now also mention particles. As any budding quantum mechanic will tell you, there is more to the existence of light and sound than waves—there are also particles.

Quantum Matter Particle Waves

It can now be understood that the brain is a resonant structure, resonating frequencies that, when "in-tune" with each other, open new pathways or networks of neurons. Our own thoughts are in fact resonances that are firing across these pathways, so balancing out and amplifying these resonances by bringing them together, as does Obrien and Hopking's Brainwave Conditioning System, and Monroe's Hemi-Sync, improves our cognitive capabilities. This makes the wave effects in our brain quantum "matter particle waves" that come into resonance when excited by drugs or meditation. These matter particle waves are best excited when in unison with their environment—the world around them. Those more in tune with the environment therefore have a better chance of survival, and consequently, on the Darwinian scale of thought, are more likely to evolve. For instance, those people who use certain illegal drugs shift their brain out of phase with the world around them—they become separate from others. These "separated" people are no longer viable human beings and would not be the fittest of the species. Those who are more in tune with the resonant frequencies of the Earth and environment around them would be the fittest.

So, if the brain is made up of "matter particle waves" that open neural pathways and are more in tune with the environment around them, then I have to ask the question, what does this mean? It means that we are talking of an extremely deep level of understanding, that the human mind is part of the greater whole of the universe; it means that the mind could theoretically communicate at an unconscious level with the same resonant frequencies of our environment. It means also, with the addition of quantum entanglement (whereby particles of individuals are entangled or are on the same resonant frequency), that we could, theoretically, be able to communicate with each other, at any distance, without the need of oral or visual means: ESP.

What we are discussing here is a quantum brain in unison with a quantum universe, where all things are possible. This is not science fiction. It is known that information is processed in the brain via chemical transmitters, which pass on energy information via neurons. One neuron transfers its particular resonance to another neuron by turning its wave energy into a particle, and vice versa. This is a quantum brain. We also know that the vibration of electrons inside our brains produce electromagnetic discharges that emanate outwardly into the environment in all directions.

We shall discover in the next chapter that this system is not solely the domain of the brain. We shall discover that the Earth, and the universe around us, resonates at a specific frequency on the ELF scale, and that via quantum particle wave phenomena we are perfectly capable of understanding what the environment around us is saying. More than that, we shall discover that we can influence this environment when we become superconscious.

Chapter 9
Mind the Earth

e discovered in the last chapter how the brain has certain resonances or frequencies. I found that one particular area, namely alpha-theta, actually causes the effects required for the trance state, and that drugs, dervish, isolation, or meditation has actually aided mankind in achieving this specific resonance to enable the opening up of the mind or Gateway. I found that investigating this specific area, that we have called the Holy Grail Frequency, subjects actually have peculiar "otherworldly" experiences and *believe* that they are "transported" to other worlds.

But I wanted to attempt an experiment myself, in isolation. I wanted to truly see if the experience or effect could indeed be manufactured. I knew I could not produce a true scientific and objective experiment, but nevertheless I wanted to explore the mind. To this end, I found an anonymous but willing subject who decided to be the guinea pig, and I began my preparation. I knew a few shops in Glastonbury, England, where there were specific items I wished to purchase for the experiment, so I took a magical mystery tour.

Glastonbury is a marvelous place to start any journey, being the home of Holy

Wells, said to hold the Holy Grail itself, and Joseph of Arimathea's Hawthorne Tree (even if it isn't an original). King Arthur is said to have been buried there (he isn't), and the seemingly entrenched tourists give the place an air of the New Age (or Old Age, these days). It was because of this New Age presence that certain shops have sprung up throughout the years, and there were quite a few here that I needed to visit. It's a little like a trip down Harry Potter's Diagon Alley. I finally ended up in a back street crystal shop, where I bought a large quartz crystal block at a haggled price from a pushy crystal salesman. This quartz, I knew from my research, had the electro-magnetic qualities I needed and that had been used by the ancients, whether in the form of granite or pure quartz.

I then moved up the main hilly street and past the Christian church on the left, just as the heavens decided to give me a shower. Quickly I jumped into the first doorway I could find and discovered it was just what I was looking for. I needed some esoteric literature, Buddhist in flavor, for my experimental subject to read during the experiment. This was in order to some way ease the mind into the metaphysical realm—as my subject was everything but spiritual in nature.

Next I traveled back to my home, and my subject took a few days out. He began a water-only fast. This element I knew to be part of the ancient preparation also. He then began to read the Buddhist literature I had bought, and kept himself apart from as many people as possible. This was an isolation technique. Each night he slept uncomfortably with the quartz crystal beneath his pillow, and played a frequency CD that entrained his brain to the specific "Holy Grail Frequency" or Schumann Resonance of approximately 7.8 Hz, using bineural beats.

The first few days were painful, the subject feeling an aching in his stomach and a light-headed outlook that blurred both vision and thought. Sitting down seemed to be the only thing worth doing, and even reading became difficult and tiresome. Then, as if by magic, on day three this effect cleared; he no longer had a longing for food, and an amazing clarity of mind ensued. It was like a clearing of mist. Suddenly everything around him became crystal clear. Colors and sounds were incredibly profound, and his dreams were extremely realistic and easily recalled the next morning. The hormones were kicking in.

Then, on the third night, while trying to sleep, he found that he could not fall into a deep slumber. Instead he remained on the edge of sleep, dreaming and yet aware of the dream. It was a lucid dreaming state—a trance Gateway—and he knew he was experiencing the elements I had found in history and science. The trouble was that the excited nature of actually experiencing a real element of metaphysical belief was stopping the effect in its tracks and bringing him up and into full consciousness. He realized eventually what was happening, and grew used to the effect. He began breathing in a regular pattern, and then tried to forget even about the breathing, and opened his mind to the effects that would come. Again he lowered his mind into the edge of sleep, but this time remained almost as an observer rather than

a participant. Eventually, he was floating in a strange half-dream, half-awake state.

After 10 or 20 minutes of this experience, he decided to get up and go for a walk. But there was something peculiar about his walking—it felt like walking on air; he could not feel the ground below his feet. Something inside him then told him to turn around and look at the bed. For one frightening moment he realized what had happened. There on the bed was his own body. He was having an out of body experience—something I have read so much about. The experiment was a success, and the next morning the subject took his family to a small Derbyshire town in England and enjoyed a full English breakfast to celebrate—on me of course. It was the best breakfast of his life, and not just because I paid.

I knew that the experiment could have gone further, and that other experiences could have been gained, but this adventure was sufficient to convince me that there was reality, whether in the mind or external, to the ancient beliefs. I also believed that it was too dangerous to extend the experiment without the proper scientific constraints.

This is the quantum state of consciousness where it was believed that mind and matter—being the mental (wave) realm of dreams and the material (particle) realm of everyday reality—are both superimposed as one energy.

I am now of the opinion, from the mythological, historical, scientific, and now personal evidence, that humankind has this inbuilt key to the Gateway, but needs a location or external influence to aid them. I knew that this was a key to the unconscious mind. But I also knew that there was something behind all of this that was much more profound. The various elements of my experiment all contributed to the effects, but I knew from my research that it was all related, and strongly, to the Holy Grail Frequency. The effect of fasting reduced the brain wave activity down to alpha-theta. The frequency CD entrained the brain to the same level, and the quartz crystal magnified the effect. This is the reason that such a fast response was gained, by someone who was not the slightest bit metaphysically or spiritually inclined. The subject was not trying to do anything—it just happened. His perceptions were not previously aligned to expect a certain reaction.

The whole thing came together when I asked the basic and simple question, why would this particular resonance occurring inside our brains be the key to the trance experiences and thereby the Gateway to the Otherworld?

The answer to this was simple, and already well within the public domain, and was the subject of much discussion—everybody was just missing the point entirely.

The Schumann Resonance

In the 1950s, a physicist by the name of Dr. W.O. Schumann, then a professor at the Technical University of Munich, wanted to give his students some exercises in the physics of electricity. Part of this involved some work on ball condensers. Giving the students a hypothetical situation

involving these ball condensers and electricity, he told them to imagine that the ionosphere was one ball and the Earth itself another. He then told them to calculate the frequency between the inner and outer ball.

Schumann himself had no idea what the results would be, so decided that he needed to do the calculations himself too. He came up with the answer of approximately 6–10 Hz. Amazingly, this rough calculation turned out to be the approximate resonance of the Earth itself—a perfectly natural resonance that mankind has lived with and evolved with for millions of years. The frequency fluctuates in time as energy (such as lightning) discharges, but it has now been proven to affect the human mind. This Schumann Resonance or resonate cavity on the Earth produces rhythmic waves that entrain our brains: Our brain waves and even our bio-system are affected by ELF signals from external devices or sources.

Proof that we are part and parcel connected to this Schumann Resonance comes from, of all places, NASA in the United States. NASA found that astronauts returning to Earth were reporting feelings of distress and disorientation. To counter this it was hypothesized that by emitting artificial Schumann waves in the spacecraft, the problem may be averted. It worked. It seems, therefore, that man feels stress when distanced from his Mother! We are in tune with the very Earth upon which we live. What has shocked many is that our planet's frequency level is the very same as the Holy Grail Frequency.

At the time of his experiment, Schumann had no idea of the profundity of his discovery, but reported the results regardless. Now the frequency is called the Schumann Resonance in his honor. Schumann passed on his research to Herbert Konig, who produced extensive experiments to measure the resonance of the Earth, and found a more exact measurement to be 7.83 Hz—exactly between alpha and theta.

There can be no coincidence in nature. All things are the way they are due to evolution—there is always a reason. And so, there must be a reason for humankind (and all mammals) to be in perfect frequency harmony with our Mother Earth: Our internal rhythms are affected by external rhythms. The magnetic field of the Earth and the electrostatic field that emerges from our own bodies are interwoven. It seems our minds are entrained to the outside influence of the Earth's resonance. It also seems, judging by my research, that humankind actually found methods of improving or magnifying this resonance with the use of granite and quartz crystal (and other influences). The amplification of these signals actually promotes a coherent and large-scale activity of ELF signals in the brain, making the mental effects more profound and more easily perceived.

However, being conscious of these effects is much more than just being conscious of the Earth's own resonance in tune with our own. It is the act of being conscious that allows us to also alter this reality. By being aware of our surroundings and the images we perceive while in the trance

state and attuned to the Earth's resonance, we can then make conscious decisions. These decisions have ELF signals that alter the level of activity inside our own brains, which, as we have seen, are interwoven with the Earth's field.

This is exactly what we have seen with the Shaman, who claimed that he was capable of not only going into the Otherworld, but was also able to alter reality. In pure consciousness, in which we are not aware of the trance state, we can only affect physical reality by physical means. In the unconscious world, we may perceive the unconscious realm, but we are not conscious of it, and can therefore make no decisions. In the trance state, we are conscious of the unconscious mind, and therefore the elemental connection we have at an ELF level to the universe around us and the holistic nature of that realm. We then consciously attempt to alter the dreamworld that we find ourselves in, and thereby alter our own reality. A true adept would have huge creative powers at his or her disposal—in the dream world. At a quantum level, these powers may actually come through into physical reality via the wave particle matter phenomena I discussed earlier. This is what the ancient Shining Ones called magic.

Today even physicists are coming around to this ancient magic. In *The Conscious Universe: The Scientific Truth of Psychic Phenomena*, Dr. Dean Radin of the University of Nevada finds that there is a growing belief in the interconnectedness of the field of consciousness between people and physical objects. Radin even believes that this phenomenon is capable of transcending time and space—just as the ancient Shamans once claimed. It is believed that at the subatomic or quantum level, physical reality is nothing more than energy information. This is the same level of reality that the Shamans believed they could transcend through engaging in interconnectedness with the universe via the various methods we have previously discussed. These methods I now know to be entraining the brain into alpha-theta, or the Holy Grail Frequency, through years of preparation and training to consciously perceive and affect the energy information field. Affecting reality at the subatomic or quantum level therefore realizes a physical reality change—such as the amazing feats of healing that Shamans seem to manifest. These affects could also include understanding foreign languages by comprehending the meaning of the emitted waves; levitation; out-of-body experiences; placing and extracting energy information from quartz crystal skulls; conversing with animals; and even, via transcending time and space, prophesying future events.

How can science prove such a hypothesis is true? Well, there have been several experiments, some inconclusive and others overcome with errors. Dr. Radin produced a significant experiment with random number generators. The idea goes that any random number generator will, in time, produce equal statistics. If I toss a coin, on average I will get 50 percent heads and 50 percent tails. This is the correct random statistical outcome, and proves there is no outside influence. If, on the other hand, a different outcome is produced, then outside influence of some kind is proven.

What Radin did was have a large number of subjects watch a specific television program, such as the Superbowl, to see if the group consciousness had any effect upon a random number generator. He wanted to see if the randomness of the generator was affected during the course of the program. Radin set up various random number generators in labs and monitored the results during several important programs, which he knew millions would be watching live. In each case, Radin's results showed that the generators became significantly less random during the programs than before or after.

Radin's experiments prove beyond doubt that the collective consciousness of ordinary human beings has an effect upon a physical machine. How much more powerful is the mind when charged with the ability to perceive the quantum reality around it, and even alter that reality?

It is also interesting to note that the biggest increase ever recorded in the Schumann Resonance occurred in 1987, at the same time as the so called "Harmonic Convergence," when millions of people gathered at sacred sites around the world to pray and meditate together. This gathering was brought about by an understanding of the supposed prophecies of Quetzalcoatl and the beginning of the "end times," as well as some Asian and European astrological alignments. The prophecy goes that following the ninth hell, humanity as a whole would enter a new age of enlightenment, and we would have a new era of peace. Unfortunately, as this ninth hell supposedly ended in August 1987, we are still waiting for the new era of peace. At the

same time, there was a subtle convergence of planets, which may also have had a gravitational and electromagnetic effect upon the Schumann Resonance.

What this exercise shows is the possible effect of the collective consciousness of humankind on the Schumann Resonance, or even the effect of planetary alignments. As I write this book, the Schumann Resonance is tinkering around the 11 Hz mark, although it changes quite often. Could this increase since the 1950s be an indication of the collective consciousness of mankind at war with itself, or are the planets themselves affecting our consciousness?

As I have previously mentioned, one of the most profound effects caused by the Shamans ability when in his trance state is the talent of healing. In 1999, a Russian experiment into this healing ability found some remarkable results. Psychic healers were asked to treat mice 20 minutes before they were to be exposed to lethal doses of gamma radiation. All the mice in a control group that had not been treated by the healers died, but those in the treated group showed varying degrees of death rates from 90 percent to as low as 22 percent. Not only are these results impossible as far as orthodox medicine is concerned, but they also imply that the healer can cause a healing *before* there is an actual health problem. Incidentally, the 22 percent-rate control group had been pre-healed by remote viewing psychics more than 800 miles away.

The benefits to society of such a healing ability are phenomenal. But with such huge amounts of money changing hands between pharmaceutical companies and hospitals around the globe, there is no

appetite to search out a truly *free at source* cure for any ailment.

With thousands, if not millions of years of research and healing activity by humankind, it is a remarkable situation we are in today, in which we consider the healing abilities of chemical medicines of the past 200 years to be far better than any natural remedy. Orthodox medicine is paid for, controlled by, and funds a massive corporate monster. This same monster vilifies and ridicules cures and treatments that are perfectly natural and in balance with nature, and have been developed in vast periods of time by people who were closer not only to that nature, but to the entire universe on a quantum level. This corporate monster claims that its own remedies are tested rigorously, and then issue us with huge amounts of antibiotics that weaken us to new strains of viral infections. This then leads them to have to take more public money to research stronger and better antibiotics, thus keeping the corporate cycle going in perpetuity. They claim that alternative healing and medicines are not tested so thoroughly, and forget the thousands of years that humankind has been using them. The whole thing is completely out of balance, as I discovered with the immense healing and anti-aging abilities of serpent venom in *The Serpent Grail*.

Dangerous Field

Along similar lines, but retracing our steps back to the Holy Grail Frequency, we discover that this Earth resonance is in the perfect trance frequency level—as if the Earth itself is somehow in a trance. I wondered, what would it mean if the frequency of the Earth were increased? Would this mean that our ancient Mother would rise from slumber and issue a terrible wrath upon her children? I know that the Earth is being polluted, and that the effects are now striking back at us with impressive weather fluctuations and climate change. Could this have more to do with an increase in the Earth's resonance? Could this be linked to our poisoning of the Earth? When people take drugs or poison, they change their own brain wave activity. Are we doing the same to the Earth?

Christians, Jews, and various other religions, believe that God made the Earth in six days, and that on the seventh (which is the current period), he rested. I know that in the creation of the Earth, from a scientific point of view, the planet was in turmoil. Huge volcanic eruptions, comet and meteorite strikes, earthquakes, and a frantically altering weather pattern created the Earth we now live upon. During this time the frequency levels the Earth created were massively above the current position—they were *awake*. Now the Earth is in a relative calm—it is resting on the seventh day. This lends weight to the Gaia theory of the last century, and implies a kind of consciousness that we can only guess at.

Regardless of whether the increased effects of our polluting corporate capitalism are heightening the destruction of the finely balanced ecosystem, I now know that humankind is actively attempting to directly affect the frequency of the Earth. In Alaska, there is a government project entitled HAARP (High Frequency Active

Auroral Research Program), which began in 1990, but went into full operation in 1998, and is actually emitting huge levels of ELF (extremely low frequency) signals into the Schumann Resonance between 2.8 Hz and 8.2 Hz. According to the HAARP Website (*www.haarp.alaska.edu*), its purpose is as follows: "HAARP is a scientific endeavor aimed at studying the properties and behavior of the ionosphere, with particular emphasis on being able to understand and use it to enhance communications and surveillance systems for both civilian and defense purposes." Some scientists, such as William J. Bray, believe that "It is probably true that the Navy only intends to use the antenna [HAARP] to communicate with submarines. However, the potential effects of the operation of this unit could have serious implications for human and animal health, as well as hitherto unforeseen ecological impacts, not to mention the risk of operating in a frequency range demonstrated to directly affect human and animal behavior and physical health."[1] More than this, all the major communication, radio, and television companies on the globe are bouncing their millions of signals off the ionosphere back down to Earth. It is recognized, but not understood, that what exists in this ionosphere is a kind of plasma, the most common form of matter, which is often called the fourth state of matter (the other three being solid, liquid, and gas). Nobody understands the true nature of this plasma.

Although HAARP claims that its ionosphere activities in no way "compares to the worldwide events frequently caused by the sun," it is still a fact that what the sun does with its solar flares and radiation is perfectly natural—and the Earth always finds a balance with nature. But pumping such ELF signals into the cavity between the Earth and the ionosphere will result in manmade ionospheric storms and climate change,[2] although HAARP claims otherwise. How? The Earth's resonance is no different from our own, and similar to the human brain, it too can be entrained, as can any similar signal. By emitting such signals into the cavity, HAARP and others are, inadvertently or otherwise, entraining the resonance of the Earth upward and out of a natural balance. What occurs in the brain is a cascade of waves that are entrained until the whole is "kindled," which is what will happen to the Earth. Eventually the entrained waves will cascade, and added to the massive amounts of pollution, will cause mammoth and possibly catastrophic climate changes. Geomagnetic storms will ensue, and the electromagnetic effects of these will further change the Earth.

Instead of increasing the ELF of the Earth, we should consider reducing pollution, stopping the HAARP experiments (and indeed any others that remain secret), and investigate the effects of the commercial use of the ionosphere for communications. We should in essence leave the Earth to find its own balance again. Alternatively, humankind may be forced to either live on an *awakened Earth*, or attempt to reduce the resonance by entraining downward.

If humankind has evolved with this frequency throughout millions of years, what would be the effect of changing it? Would we evolve on a more rapid basis? If so, into

what? The consequences of our input into the natural world around us will have far-reaching effects that I cannot even imagine. But the fact remains that if I affect the Earth, it will affect me. We are in essence waking up a sleeping giant, and closing the Gateway.

Chapter 10

Finding the Gateway

e are now ready to travel in space and time ourselves. It is time to travel backward and find the Gateways; to search out the clues that ancient peoples have left us. It is time to use all that we have learned to uncover the true Gateway to the Otherworld.

The problem is, as ever, where to start? History and mythology are full of stories of travels into other realms. Legends tell of great heroes and gods coming and going through one portal or another. I decided to break the continents up and go through them painstakingly, trying to uncover the true Gateways from the information I now had. In the next chapter I will run through the various mythologies of the world, and then get to the actual tracking-down of physical and ancient Gateway locations in Appendix I. But in this chapter, I decided it was a good idea to run through some of the elements for which we will be searching, and to decipher the meaning of perplexing problems that orthodox history has come up with.

Seven

One of the elements we have already discussed is the use of the number 7 in religious and mythological legends. Mircea Eliade, in the 1964 book *Shamanism: Archaic Techniques of Ecstasy*, tells us that the number 7 is of extreme importance specifically to the Shamans of Central Asia and Siberia, where the seven-spotted mushroom is eaten by the Lapp and Oystak Shamans to enter the trance state. This relates to the Oystak idea that the cosmic pillars have seven notches, similar to the seven levels of heaven seen by Judaism and Christianity—a direct relation to the Gateway to the Otherworld.

I could spend a huge amount of time expounding upon the number 7, but the fact is that it is always important in relation to the world of the esoteric and "Gateway" travel.

Center

We should also be looking for the idea of the center being the true Gateway. This should be obvious to us now, as the true center is the point between the brain's hemispheres, and the sacred location on Earth where the earth energies cross. This should then, theoretically, be imaged or manifested by the ancients in their beliefs and structures. Still, I decided that we needed to look a little deeper into the psychological and metaphysical aspects of the ancient idea of the center.

All of the emotional problems people have stem from having a divided perception, because we perceive, or *receive* the world through either one brain hemisphere or the other, and so we can only understand it from one side or the other—logical *or* emotional.

Each hemisphere acts as a filter, through which the images and meaning of our reality is received and interpreted. But not only do we perceive and receive this information about our reality through either of these filters, we also *create* our reality through either one of these hemispheres or filters. Each one of these two hemispheres is associated with the way we create and perceive the world during every moment. So, many of us create a perfectly logical and ordered universe around us, and others create a wondrous imaginative world—if we look on the bright side. The dark side has the logical subject creating his world of structured order along the lines of Stalin, and the imaginative individual perceiving that everyone is turning into monsters.

We see everything in opposites, and the particular forms or patterns we are experiencing or perceiving every moment depend on whatever side our energy is focused through. Achieving a balance between these hemispheres is exactly the process I was undertaking with Dominic O'Brien and his binaural system.

This indeed may be the reason why there is so much hatred and war in the world—because not only are we divided against each other, but we are also divided within ourselves. If we were all "balanced," in left and right brain waves, then we might be able to see the other person's side of the argument.

I then thought about the whole thing for a moment. All of this is simply telling us that we are living in an illusion of our own making. Nothing that we see, hear, or experience is ultimately real, and neither is anything we say or do. This is the Eastern concept of Maya, that the material world, the physical world, is illusion.

Add to this the idea that all things are basically empty—that is, the atom is void of much content—then we are simply manifesting illusion because we are divided. If we were fully balanced and saw the logic and emotional, left and right, then we would see the full reality, which begs the further question: If we can only see the real world when we are in balance, and we can only see into the Gateway when we are in balance— then must not whatever is in the Gateway be reality, and not the imagination?

If this were true, those mystics and Gnostics we have burned and hanged throughout the centuries for their madness were in reality sane, and it was we that were mad all along. Now, when one takes a look around at the wars, disputes, hatred, lust, and greed we have sown in our wisdom, then one seriously has to wonder which side of the Gateway one wishes to be on.

It seems then, that the true insight gained by the Shaman on his or her journey into the Otherworld is insight we ought to listen to and not deride.

Other World Centers

We can also see this center location in another extract from Mircea Eliade's *Shamanism: Archaic Techniques of Ecstasy*:

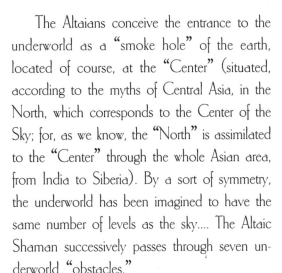

The Altaians conceive the entrance to the underworld as a "smoke hole" of the earth, located of course, at the "Center" (situated, according to the myths of Central Asia, in the North, which corresponds to the Center of the Sky; for, as we know, the "North" is assimilated to the "Center" through the whole Asian area, from India to Siberia). By a sort of symmetry, the underworld has been imagined to have the same number of levels as the sky.... The Altaic Shaman successively passes through seven underworld "obstacles."

This "smoke hole" of the earth that Eliade tells us about could be a fissure, and implies strongly that it was on a fault line, which we know to be an area with strong and unusual electromagnetic properties, thus improving and magnifying the ELF effect. The North, and therefore Center aspect mentioned, is also interesting in relation to the mention in the book of Enoch, in which the Watchers of Sumeria go north in order to measure and build their great megalithic monuments—they are basically finding the sacred center location of energy convergence. The fact that the Underworld has the same number of levels as the sky implies the wisdom of Hermes and the much-overused statement, "as above, so below." The passing through seven obstacles is seen in other cultures as well, including the story of Salome in the dance of the seven veils, and with Ishtar, the great Queen of Heaven. It is also seen in various stone alignments (see Appendix I), where great granite blocks are placed along a sacred pathway.

The center of the labyrinth is also of importance. The labyrinth is seen world-wide, and is a true pathway to the Otherworld. More often than not, the labyrinth is seen as an element of the Mother Goddess, and it is no surprise to find that the Underworld was symbolically depicted in a feminine way as the Mother Earth. This is seen clearly in the mounds of the world being the great womb-like entranceways to the Mother. The labyrinth is often sevenfold, and depicts the mystical journey to the Otherworld—a symbolic transformation from death to rebirth in the womb. The Hopi Indians say that it is the symbol of the Mother Earth, and that it is like the kiva (see Appendix I), which is their entrance to the Underworld. In Buffie Johnson's book *Lady of the Beasts*, we are even told that the labyrinth was presided over by females.

Often labyrinths were placed at entrances to caves (such as in Minoa), which we know were symbolic of Gateways. The most famous labyrinth in the world, at Chartres Cathedral (see Appendix I), has a rose at the center, thought to represent Mary, the Mother of God, and also symbolic of a hidden secret. It seems then, in order to traverse the labyrinth and actually make it to the center, one must to gain access to the Otherworld.

In essence, the center is located where there is a fault, or earth energy, which we now know to be electromagnetic ELF signals—energy information. The key to the Gateway is through seven levels of consciousness, or alternatively through attaining the harmonious level with the frequency of the Earth. But it is also gaining the center, balancing our own minds.

Trees

We find many stories of great trees, which are cultural elements of the axis mundi—the fixing of energy to a specific location. Probably the most famous of these is the Tree of Life, or the Sefirot. This is more properly the Babylonian Tree of Life, with the sacred fruit only to be eaten by the gods, and which became the Tree of Life in the Garden of Eden and the Asherah trees of the Temple of Jerusalem—a location where one could access the divine, otherwise known as a Gateway. Later it was taken over by the Kabbalah, and became a method of initiation similar to the chakra system of the Hindus. The term *sefirot* comes from the Hebrew word for *sappir*[1] or sapphire (which forms into a pyramid), and loosely means the "radiance of god," or the "shining one," an allusion to the trance one must achieve before travel to the Otherworld is beneficial. In fact, this sapphire came from the Otherworld of heaven, from the very seat of God. In Jewish mysticism the true element of the Sefirot is Da'ath, "the secret sphere of knowledge on the cosmic tree."[2] This is the very knowledge believed to be obtainable when in the Otherworld; it is "the omniscient or universal consciousness of God, which, properly speaking, is not a Sefirah, but a cognitive presence of the One in each of them."[3] According to Dion Fortune, "When working with the tree either to call down the greater knowledge of the superhuman universe and its infinite organization, or to bring our self up the tree from the lower sephirah for spiritual upliftment and higher perspective, all energy must pass through Da'ath on its way into matter or

disintegration into the hypertext of the universe."[4]

Colin Low tells us more about the Da'ath:

In the 17th century, Nathan of Gaza circulated a curious document, the Sepher ha-Sha'are ha-Daath. He described this as a commentary on the two chapters of the Book of the Allazred, an ancient history of the world. The title means the "Book of the Gates of Knowledge." The word for knowledge, da'ath, has a technical meaning. When the Bible was translated into Greek, the word da'ath was translated as gnosis. Da'ath has a very peculiar status in Kabbalah, being a kind of non-existen[ce], a nothingness. In modern Hermetic Kabbalah it is sometimes represented as a hole or gate into an abyss of consciousness.... [A]n infinity of gates open, each one a gateway to a mode of being. These are what Nathan is referring to as the "Gates of Knowledge."[5]

So the Jewish mystical Kabbalah, with the Tree of Life, has the secret element of the gate through which we can gain a superhuman element of consciousness.

The true union of opposites (the left and right hemispheres) we spoke of earlier also is seen when we understand that this term *da'ath* was translated as "gnosis" in Genesis, and when Adam *knew* (gnosis) Eve, he really knew divine union and the knowledge gained from the Tree of Life. So in effect, Da'ath is simply knowledge gained via connection to the divine, by being in a mental state or trance at a fixed (tree) location where the energy (serpent) can open one up.

Hathor and other goddesses were often depicted reaching from a tree to give food or provisions to the dead in the Otherworld—the tree was therefore a portal, because it marked the sacred location for those adept at using it. As a bird, the soul or *Ba* of the deceased was attracted to the tree and nourished by it, as we would expect in this scenario. Burial, in this respect, was therefore made in the trunk of a tree, as a symbol of the portal into the afterlife through the Mother Goddess.

There is little difference in other parts of the globe. To the Celts the tree was the all-provider, and was linked to the Druid and Shamanic beliefs in the Otherworld, and this has come through to us in tales of Robin Hood, who was himself originally based upon Otherworldy creatures.

The Celts believed that the tree was a connection to the world of the dead and of the gods. Wood from sacred trees manifested magical properties, and even the script of Ogham was made up of symbols of the various kinds of trees—enacting a spiritual element of the Otherworld in the sacred writings.

One of the most sacred trees in Europe was the oak, which was seen as the World Tree or axis mundi. It was the doorway to the Otherworld, and we can see this in its Celtic name, *daur* or *duir*, which is the origin of the English "door." Many folktales abound regarding oak trees, and even today areas of Ireland still have tales of people falling asleep beside an oak tree, only to find themselves transported into the Otherworld of the fairies—in sleep. Trees, in association with serpents, often guard sacred treasures or springs and wells. They are said to carry messages to the Otherworld, and people tie notes or votive offerings to their branches to be carried off as a message to ancestors or gods down the trunk and into the roots within the Underworld. The Green Man (and woman) of Europe is brought into our vision only through the portal of the tree.

Pliny, the Roman historian of the first century AD, tells us that the Druids worshiped in groves of oak trees. Strabo tells us the same thing of the Galatians. We even learn that the Druids of Gaul ate acorns (from oak trees) to divine the future and access altered states of consciousness.

Today, people still take branches of trees into their homes as tokens of good fortune from the people or gods of the Otherworld. But why would the oak be so important as a symbol of the Gateway to the Otherworld? Well, we do know that the second-century writer Maximus of Tyre described the Celts as worshipping Zeus, or more likely their version, which was Taranis, in the symbol of an oak. Also, we know that in Anglo-Saxon times, Thor was known as Thunor (hence thunder), and sacred groves of oak trees were dedicated to him. This tells us something about the oak: Taranis, Thor, and Zeus were associated with lightning and thunder, and the oak is said to attract lightning, hence it became an earthly portal for the lightning flash or "shining" of the gods—a visual representation of the energy they perceived. It was the point at which the gods (specifically Thor, et al.) connected with our world, from seemingly nowhere and out of "the black"—as it generally goes very black

when such storms emerge. As we can see in Appendix I, with relation to Machu Picchu and other places, this belief in lightning being the connection of the gods to the physical plain of existence is universal, and was actually aided by placing tree poles on mounds or granite stones on hilltops—in addition to finding locations on the earth where there were peculiar energy effects, such as fault lines. The ancients were literally drawing down their gods to and through the Gateway. Indeed, in Shamanism those who survived such a lightning strike were themselves somehow deified and often became Shamans. Now we have the lightning strike being seen as a symbol of illumination, and the world tree seen to be growing from the world mound.

Of course there are other reasons the tree is seen to be symbolic of the Gateway or portal: The branches of the tree reach high in the sky and almost worship the sun, whereas the roots stretch underground into the Underworld and worship the darkness. This again matches the Hermetic "as above, so below" perfectly with the serpent also being seen in the roots of the tree, such as the Yggdrasil of Scandinavia.

Another tree to be found in sacred places is the hawthorn, which grows on top of wells and springs sacred to the Otherworld, and is always guarded by a watery serpent. In Celtic lore the hawthorn is also a Gateway to the Otherworld, and has the protective element of thorns. It is seen as a powerful manifestation of the duality or opposites of the male and female—the left and right hemispheres of the brain and the converged energies of the earth. It is often used as the basis for the May Pole, around which people must circle

to raise the powers from the Otherworld by wrapping their serpentine strands of red and white (opposites) around it. In this way, and no different from the circumambulation of the kaaba at Mecca, the ritual creates a dot (the pole) at the center of the circle (the people). The kaaba is a large square stone, a remnant from star and meteorite worship, and with the circle around it we have a perfect union of earth and heaven, the circle and the square. The hawthorn is also, by folk tradition, the tree that Joseph of Arimathea brought to Glastonbury as a symbolic representation of his power over the Otherworld, firmly establishing himself as a true Shaman of Christ.

The tree itself usually has white flowers and red berries—mirroring the colors of duality so often used in ancient literature and alchemy. This duality is also shown in the fact that the wood was used to make a marriage torch—the flame uniting the couple. In Teutonic lore the wood was used for the funeral pyre—enabling the dead to rise to the Otherworld in the flames of the sacred tree. It was believed that this connection came about because hawthorn trees were said to attract lightning strikes.

In Ireland the hawthorn is a fairy bush, and of course fairies were from the Otherworld themselves.

The folklore of the hawthorn is rich in tales that relate to the Gateway. Witches are said to be able to turn themselves into a hawthorn tree, an indication of their ability to slip into the Otherworld. As we saw in an earlier chapter, Witchcraft itself is nothing more than an adaptation of earlier Shamanic beliefs.

Solitary hawthorn trees grow on hillsides and are even implicated in a Druidic trinity of trees—the oak, the ash, and the hawthorn. In Judaic tradition the burning bush through which God spoke to Moses was the hawthorn bush or *Crataegus pyracantha*. This bush was, again, on a hillside, and God speaking through it implies that it was a point of connection to the Otherworld or heaven.

I briefly mentioned earlier Yggdrasil and the ash, which are one and the same. This Viking tree was said to grow alone on an island, with its branches reaching into heaven and its roots extending to the four corners of the globe. It was to this tree that Odin, like Christ, was crucified as a sacrificial offering, during which he lost one eye—something profoundly Shamanistic. Not surprisingly, we also find that this ash was at the very center of existence.

In Greek mythology, Hesychius in his *Lexicon* told us that the "seed of ash" was the race of men, and this saying has puzzled scholars ever since. When Chronos overthrew Ouranos, the giants, furies, and Meliai were formed. The giants are the men of renown, the Watchers or Shining Ones of old that I discovered in my other works. *Meliai* simply means "ash trees," and they were the people who can be found in caves on ancient Crete nursing the infant Zeus. All of this simply implies that the original men were born from the Otherworld via the ash, or portal. Indeed, the first man in Germanic mythology was called Ask (ash).

To some, the ash is also the producer of Manna, seen in the Bible as issuing from heaven—the Ash is therefore the Gateway through which God provided sustenance,

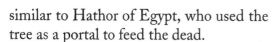

similar to Hathor of Egypt, who used the tree as a portal to feed the dead.

We must also recall that the Buddha was himself enlightened under the Bodhi Tree, which now is seen as a Gateway to Nirvana, and that Christ was crucified upon the tree to then enter the cave to the Underworld.

Other Clues

Other clues to watch for are the stories revolving around any given location. These legends may involve certain aspects that reveal the use of the location, such as mystical experiences or time distortions, much akin to alien visitations. These psychotropic experiences are evidence of Shamanistic activity at that location. Clues can be things such as dreaming (lucid dreaming), a journey or obstacles to overcome (seven levels of consciousness), descent (into the Underworld), wonderful food or drink (heightened senses), and ritual preparation (not optional without the aid of modern binaural techniques).

Certain places are said to have a demonic or devilish presence, and this is often nothing more than Christian propaganda against the old ways. Alternatively, they could also be stories of "failed trips," such that the Shaman or initiate has not prepared correctly for the journey and sees or experiences what we know today as a "bad trip."

Physically we should be noting the presence (or previous presence) of granite, quartz crystal, trees, mounds, and caves, as well as rock art depictions of the ancient Shamans, and the presence of sacred watery spots such as wells, springs, and lakes.

In the next chapter we will examine the various myths of the Otherworld for further clues, and then we will be fully prepared to track down the specific locations of the ancient Gateways.

Chapter 11
Otherworld Myths

hapter 10 focused on the clues that would guide us to the world's real Otherworld Gateways; in this chapter I shall run through the myths of the world and consider them in the light of the scientific evidence we have seen so far. Now, with the understanding that what the ancient Shamans and mystics were claiming with regard to their "trips" into Otherworlds might indeed have some truth in it, we will begin to see the myths of this Otherworld in a unique and different way. We will understand the world in a way only the finest spiritual avatars have done.

What we shall find is that the real or even mythological locations of these Gateways are no different from the "centers" of the world as found in many cultures of the globe. The word *pyramid*, for instance, means, "fire in the middle or center," and indeed it is to be found at the center of the earth's landmass. This "center" has a double meaning for several cultures, as the center of the self, not just the world. But more than this, it is the central location in the mind, the balance required to attain true enlightenment, manifested here as physical or mythological places that are also at the "center."

Center of the world ceremonies are to be found in many cultures associated with sacred places or objects. The center of the world is not in this context, conceived geographically or geometrically, but rather as a place or the place forming the sacred heart of reality, differing in kind from ordinary everyday reality, but giving form and substance to everything that is real. Because of its sacred nature, there is no inconsistency in the recognition of more than one such center. In different cultures in China and India, for example, a large number of "centers of the world" may be recognized. These symbolic centers take on many forms: whole sacred cities; the cosmic tree; the bridge or ladder; also sanctuaries, temples, and cathedrals, even houses. In certain traditions (e.g. Tantric schools), the center may be located within the human body.

The center of the earth is the place where the mundane and the supernatural unite and communication between the human and the divine takes place. During, and as a result of, ceremonies associated with the center, sacred power may be generated and spread abroad. Its importance is underlined by the imagining of the axis mundi in many traditions and in various forms—intricately woven fibres, drums, the "cat's cradle" of children's games. Also often associated with it are certain sounds or music, to symbolize the crossing from one level of reality to another.[1]

There are a few interesting elements in this short extract from the early 20th century *Book of Ceremonial Magic*. Firstly, the fact that there are many centers, both within the mind of humankind and the geometrical earth. As the text says, there cannot be many centers to each of these; there can be only one. It cannot be literally true that there are many "navels" of the earth—there is only one, and that is at Giza, which is at the center of the earth's landmass. There cannot be many different centers in the mind or body of people either. So what is all this talk of many centers? Well, in each place the sacred ceremony was talking about *the* center, the place between the left and right brain hemispheres of logic and emotion, where there is perfect control, and also the location of convergent earth energies. This ceremonial language and ritual, spoken of as if it were part and parcel of the earth and the human, is truly talking about a center that can be almost anywhere, as long as the energy is fixed. For greater effect though, it should conform or be made to conform to the energy grid that we have been discussing, such as the Oracle at Delphi, which was also a navel of the earth, located on strategic fault lines, altering the electromagnetic interaction with its surroundings. The text also makes it clear that ancient mythology truly fixes this central location to be the place where the "mundane and the supernatural" come together; it is the "crossing from one level of reality to another." The center then is the true location of the Gateway, and it is to this place, physical or otherwise, that we must look.

Classical Otherworlds

In Roman and Greek mythology it was believed that the entrances to the Otherworld were to be found in very real locations—a belief with which I agree, as man has from time immemorial made manifest the internal world. The Roman versions, for instance, were called mundus (literally, "the world"), and the one in Rome itself was known as Mundus Cereris ("World of Ceres," for Ceres, a goddess of the Otherworld), although the precise location is now lost (or hidden) to us. This mundus in Rome was a pit, capped by a stone known as lapis manalis. On three specific dates in August, October, and November, the lid was lifted to reveal the Ostium Orci or Gateway to Hades and release the spirits of the Roman dead. These dead were considered now to be divine, and needed appeasement, so special holidays were created for just such a purpose. These spirits, known as Lemures, appeared at night in grotesque form. "They were placated by the Lemuria, held annually on the 9, 11, and 15 [of] May, when the head of the house would purify his hands and scatter black beans to appease the lemures."[2] Amazingly, tradition states that this observance was instituted by Romulus after he killed his brother Remus—a literary device for explaining the splitting of the opposite principles of the mind, which require uniting to obtain access to the Otherworld. It is also the same reason that offerings were made in equal proportion, such as in Virgil's epic poem *Aeneid*, in which Aeneas has to give the magical number of seven bullocks and seven ewes—the equality of the male and feminine principles.

There are clues here to the physical locations of the portals. Firstly, lapis manalis was a large stone placed over a pit to keep in the spirits of the Otherworld. Aspects of this stone lid can be seen throughout physical archaeology in the cairns and cists of Europe, and in religious writings, such as the stone that was rolled back from the tomb of Jesus. The lids or large granite blocks found above so-called tombs in Europe and elsewhere are no different in this respect from the cave that Jesus was supposedly buried in. This cave was just another entrance to the Otherworld, and Christ was the symbolic and ultimate avatar of Otherworldly travel. There is little wonder that Jesus is therefore seen as the "sacred heart," which is a term we saw used in the *Book of Ceremonial Magic* extract for the center.

We also find from Roman mythology that Lemuria is really the ritual surrounding the appeasement of the Lemures, the spirits from the Otherworld. The word *lemures* was later misused, and became a mystical land similar to Atlantis. Maybe, therefore, Atlantis was nothing more than a mystical vision of the Otherworld, and was also changed in time into this physical place we are all searching for. The fact remains that Atlantis was supposed to reside between the Pillars of Hercules to the west (the land of the setting sun on the horizon and therefore between night and day), and to have had seven levels or layers—all elements we are now familiar with in the search for the Otherworld.

A great many oracles in both Roman and Greek mythology appear throughout time, and all reside upon portals or Gateways to

the Otherworld. It is from the other side that the oracles gain their divine and significantly opportunistic revelations and authority. These oracles reside on our side of the Gateway. Only the special individual, such as the age-old Shaman, could gain access to the Otherworld. The rest of us would of course have to be dead. But even death would not guarantee entrance, as there were always obstacles: Charon, the Greek ferryman of the River Styx, would not take any soul that had not received proper burial in the ground. Even then, the dead soul would have to pay the ferryman with the coin that had been placed beneath his or her tongue during the burial rights.[3]

To gain insight into the world of these oracles I need to quote the archaeologist Sotirios Dakaris concerning his journey into the Thesprotian Oracle (in Thesprotia). He describes "...a dark labyrinth with three arched doorways barred with iron...oblig[ing] the visitor to follow a complex path through murky corridors which gave him the impression of wandering through the gloom of Hades.... [E]ach visitor, before passing [the] gate apparently cast down a stone in order to protect himself from the evil influence of the spirits...."[4]

Dakaris goes on to describe an amazing labyrinthine complex below ground, making the whole Underworld become real and physical. This is ancient humans, manifesting the mystical world they had come to understand truly existed. It was not *just* a magical trick to delude people into paying money to the coffers of the oracle; it truly must have begun with the desire to create a Gateway to the peculiar world that mystics could access on sites such as

Thesprotia. Tiny elements of truly prehistoric rituals survived in ancient Greece, such as the offering of stones, and still survive today. Stones are placed in sacred piles as markers of respect for the location, a tragic accident, or some other special reason, across the world. This is a continuation of a much more ancient practice we can only guess at today.

We also find that the visitors to these oracles were fed not only a psychological concoction, but also a diet to match. Fruits, beans, barley, wheat, and lupine seeds have all been found on oracle sites. When eaten when they are green, the broadbean and lupine seed, for instance, can cause one to relax almost to the point of sleep, and induce hallucinations. Some have suggested that these hallucinations are purely caused by chemical reactions within the brain, and this may be true. However, as we have seen already, by taking the brain down into the area between alpha and theta frequency, these ancient drugs may have been inducing the trance state, and therefore these ancient procedures were indeed controlling the effect every step of the way. The oracle and her aids were truly a classical manifestation of the Shaman guide. The question will forever remain, did the guests really visit the Otherworld?

What is fact (and has also recently been found to be true of several Mayan pyramids), is that beneath these man-made Oracle temples are further prehistoric caves. These caves were seen by the ancient Greeks and Romans as the real physical and mysterious portals to the various Otherworlds, and this is the reason they expected the spilled libation offerings to drip into Hades.

The latest discoveries of caves below Mayan pyramids has spurned on those who believe in a physical Underworld that truly exists under our own. They call this place Shambhala, Agharti, or Shangri-La, the ancient Buddhist paradise described in *Lost Horizon* by James Hilton. In the popular book *The Lost World of Agharti: The Mystery of Vril Power*, author Alec Maclellan tries to prove that there was, and to some extent still is, a world below our feet, made of tunnels, cities, and possibly a whole civilization. Agharti, Maclellan claims, is in or at least near Tibet, and is connected to the rest of the world by a series of fantastic tunnels. These tunnels and their portals are guarded from the people of the upper world by powerful and highly advanced underworlders. As daft as this theory may sound, the evidence that Maclellan stacks up is interesting—though not overwhelming.

These beliefs in a real, physical Underworld are nothing new; in fact, they are hundreds, if not thousands of years old, and are based upon the same original cause. Athanasius Kircher, alchemist, mystic, and writer, even wrote a book on the subject in 1665, entitled *Mundus Subterraneus* (*The World Below*). In fact, it is relatively true to say that most people interested in the esoteric, throughout time, have found themselves led to the door of this physical Underworld, and for good reason, as we shall see.

There is a subtle clue in the words of the early 19th-century writer and chief justice of Chandernagor, Louis Jacolliot, when he said, "This unknown world, of which no human power, even now when the land above has been crushed...could force a disclosure.... Those who dwell there are possessed of great powers and have knowledge of all the world's affairs. They can travel from one place to another by passageways which are as old as the kingdom itself."[5] These powers spoken of here and elsewhere are a form of the infamous "Vril power" said to have been developed by the civilization of Agharti. It is a mystical and mental power, enabling mind control and Shaman flights of fancy. In essence, the power of those from the Underworld is nothing new; it is nothing more than those powers that have been attributed to the fairies and Witches of times gone by. It is no more than the fanciful additions of the imaginings of humankind onto what was and is a perfectly human, evolved function of the conscious and unconscious mind. Indeed, the people of Agharti were even said to have special Vril Staffs, with great and mysterious powers, similar to those of Merlin, Aaron, Moses, and hundreds of other Shamanic god-men of the past. These staffs were even said to be perfect antigravity conductors, enabling the user to lift hundred-ton blocks without effort, giving rise to speculation concerning just how the Great Pyramid was built. This is a clue to the true nature of these Underworld masters: Their magical staffs were said to be used to help build temples (such as the Hebraic Shamir), and yet these "temples" are nothing more than ourselves, and if we are the true temples, then we have no literal stone to carry—just our own burdens.

One of the proponents of the physical Underworld and the power of Vril was Joseph Alexander Saint-Yves d'Alveydre. Born a Parisian in 1842, he grew up on Jersey and eventually married fortuitously, thus enabling him the life of luxury precious few of us are allowed. He learned several languages and astronomy, and gathered together a considerable library of books. While engaged upon this journey of discovery he went deeper and deeper into the world of the esoteric, and eventually others had difficulty relating to him—which is why his metaphoric language has been taken literally. He published his ideas on the Underworld in various articles and in the book *Missionary*, in which he informed the world that his knowledge had come to him from an emissary of Agharti. Although there are stories of visits from strange-looking men of the East, they were not emissaries of Agharti as most would see it. They were instead teachers from India, who were spreading their own clever propaganda about a culture that was under seemingly constant threat. Agharti, they said, was a place of millions, with powers to terrify the most stalwart of nations. To prove this, the Indian teachers showed various Westerners the tricks of the trade— meditation, Tantra, philosophy, and their ancient Shamanic techniques as a finale. Joseph himself claimed that many of his ideas came to him through trance! As soon as much of this information was spread, there was no stopping its growth, and imagination fanned the flames.

There are telling stories of the power actually seen performed by these mystics of the East. One writer, Ferdinand Ossendowski, born in 1876 a native Siberian, grew to become professor of geology at the universities of Petrograd and Omsk. Following several expeditions to Tibet and Mongolia, he became convinced that these mysterious religious people had some kind of strange power, and he even met up with a lama who told Ossendowski all about the King of the (Other) World. Apparently, one of the Buddhas and the Tashi Lama actually received a message from this King of the World, written in symbols and signs upon golden tablets. But no one could read the symbols, so the Tashi Lama put the tablet upon his head and solemnly prayed. It seems that the thoughts of the King of the World came down from the golden tablets and penetrated the lama, and without ever having understood the symbols, he seemed to know what they meant. This concept is strikingly similar to the crystal skull method of passing on information we explored earlier in the book.

Annwyn

Annwyn is the Welsh term for the fabled Underworld of the Celtic myths, accessed through the tumuli or mounds scattered across Europe and associated with the Irish sidhe or fairy folk (the Shining Ones). These sidhe or Tuatha De Danaan were literally driven into the side of the hills by the Milesians (modern Irish), and once there, divided up the Underworld kingdom into their new homes. This makes a lot of sense, as the Pagan Celts are thought to have believed in reincarnation, as did the modern Druids, hence the spirits of the Underworld would rather be the spirits of the Tuatha De Danaan, and not of the dead. Now the doorway or Gateway to the underworld is opened only on the days of fire festival (the internal fire of illumination enabling the opening of the Gateway), such as Beltane or Samhain.

In the Mabinogion, the epic Welsh collection of stories from at least as early as the 10th century AD, we find Pwyll Pen Annwyn, an infamous character of the Underworld who will give us further clues to the beliefs of times gone by. Firstly we need to look at the etymology of *Penn* or *Pen* and *Annwyn*.

I had already come across *pen* before, when I investigated Arthur *Pen*dragon and the *pen*tacle. It means, in relation to Pendragon, "head," "first," or "leader," but it can also mean "summit of a hill" or even the number 5. *Annwyn* can have two related meanings: Firstly it can simply mean "the very deep place," which is peculiar when we find that Annwyn is often associated with very high places such as hills and mountaintops. Alternatively, it can mean "the none-world." This none-world can be nothing more or less than the Otherworld.

So this Underworld character, Pwyll Pen Annwyn, was the leader and head of the Otherworld. He was also both good and bad—or, more to the point, helpful one moment and a hindrance the next (although there are also concepts that there were two gods of the Underworld). Now, this god of the Underworld protected the cauldron, seen as a portal to the Otherworld by our ancestors. Men killed or injured in battle would step into it and be reborn anew. In balance with him was the goddess Sovereignty, who held a special cup. The king of the material world would have to please the cauldron god in order to retain power and authority—which was the cup of the goddess Sovereignty. What this tale is truly telling us is now simple to decipher: In order for us to be truly masters of our own destiny, both in this life and the next, we must achieve the balance in our "head," and then wisdom (the goddess) will be ours. These are truly the "spoils of Annwyn" spoken of in the poem of Taliesin, and the cup of Sovereignty is nothing more than the Holy Grail—especially when we consider that King Arthur and his men traveled to Annwyn to find the sacred cauldron (an alternative form of the Grail). In essence, this is the story of two things: It reveals the beliefs of the Pagan Celts, in that they saw their power and that of their king coming from the Otherworld, and that this Otherworld was to be found within the balance of the mind (head/pen). No wonder then that the "pen" is mightier than the sword, for it can truly "spell."

This Celtic world has been perceived in many ways. As Annwyn it is likened to Avalon, hence the reason for believing in Arthur's return (the return of balance). As *Caer Siddi* ("shining mound/castle") it is the whirling or revolving castle, a concept perfectly in tune with our thoughts in this book. Stonehenge was even called Caer Siddi, it being the best location for the "third eye" to perceive the whirls of color from the electromagnetic spectrum. As *Caer Feddwid* it is the place of sparkling or shining wine, which offers intoxication. Again, this is another allusion to the effects required and indeed created when attempting to enter trance, illumination, and superconsciousness.

Hy Brasil

There are many ways of spelling *Hy Brasil*, but all relate to the legend of this Blessed Isle of the Otherworld, which appears in a fog every seven years. Hundreds of researchers and explorers have believed this to be a real, physical location, and it even appeared on maps, giving rise, according to some, to the name for Brazil. In reality, Hy Brasil is no different from Annwyn or the land of the Sidhe, in that they are internal processes; it is one of many "islands" that our heroes of this internal process (such as King Arthur) can travel to and attempt to overcome obstacles. And how do we find these places? It is believed that by looking we shall not find, and most tales tell of heroes who accidentally discovered these Blessed Isles, when they were going "nowhere." Again, this all fits perfectly well, because we have already found that by *trying* to access the trance state properly we shall fail—it is something that must be *allowed* to come.

Sheol

This is the grave of Judaism, also known as Hades and hell (gehenna), and is a place of the Underworld—not necessarily eternal punishment. The Old Testament claims that this is the place where the soul goes and the body returns to the earth as dust (or goes to the pit, known as *shachath* or *bowr*). However, Job in 33:18 states: "He keepeth back his soul from the pit...." In 33:22: "Yea, his soul draweth near unto the grave...." In 33:28: "He will deliver his soul from going into the pit, and his life shall see the light."

And in 33:30: "To bring back his soul from the pit, to be enlightened with the light of living" (the Masonic Bible). What we actually have here is Job's *soul* being saved from going to the pit—not his body—so we have a contradiction. We are also told that he shall be saved and will gain enlightenment itself.

A further contradiction is then found in Numbers 16:30: "But the Lord creates a new thing, and the earth opens its mouth and swallows them up with all that belongs to them, and they go down alive into the pit..." (New King James Version). Here we have it distinctly laid out before us that people can go to the pit while alive. The text continues (this time taken from the Masonic Bible): "And it came to pass, as he had made an end of speaking all these words, that the ground clave asunder that was under them: And the earth opened her mouth, and swallowed them up, and their houses, and all the men...." (An interesting aside here is that the Old Testament makes it quite clear that this portal to the "pit" was seen as feminine—"opened her mouth.")

The confusion is still with us to this day, as many see this pit as being a place of torment, that the spirit of man is sent either to the heavenly realm to be with Jesus, or to that place of hellfire and damnation below. And yet the Bible tells us that all spirits return to God and all souls go to Sheol, the pit. Various poor or purposeful translations of the Bible have not helped with clarification: In the King James Version the word *hell* was used for Sheol when speaking of nonbelievers, and *grave* was Sheol for believers.

The fact remains that nothing spoken of in the Bible is any different from the other beliefs based around the Shamanic Otherworld. It is a place that we can visit to speak with the spirits of the dead or the deities, similar to the Celtic Tir nam Beo (Land of the Living), and Just as Jacob wishes to in Genesis 37:35: "For I shall go down into the grave [Sheol] to my son in mourning" (New King James Version).

Indeed, we can even use the word *sheol* to discover hidden elements of the Bible and show the relationship to the process of the ancient Shamans. In Jonah 1:17 we find that Jonah was really a Shaman entering the Otherworld for three days and three nights. "Now the Lord had prepared a great fish to swallow up Jonah. And Jonah was in the belly of the fish three days and three nights. Then Jonah prayed unto the Lord his God out of the fish's belly, and said, I cried by reason of mine affliction unto the Lord, and he heard me; out of the belly of hell cried I, and thou heardest my voice...yet I will look again toward thy holy temple.... I went down to the bottom of the mountains.... When my soul fainted within me I remembered the Lord" (the Masonic Bible).

This Otherworld is known as the belly of the great fish. Jonah is in fact Oannes (Joannes/Jonah), the fish god associated with Dagon. Oannes is also the same as the Hindu Vishnu (fishnu), whom I knew to be linked with the serpent and altered states of consciousness: The sun as a serpent would sink beneath the horizon and become a fish. *Dag* means "fish" and *On* means "sun," so Dagon is therefore the "nighttime serpent sun"—otherwise known as the "Black Sun" in various esoteric traditions. The black sun is a symbol of the Underworld and the unconscious—the collective unconscious attributed to psychologist Carl Jung. These ancient, legendary creatures are nothing more than aspects of our own journeys into the unconscious world—water itself was this place of the dead. Nothing but those creatures, which would become symbols of the greatest of deities, could survive in water.

Water, in scripture, was a symbol of the first death, just as it was with the watery Sheol of Jonah. And in Job 26:5 we find that "Dead things are formed from under the waters, and the inhabitants thereof."

Humankind offered their greatest treasures to the water, to be guarded by the sub-aquatic deities on their behalf. It was the amniotic fluid of the World Mother, and only those born again from this special water could truly be called special—hence baptism. This sacred ritual is thousands of years old, and in truth means to be submerged in wisdom (*baph*="submerge," *metis*="wisdom"). Jesus, when he was baptized by John, was being born of the waters of the mother into true wisdom—the wisdom of his own divinity. This same wisdom is for all of us.

Here, in Jonah 2:2, we see that this watery abyss, or indeed the fish within, is equated with Sheol: "I cried out to the Lord because of my affliction, And He answered me. Out of the belly of Sheol I cried, and You heard my voice" (New King James version). Jonah was the Shaman entering the Gateway of the Fish Lord and gaining power to do the Shining Ones' (Elohim) bidding through the empowerment from the Otherworld.

So, as far as the Bible is concerned, it was believed that the Otherworld was not only a place to which the spirit returned, but also a place that could be entered while still alive. This is the belief that the spirit (the superconsciousness) lives after death, and that, via our superconsciousness, we can access this same place while alive. So, the spirit is our superconsciousness, and it is separate from our bodies.

Sheol, hell, Hades, or the grave—are all places in darkness or black, because we cannot see them in consciousness. They all have meanings related to "sunken," "holes," or "caverns," and are therefore (in my opinion) nothing more than the void through which we must pass to enter the Otherworld. This is why the grave is seen as a waiting place before entrance to heaven. Indeed, the spirit is truly weighed here, as those found to be unworthy, as in any bad trip, will begin to see their own darkest fears—they will enter their own personal hell.

These locations are then physically manifested by man's ingenuity in great buildings and tunneling projects scattered around the globe. The greatest to the Jews was their temple at Jerusalem, which was nothing more than a sacred geometrical cube following specific mathematical equations mirrored in the Ark of the Covenant and the coffer in the Great Pyramid (see Appendix I).

Jacob's Ladder at the Kykoss Monastery, Cyprus.

Jacob's Ladder

"Now Jacob went out from Beersheba and went toward Haran. So he came to a certain place and stayed there all night, because the sun had set. And he took one of the stones of that place and put it at his head, and he lay down in that place to sleep. Then he dreamed, and behold, a ladder was set up on the earth, and its top reached to heaven; and there the angels of God were ascending and descending on it." Genesis 28:10 (New King James version).

Jacob then goes on to say that this place was awesome, and that surely God was in it. But, more than this he says, "This is none other than the house of God, and this is the gate of heaven." (Genesis 28:16).

To the Kabbalist, Jacob's Ladder has now come to be a powerful alchemical vision that is another way of expressing the site of the superconsciousness—the vision of the subatomic elements brought on by or aided by the laying of the head upon a stone. Folklore and traditions have now erupted around this stone, due to the importance many have seen in it. According to some, it was taken to Egypt or moved around by the Israelites, or even that it was the stone of the Tuatha De Danaan. To others it also became the stone of destiny, upon which the kings and queens of Great Britain have been crowned.

Babylon

The term *babel* means "confused," and gave us the name of Bablylon, the once-great city in Iraq. There are other meanings of the word: *babil* is Assyrian and means "gate of God," and *babili* may mean "gate of the Gods," explaining the supposed building of the Tower of Babylon to reach God. Babylon is known by various names in the Bible: Shinar, Sumer, land of the Chaldeans, and Akkadia. As E-Saggila this place was simply "the place of the lofty head," which has connotations all of its own, as we know. Located in Mesopotamia, that fertile plain between the Tigris and Euphrates, Babylon has become famous due to the biblical mutterings

from Revelation, but more so from the Old Testament story of the building of the tower.

The Tower of Babel, as it is often known, was being constructed by the people of the earth at Shinar to reach heaven: "And the whole world was of one language, and of one speech. And it came to pass, as they journeyed from the east, that they found a plain in the land of Shinar; and they dwelt there. And they said to one another, Go to, let us make brick, and burn them thoroughly. And they had brick for stone, and slime had they for mortar. And they said, Go to, let us build us a city and a tower, whose top may reach unto heaven; and let us make us a name, lest we be scattered upon the face of the earth" (Genesis 11:1).

This is most revealing. They came from the east—the land where the sun rises—and moved toward the west—the land where all such Otherworlds reside. But there is more to come, because the Lord gets worried that somehow the erection of this building will bring too much knowledge: "And the Lord said, Behold, the people is one, and they have all one language; and this they begin to do; and now nothing will be restrained from them, which they have imagined to do" (the Masonic Bible).

Babel was therefore some kind of construct that would enable these people to converse with the other side. *Shinar*, incidentally, is related to *Eshuana*, and means to be empowered by the sun (electromagnetic energy), which relates to the words of the historian Herodotus, who wrote about the tower in the following way in

The History of the Persian Wars: "...the sacred precinct of Jupiter Belus, a square enclosure of two furlongs each way, with gates of solid brass.... In the middle of the precinct there was a tower of solid masonry.... The ascent to the top is on the outside, by a path which winds round all the towers." Jupiter Belus is none other than Baal of the Bible, a solar deity.

God, just as in several other stories seen in India, Central America, and even Africa, did not like this attempt to enter heaven, and so he confounded the languages of the people. This is the point in the supposed history of humankind at which we stopped understanding each other. This myth is seen on several continents, in different languages, and even in connection with a pyramid. Is it possible that the great pyramids of Egypt are not really tombs of the pharaohs (who ought to, in truth, be buried below ground, not above it in a pyramid)? Is it possible that they are really towers toward the heavens? Gateways? This confusion of languages reflects the separation and division within our own consciousness that we need to draw back together in order to be able to reunite through the Gateway with the universal creative principle—the collective superconsciousness.

Nierika

Nierika is the "mirror" or "face of the deity" of the Huichol Native American tribe residing in Mexico. This is the void through which they pass to access the "transpersonal realms." It is symbolized by a five-directional cross: four for the cardinal points, and one for the infinite center, the midpoint, or void—in essence, the fifth points toward the secret Gateway. In the same way, the Chinese have the Pi, a jade disk with a hole in the center associated with heaven and the swirls in a pond.

Water

As I have already mentioned, this point between the worlds was symbolized by water, and it is for this reason that spirits (especially serpentine and feminine) are said to reside there. This is also the reason that baptism is done properly by full submersion within water: By entering and then returning from the Otherworld, one has truly been blessed and seen the truth. In Celtic traditions, this water element has come down to us through the Halloween (Samhain) pastime of bobbing for apples in a barrel of water. Firstly, these apples were the fruit of the dead (or spirits), offered via the portal of the water—they gave immortality. They were also the fruit of knowledge—the kind of knowledge that can only be gained during this "enlightened" state. It is a symbolic representation of travel to the Otherworld to return with fruits or treasure, just as King Arthur or the Shaman would visit the Otherworld and bring back healing or prophecy.

I have already pointed out that caves were seen as entrances to the Gateway, but within these caves the ancients would find the dark water of the Mother Goddess as little pools of natural mineral water, and these were truly seen as the Gateways, giving rise to the many stories and myths surrounding the caves. These caves were also

the progenitors of the physical Underworld myths such as those of Agharti and Shambhala.

❡❡❡

There is no wonder that we have believed in a world beneath our feet, especially considering the large amount of caves scattered around the world, both natural and man-made. In time, these caves, as wombs of the Mother Earth, were extended along complex, sacred geometrical layouts. This sacred geometry is based upon perfectly natural patterns we can find in everyday items such as leaves or flowers. It is also to be found in the very subatomic particles that make up everything in the universe.

There is a pattern, which ancient people understood, and which they knew or intuitively discovered, that would enhance the mystical experiences of the in-between state. These sacred geometrical shapes followed the golden ratio of 1.618, and the materials utilized in their creation were also carefully chosen. Eventually man developed the most perfect of caves, which followed these sacred geometries more perfectly than ever before. This "perfect cave" had material collected from more than 600 miles away, because it needed the physical properties of granite and limestone, both of which contain the all-important quartz.

One example of this most perfect of structures was the world's largest, was right at the center, and is still the most enigmatic and mysterious structures on the globe. It is the subject of the next chapter.

Chapter 12
The Great Pyramid

lthough I have covered a lot of ground with the Great Pyramid in Chapter 6 and others, I decided to leave my conclusions on its real purpose to this point in the book. The vast amount of knowledge I had built up in the course of my investigation lead me to new revelations regarding the specific purpose of the pyramids in general, and now is the time to speak of them.

According to standard, orthodox Egyptology, the pyramid complex on the Giza plateau comprises the funerary structures of the three pharaohs from the fourth dynasty, approximately 2575–2465 BC. The

Great Pyramid is attributed erroneously to Khufu (Cheops), with the other two being those of Khafre (Chephren) and Menkaura (Mycerinus).

Author Miroslav Verner, writing in *The Pyramids* stated: "To suppose that the pyramid's only function in ancient Egypt was as a royal tomb would be an oversimplification." This is now truer than ever, and I believe that the idea of the pyramids, or more specifically the Great Pyramid, being built solely for burial purposes of the given king is a farce. It is simply unimaginable that so much effort was made to build a structure of such gargantuan proportions,

The Gateway of Karnak, Egypt. (Photo courtesy of John Bodsworth.)

purposes instead of or in addition to the established theory. The body parts discovered within the pyramids may be pharaonic remains, or they could just as easily be more modern burials, the bodies placed within the pyramids at a later date. A similar practice is found in the burial mounds of Europe and elsewhere. Here, the burial mounds, as sacred images of the primordial mound or World Mountain, were Gateways to the Otherworld, and for centuries progressive generations would cut into them and make fresh burials. This practice does not take away the purpose or meaning of the mounds as Gateways to the Otherworld—in fact, it was part of the main purpose.

Were these great feats of human ingenuity and skill done only for the purpose of encasing the carcass of one man? No. I will show in the following pages that there was much more to it. In fact, if the pyramids were built for just one man, then why did Amenemhet III have two pyramids built, one at Dashur, which contained his granite coffer, and one at Hawara with a quartzite coffer? The unifying element of these two pyramids that struck me was the material used for the coffers—granite and quartz, which as we have seen are key to the whole Gateway scenario. Some researchers claim that one of these was a cenotaph (the word comes from the Greek *kenotaphion*, meaning "empty tomb"). It is even more remarkable that a tomb would be built empty, and the reason given by Egyptologists is simply that it would confuse the tomb raiders.

with such amazing astronomical alignments, with such perfect precision, by thousands of human souls, all for the singular purpose of burying their god-king.

In all the pyramids in Egypt, not one has contained the complete body of a pharaoh. There have been parts discovered—a supposed mummified foot at Djoser, fragments of a mummy in the pyramid of Unas and Pepi, an arm and shoulder at Teti, and a skeleton of a young woman in the coffer of the pyramid of Menkaura—but never a full mummified body of the pharaoh that was supposed to be buried within. Egyptologists claim that this was due to the tombs having been raided throughout a vast period of time. This may be true—or it may be that pyramids were used for other

The only so-called evidence that the Great Pyramid was built for Khufu is scant, to say the least. Herodotus, the infamous

Roman historian, visited the pyramids in 443 BC and claimed that Khufu was buried *underneath* the pyramid, not in it. This was 2,000 years after the supposed burial. We simply cannot believe Herodotus's interpretation.

The next piece of "evidence" is extremely controversial, as it relies upon some difficult to see, let alone decipher, "inscriptions" on a funerary complex near the Great Pyramid purported to be "in the time of Khufu." Again, and lastly, in the pyramid itself, the hieroglyphic symbol for Khufu was discovered as a quarry mark by archaeologist Richard Howard-Vyse, who is now believed to have forged it under pressure of competition from contemporary foreign archaeologists—namely the Italian Caviglia.

So, we are left with an inscription *near* the pyramid, a fake hieroglyph, and a more than 2,000-year-old text based upon hearsay. This is hardly evidence for the Great Pyramid as the burial place of Khufu—or for anything else—although it is perfectly possible that Khufu was buried at this "special" place, and that later a pyramid was constructed there. Such unproven nonsense has pervaded Egyptology ever since, and the pyramid itself remains an enigma. Until now.

The Great Pyramid of Giza is to be found at the center of the earth's landmass (30° north, 31° east)—both north–south and east–west. It is in the perfect location—at the center—for collecting the earth energy we have been discussing, and as Tesla proved with his experiments on resonance, as we shall see, it is also the perfect shape and size. To add to this, the two materials used were also perfect, as I shall explain.

But first we need to take a foray into the world of Tesla.

Nikola Tesla

Nikola Tesla (1856–1943) was an eccentric and brilliant inventor who managed to harness the alternating current we use today, as well as radio, florescent lighting, and much more. Tesla believed he could send waves of electricity directly to our homes through the earth and/or ether without the use of wires, and without harming anyone along the way, by simply applying a subtle push-pull resonator. And he did.

Tesla successfully sent electricity 26 miles away and extracted it using what he called a "magnifying receiver." This is an incredible thought, that energy waves, even extremely low frequency waves, could be sent around the globe and then picked up and understood or used. In fact, Tesla even tuned in his pyramid-shaped magnifying transmitter to the resonance of the earth, and found that his coworkers were becoming ill with symptoms of "extreme tension of the nerves."

Tesla discovered that "The Earth was found to be literally alive with electrical vibrations, and soon I was deeply absorbed in this interesting investigation." Tesla continued and revealed his feelings: "My first observations positively terrified me, as there was present in them something mysterious, not to say supernatural." I can now say that this mysterious presence Tesla stumbled upon within the resonance of the earth was the akashic records, the collective mind. As Tesla said, "It was some time afterward when the thought flashed upon my mind that the disturbances I had observed might be due to an intelligent control."[1]

It would be many years later that Schumann would discover the resonance of the earth and prove that it had its own wave-particle pattern, and that it can be altered by the surrounding universe, the collective superconsciousness, and any number of other external influences. How does it do this? There is a theory that the universe is a standing wave being pushed and pulled by some impulse (thought?). This

Recreation of the energy vortex discovered through Kirlian photography by Dr. Dee J. Nelson and his wife in 1979, using a Tesla coil. Note the double helix spiral or serpent-like effects of the electromagnetic waves; similar effects are caused with cones, hence the reason for the cone shapes utilized by the ancient Shining Ones.

impulse (similar to our thoughts, which seem to create wave-particles) pushes and pulls the standing wave, which then does the same to its neighbor, and hey presto light can travel across the universe as a wave cascade, without loss of energy—a perpetual motion. Our thoughts affect the surrounding standing wave in the same manner. Maybe what Tesla had discovered in these "vibrations" that were "disturbances" and seemed to have "intelligent control" were really the living wave-matter-particles of us all pushing at the boundaries of an expanding universe.

Tesla had discovered "intelligent" signals by pure accident, and stated the case. Unfortunately, through circumstances outside of his own control, he never did get around to seriously working on the phenomena, and no one since has had the intelligence or will to see the issue through. What Tesla did discover was found within the ELF field, the low frequency bandwidths. Many people, not least of whom are SETI (Search for Extra Terrestrial Intelligence), are out there looking on the megahertz level, when they should be redirecting their search back down to earth and to the extremely low frequency, before the mobile phone masts completely engulf us.

What struck me was that Tesla's receivers were great towers with pyramids on top, and his insistence that being at the center of the land mass (dependent upon where you are) would be far more beneficial to the purpose of the machinery.

So, Tesla discovered the resonance of the earth, and that this resonance had intelligent attributes. The resonance of the earth is in the same 0–40 Hz spectrum as

the human "mind," the same mind that is constantly emitting signals into the environment around it. These signals are much more than just waves; they are also particles—they are therefore matter.

We see stars in the sky, little lights flickering billions of light years away. Many of these lights are no longer there; they are stars that have died, and yet we still see the light. We now know this light to be wave-matter-particle; we know it is the continued life of that star. We ourselves, as part of the laws of chaos and order, are no different from those stars. We are also putting out signals, which will continue as wave-matter-particles, *even after we have died*. These signals are ELF signals, and are caught up within the Schumann resonance (37 miles above the earth), creating a whole. Are these the signals of our spirits? Are these the signals we are ourselves placing into the great collective superconsciousness of the akashic records? Do these wave-particles that Tesla discovered represent the sum of humankind and indeed all life on earth? Is Gaia, the Mother Earth, truly alive and conscious as the collective mind?

Amazingly, Tesla described these electromagnetic signals as stationary, parallel circles forming on the surface of the Earth. These are no different from the circles people have been perceiving and materializing here on the earth for thousands of years, as stone circles, rock art, and all manner of mysterious artifacts. And where would the most powerful, collective electromagnetic current collect other than at the center of the landmass? As the great

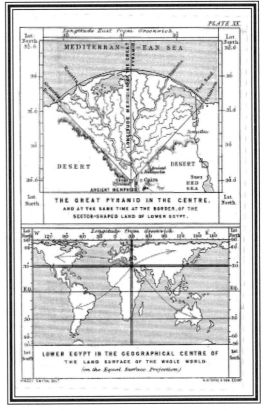

The location of the Great Pyramid at the center of the Earth's landmass, according to Piazzi-Smith.

and mystical word *om* turns from a circle into a square as it reaches "mmm," so too this great collection of human thought and quantum emotion turns into a square base at the Great Pyramid in Giza.

So, the Great Pyramid, at the center of the earth's landmass, and as a perfect shape for receiving the resonance of the earth, simply must have a better reason for existing than as a large coffin for one man. Let's break it all down and move through the various elements one piece at a time.

The Great Pyramid

This pyramid is composed mainly of solid mass, with the interior spaces being the Descending and Ascending Passages, the Grand Gallery, a subterranean chamber, an unnamed chamber, and the King's and Queen's Chambers. The King's Chamber (so named by Arabs who attempted to raid the tomb, but found it empty) is 10.46 meters east to west, 5.23 meters north to south, and 5.81 meters high. This is an architectural 3-dimensional representation of the golden mean, or Phi—a sacred geometry known well before Pythagorus.

The sides of the Great Pyramid line up almost exactly with the cardinal points on the compass, with an accuracy that would defy today's builders, leaving a fifth point on top, which we saw in the previous chapter to be symbolic of pointing towards the Gateway. The dimensions of the Earth can be calculated using the dimensions of the pyramid, it being a scale model of the hemisphere with information on the latitude and longitude of the Earth.

The very foundations of the pyramid also defy modern building techniques, as it rests perfectly level, with not one corner of the base more than 13 millimeters higher or lower than the others. When we remember that the base covers 13 acres we can suddenly understand just how this was an incredible feat of human engineering.

The King's Chamber is made of solid red granite transported from the quarries of Aswan 600 miles away. There has to be a better reason than simply lining a chamber for the ancient Egyptians to have undertaken such a task, transporting at least 50 tons of red granite for such a huge distance. We have already discussed the unique properties of granite in previous chapters, so we should be able to grasp the importance of this material. But there were more interesting uses of granite in the pyramid that caught my eye.

In the King's Chamber itself there is a coffer thought by Egyptologists to be the remains of Khufu's sarcophagus. Nothing was ever found in the coffer, and neither was there a lid. The coffer is too big to take out of the corridor leading to and from the chamber—indicating that it must have been laid inside as the building was erected around it, which is in opposition to the funerary custom of the period. There is not the slightest piece of evidence to suggest

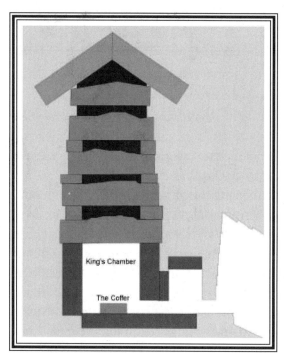

The King's Chamber in the center of the Great Pyramid (modeled after Charles Piazzi-Smith's research).

The sarcophagus from the King's Chamber in the Great Pyramid.
(Photo courtesy of John Bodsworth.)

that Khufu was ever laid to rest in this 3-ton granite container. There is nothing. No funerary implements, nor embalming materials. Not a scrap. And yet, short of any other ideas, the orthodox theory remains that a building with 2.3 million blocks, weighing between 2.5 and 50 tons each, of perfect size and orientation, was built for one man to be buried within. In addition, we must remember that not one of the fourth-dynasty pharaohs put their names upon the pyramids supposedly built for them, whereas from the fifth dynasty onwards official inscriptions are in their thousands.

So what is the truth of the Great Pyramid? Well, firstly I decided that I should run through some of the theories that have been put forward, and some of the more esoteric beliefs that related to my own quest.

There are legends and traditions that claim the King's Chamber to be a place of initiation. I would in part go along with this theory, especially in relation to the rituals required or made surrounding the Gateway mythology. There are also many stories of individuals who have felt peculiar presences or had mystical experiences within the chamber. There is also the tradition that Napoleon himself actually refused to express what happened to him in that enigmatic place, reportedly saying, "You would not believe me if I told you."

According to these popular modern folktales, the coffer itself is the center of the process or energy vortex. Writer C. Dunn, in his book *The Giza Power Plant: Technologies of Ancient Egypt*, goes so far as to say that the Great Pyramid was a huge geomechanical power plant that responds to the earth's vibrations or resonance and transforms it into energy. Dunn conjectured that the geometric and physical design of the chambers inside the pyramid turned it into a large transducer, and he has produced a highly scientific analysis of the subject. So there is now scientific experimentation in addition to these folktales, as we shall see—but with a very different purpose.

On the medical and scientific side there are stories of amazing healing, as we saw in Chapter 6. In the 1920s, Antoine Bovis discovered that the heat and humidity of the King's Chamber reduced the decay rate of dead animals—something still denied by orthodox researchers today. Bovis went on to construct a small-scale pyramid and oriented it in the same fashion. He placed a dead cat inside and found the result to be the same. Following this, in the 1960s, U.S. and Czech researchers repeated the process and achieved the same results.

The following is from *Yogalife* magazine in Autumn 2003, written by Dr. Prabhat Poddar, director of the Geobiology Research Center for Applied Scientific Research, originally from an article appearing in *Architect and Design* in July 1991. The article points out that there are often two kinds of phenomena observed: There is seemingly a concentration of energy passing through the vertical axis and apex of the pyramid, roughly one-third up from the base. There is also a spiral energy coming from the top. Poddar points out that unusual phenomena also occur, such as food not spoiling, but instead dehydrating. Milk becomes cheese; blades and knives get sharper; grains germinate quickly and grow faster and more healthy; water kept in pyramids acquires healing properties, and even people who remain inside are often cured of certain diseases and health problems. A pyramid placed inside a room seemed to clear the air and eliminate noxious smells. As Podhar said, "Mathematically pyramids are projections of hemispheres, and the famous Pyramid of Cheops in Egypt, in its proportions and location, is perfectly related to the dimensions of the earth.... [W]hat about the effect on us of other shapes, proportions, volumes, orientations, materials used in ancient and modern architecture?"

In the ancient Egyptian language of Khemitian, the pyramid was known as *Per-Neter*, which can be translated in two ways—"House of Nature," or more importantly the "House of Energy," remarkably similar to *pyramid*, which means "fire in the middle." It is interesting to note that "nature" and "energy" are interchangeable in this way, indicating that the Khemitians truly saw the energy as from nature itself (herself). In addition, the word *neter* (*NTR*) also means "neutral," which is the position one has to be in to gain entry into the Otherworld—balance between the left and right hemispheres of the brain. Another title for the Giza area is *Rostau*, which means "Gateway," and is sacred to Osiris and his progenitor Sokar, the God of the Underworld. In the Book of Am-Duat, Sokar inhabits a place of the dead that even

Ra, the sun god, cannot access—this is therefore a place of darkness or black. Sokar can also be seen in the representations of the fourth and fifth hours of the Duat, standing upon his mound within what seems to be a hill topped by a black conical symbol of some sort—the philosopher's stone? Incidentally, and perfectly related, the only way that Ra can traverse this mystical realm is by taking the form of the snake!

According to Reginald Aubrey Fessenden, author of *The Deluged Civilization of the Caucasus Isthmus*, the term *Rostau* is again a literal translation of *E-kur* or *Akur*—meaning the "great mountain" or "great house." These appellations make obvious reference to the Great Pyramid, which could be referred to as the "great house" and the "great mountain."

Writer Zecharia Sitchin, in *The Wars of Gods and Men*, tells us that the Sumerians also called their Ziggurat temple in Nippur (a truncated, stepped pyramid) Ekur, a "house which is like a mountain," but quotes a poem that exalts the goddess Ninkhursag as the mistress of the "House with a Pointed Peak"—a perfect pyramid. This is interesting in that the Sumerian goddess Ninkhursag is synonymous with the Egyptian goddess Isis. The Inventory Stele—said to have been written by Khufu—states that the Great Pyramid was dedicated to Isis.

The Akhu or "Shining Ones"—variously named "ancestors," "sages," "ghosts," or "spirits," can also mean "astral spirits," as associated with the stars. As for the serpent link, there are many ancient Egyptian illustrations showing human figures on the backs of feathered serpents about to ascend to the stars. This gives us a clue as to the nature of their special abilities associated with an initial core experience by which they also attained their knowledge and wisdom. This is further supported by the definitions of *Akhu* provided by Sir E.A. Wallis Budge in his *Hieroglyphic Dictionary*: "to be bright," "to be excellent," or "to be wise" and "instructed." In brief, the Akhu were a shadowy brotherhood, an enlightened and highly intelligent group of individuals who seem to have understood all the sciences associated with mathematics, astronomy, physiology, and metaphysics, and had encoded their knowledge in certain monuments and buildings—one of them being the Great Pyramid of Giza. These were the very originators of the deities such as Thoth and Hermes, who would enter the world of secret societies and become all-important.

So, why would all three meanings of the Giza area and pyramid, in addition to the myths, relate to the Otherwordly theory if it wasn't correct? Why would the people associated with this area be deemed to be special "bright" or "shining" people if not for their seeming ability to access the illumination and hence go through the Rostau or Gateway? With the use of large quantities of granite encasing the King's Chamber and the five huge granite blocks resting above it (for which Egyptologists can give no reason),[2] we have here a kind of peculiar resonating magnification machine tuned into the human mind. But what is the machine for? I would like to forward the following hypothesis.

First I must lay out some background information: The only thing found in the coffer was salt. This was not from embalming, as there was never a body in the pyramid.

We have seen how water was the final Gateway—one must past through it, within the deep recesses of the cave, in order to enter the Otherworld. Salt is the mineral used to help us float.

So, the individual, resting in this perfect sacred-geometric coffer, with internal dimensions to match the Ark of the Covenant, would be in total blackness within the "fire in the middle" situated in the Gateway of Giza (Rostau). This great mountain of limestone and granite contains huge quantities of quartz, which when vibrated gives off an electrical and magnetic energy that has been shown to resonate at the same level as our minds. The earth actually entrains our minds to the resonance of the collective superconsciousness, and we tap in on a profound level. But much more than this, as Shamans the world over have claimed,

by using this powerful superconductor of the superconsciousness, the ancient priests or Khufu himself could enter the Gateway to the Otherworld and actually control elements on the other side. These elements would be subatomic energy particles perceived in the mind's eye through resonating at the same quantum level as the earth (our Holy Grail Frequency)—to be conscious of the unconscious but perfectly natural world. To be conscious of the world of subatomic particles, which make up everything. To actually alter these energies through our own thoughts.

Now we have a better reason for building such a massive edifice at the center of the world. Truly, humankind has wanted to journey to the center of the earth for many thousands of years, but for very different reasons than previously imagined.

Chapter 13

The End Is the Beginning

ust as in the image of the ouroboros—the serpent that eats its own tale—this is not just the end, but also the beginning.

It is a time for us to make a new start with our understanding of what in fact life is all about. We can only truly ever do this with knowledge, and as this grows daily, we must, or should, reappraise our own unique perspective on the reality in which we live. One of the most profound elements we simply must come to understand is quantum physics, and the whole and seemingly peculiar area of the subatomic world.

Quantum World

What I always find to be most enlightening is the fact that at every level—whether micro or macro, whether big planetary movements or the actions of the electron, whether the pattern of microscopic silicon dioxide or the human-conceived Egyptian pyramids—there is a universal pattern, a constant throughout, regardless of size, and even regardless of whether or not the structure or pattern came from within our own mind or from nature. For it is a fact that the very nature of human engineering

The ouroboros serpent in control of time, in St. Giovanni, Rome.

springs forth like a gushing well of seemingly sacred power to bring us manifested material geometry that itself is fashioned truly by the very universe within which we exist. In essence, we are truly one with the whole. We are brought to life within the womb of the universe, and we grow there. We are physically in ratio with the world upon which we live, and our emotions even follow the very basic patterns set out within the incredibly complex, and yet ultimately simple order. Why is there such a profound and beautiful nature, and why are we conscious of it (although not all of us, all the time)? The answer to all of this lies within the quantum world, and it is a world that remains difficult for everyone to comprehend. It is a world that, like all others, follows certain rules. But it is also a world very similar to the human realm, as it also has uncertainty principles—no photon will always do exactly as predicted.

So, we need to spend a while understanding the simple aspects of the quantum world, and more specifically, quantum entanglement.

Let Us Entangle

Firstly, to understand quantum entanglement we must understand a few other concepts. The first one is the wave. We should all know what a wave is by now; it

is exactly like the ripples upon water, and are the same for light, sound, and all manner of transmissions. When two wave patterns come together they can either grow (constructive wave), if they are the same height; they can trough, if two low points in the wave coming together; or they can even cancel each other out (destructive wave), if a high wave of height x, hits a low wave of height -x.

In the early 19th century scientists believed that light was brought to us as particles, until scientist Thomas Young demonstrated with his "double slit" device that light was also acting as a wave because it was interfering with itself—similar to the constructive or destructive waves we just discussed.

It was also believed that the smallest possible building block of matter was the atom—it being the smallest particle of any element. But then science discovered even smaller particles (or elementary particles), and we now enter the subatomic world. In this world the nucleus of the atom was found to be made up of elementary particles called protons and neutrons. Also found was the electron, which travels around the nucleus like the moon around the Earth. The trouble with the electron was that we can never know the precise momentum or position of the electron at any time—this is called the Heisenberg uncertainty principle.

What is known is that the path (known as the shell) of the electron depends upon the energy of the electron, and all electrons in any path (shell) have exactly the same amount of energy. It was once believed that electrons could move from one shell to another, losing or gaining energy in order to do so. However, it has now been theorized that the electron exists in a virtual state as a probability wave spread "throughout all of space. The electron only manifests in its spacetime location when a conscious observer makes the measurement."[1]

Physicists say that these electrons are defined by terms of probability rather than fact, and that that electrons are basically restricted to "quantized orbits," in that they could, theoretically, be in orbits thousands of miles away from the nucleus, but that it is "probably" more likely to be close to the nucleus around which it orbits, especially if we attempt to observe it. Electrons can jump or "quantum leap" from one shell to another, according to the Heisenberg uncertainty principle.

Now, how does the electron manage to leap? Well, there are things called "force carrier particles," or photons, and they act rather like a carrier, helping the electron reach its preferred shell—they are responsible for electromagnetic interaction. This is how energy (or information) is transferred, via the electromagnetic interaction of the photon with the electron, hence changing the makeup or energy/information signature of the particle, within which lies the electron.

Now, this interaction can happen in two ways: photons acting as forces upon electrons "within" the atom, causing the electron to bind with an atom nucleus; and photons acting as forces upon electrons "between" atoms, like two bodies coming together—and all this within electromagnetic waves and fields. Now, the unit of energy these electromagnetic waves carry are called quanta (hence quantum), and following this forward, a photon is really an electromagnetic wave carrying one quanta of energy, and this "behaves as a wave and particle, depending entirely on the mindset of the experimenter. There is simply no fixed objective state, as Newtonian physics presupposed."[2]

The next part of the puzzle is to understand particle spin. This is similar to the way the Earth spins around its axis, and is called "intrinsic angular momentum," in that the particle will spin as it is meant to. Photons, on the another hand, spin, but with a difference: In the case of the photon it must spin in relation to the direction in which it is traveling—it is impossible to change one without the other. As photons travel at the speed of light, then they spin only left-handed or right-handed—forward or back.

Spooky Action at a Distance

At least, that is what Einstein called it—the fact that one particle could affect another particle immediately, whether they were next to each other or on the other side of the universe.

Now how this is achieved is the really interesting part. When a photon is passed through matter it will be absorbed by an electron, which will then, at some point unknown, re-emit the photon. That's not the interesting bit though, this is: If, for instance, we choose a crystal structure to emit photons into, we get an effect that is the answer to all our issues regarding quartz and granite (in fact it is pretty common in crystals in general, just better in some than

others). Crystal structures actually improve the likelihood that the photon will "decay" (split) into two photons of lower frequency (longer wavelengths). As the total energy of the two new photons must match that of the original photon, the observed fact is that the two new photons are actually linked—quantum entanglement via the crystal. So, crystal entangles photons.

Entangled God

I took a break from quantum physics for a day while writing this book and drove out to Lichfield in Staffordshire. I enjoyed a day out at the beautiful and esoteric Lichfield Cathedral, with its marvelous façade and ornate decorations. This time it was a warm, sunny day, and I sat on one of the wooden benches outside the main entrance eating ice cream and taking in the typically quaint English surroundings. Then something struck me. There is a picture of Jesus just beneath the main arch, quite old and worn, but easy to make out. He is residing within the Vesica Piscis—the upright oval or almond shape reminiscent of the female vagina and seen as the portal into and out of another world. This image is created by two overlapping circles—two worlds colliding and creating the Gateway or World in between.

I thought to myself, this Vesica Piscis is in the entranceway of this wonderfully mystical building for a reason. The Piscis is, of course, pisces, the fish, and this is the being associated with accessing the Otherworld—just as Jesus and Vishnu had been termed "the fish." If this Vesica Piscis was the shape of the portal or Gateway, I thought, then there would be some wonderful relation with science if it were true. I have been on record several times stating that I believe that if something is inherently true, then it will be true on many levels—and in this case I was in that sudden moment of bright sunlight inside my own mind, convinced that there would be some relationship here to quantum physics. I finished my day visit and returned to my work.

I sat at my desk surrounded by books, cameras, computers, and all manner of ancient junk. Then I thought to myself, if humankind can enter the Otherworld within the mind via entangled photons with our own thoughts, then the image of the Gateway would be the same as entangled photons. It would of course be a huge leap of the bizarre to find that an image of entangled photons, assuming anybody could see such a thing, would look like some religious motif of the Gateway. Well, I was about to enter the world of the bizarre.

What I found was an image of entangled photons as produced initially by Anton Zeilinger at the Institute of Experimental Physics at the University of Vienna. This image shows two concentric circles merging into each other, like dropping two pebbles into a still pond at exactly the same time and watching as the ripples merge. It is exactly the same image as the Vesica Piscis, which is an almond shape created by the very same sacred geometrical pattern witnessed here at the lowest (smallest) possible level that humans can observe, but at the level no ancient would have been able to observe in full consciousness. I can

Concentric rings, used for meditative purposes and to access altered states, on a jug from Kykoss Monastery, Cyprus.

only thereby assume that this is a universal pattern, or that it was viewed when within the unconscious state in the same way that DNA was observed by Crick and Watson when "under the influence."

What I do now know is that the image of the Gateway, the Vesica Piscis, is amazingly seen at the subatomic level of entangled photons. I also know that entrance through this Gateway was gained via another dimension entirely, which I propose was through the quantum entanglement of the "mind's" (not necessarily therefore the "brain's") photons with those of the whole or holographic universe. There will be more on this soon.

What I also now know is that crystal is a launching point for achieving this entanglement of photons—with very low frequency levels (ELF or even the Holy Grail Frequency we discussed earlier)—and this relates us back to the crystal skulls we discussed earlier in the book. Could they be quantum communication devices, enabling the entanglement of photons, the ordering of energy/information, and the magnification of the same back into the mind of the user through ELF (Holy Grail Frequency) waves?

A Sacred Constant

There was something about all of this that proved a universal constant, a geometrical pattern. The Vesica Piscis is well known for being created using sacred geometry, and now modern science had found the same amazing shape in entangled photons. But what of that other Gateway, the Great Pyramid? This I knew be the most perfect structure ever built for my hypothesis. Was there any relationship between the Vesica Piscis and the Great Pyramid? The Great Pyramid is also created using sacred geometry—the approximate 52° angles of the sides, among many other facts, prove this to be the case. So, there should be some relation. Well, there is: The angles of the Great Pyramid actually fit within the sacred geometrical diagram for the creation of the Vesica Piscis.

What does this imply? Simply that both images created for the Gateway, across cultures, are of the same sacred geometrical and mathematical pattern. They are related to the very pattern and structure of the universe in which we live, just as we are.

Something Fishy

Even the fish symbol of Christianity is linked here. This infamous secret symbol of the early Christians was known as *Icthus* (*Ichthys*), which simply means "fish," but was used as an acronym for *Iesous Christos Theou Uios Soter*, or *Jesus Christ the Son of God, Savior*. But this is where the Christian propaganda must end, for the word, in fact, also means "womb," as was seen across ancient Greece. The reason for this is simple: The true Ichthys was the son of the sea goddess Atargatis, originally a minor Canaanite goddess of love, who is serpentine in nature, as she is depicted holding snakes and a lotus while standing on a lion (just as was Hathor in Egypt, who is also linked to serpents). Ichthys was therefore the son of the Otherworld via the womb or Gateway of the serpentine energy—at least this is how our ancestors perceived it. He was the inner sun, the shining element we can all achieve if we so desire, and his symbol was therefore reused by the Christians for their own "Sol Invictus." Not surprisingly, the same symbol was seen as the vulva of Isis, the queen of heaven, who was the Egyptian version of Atargatis.

This Christian fish symbol was also later seen as the Mitre hats of Bishops, which in fact derived from this ancient fish-centred religion, which also has links with the Jonah (Oannes) cult and its Mesopotamian origin. Bishops wore these hats in order to be able to enter the womb

of the mother goddess as Shamans. In the Temple in Jerusalem, some priests even wore phallic hats for the same purpose.

The fish symbol we see today on the bumpers of thousands of Christians' cars is truly a very ancient and very Pagan device, used and seen as a symbol of the deity who passed through the Gateway or "womb of Atargatis," the Queen of Heaven. It is a perfectly natural and geometrically derived image, linked with the Vesica (vessel) Piscis (fish) and the Great Pyramid's angles.

There is no wonder that communication across these universal and perfectly natural patterns is possible. As we have previously seen, these macro patterns are found at every level, no matter how tiny we go. Quartz crystal grows at the same ratio as the Great Pyramid (52°)—is it not therefore the case that even smaller images will be found to have this sacred triangle? Either way, one thing is sure: Our ancestors created these two symbolic devices from within the structure of the universe as concepts they had visualized as Gateways into the Otherworld.

It seems that not only is this "communication" between entangled photons across dimensions possible, but it is also possible (and probable) that "communication takes place outside of spacetime."[3] That is, quantum entanglement transcends the very spacetime reality we find our conscious brains in. And when, as we have seen, we observe the electron appearing because we have consciously observed it, the electron in fact "materializes in zero time," as author Michael Talbot put it. He continues, "Such fundamental non-locality reveals the breathtaking interconnectedness of the cosmos. The physicist David Bohm coined the term 'Holoverse' in which he said, 'the entire universe has to be thought of as an unbroken whole.' In it, space and time are manifestations of what Bohm calls the 'explicate' order, no more than one special case within a generality of implicate orders that enfold. More extraordinary still, while the human mind, as we know it, requires to be enfolded in physical reality, at the same time it appears to enfold and contain the totality, just like a hologram. This is known as a tangled hierarchy."[4]

The Holographic Universe and the Holotropic Mind

In his book, *The Holographic Universe*, Talbot explains the theory surrounding one of the most amazing discoveries in modern theoretical physics. It seems that research physicist Alain Aspect of the University of Paris in 1982 discovered that "under certain circumstances subatomic particles such as electrons are able to instantaneously communicate with each other regardless of the distance separating them.... Somehow each particle seems to know what the other is doing. Since traveling faster than the speed of light is tantamount to breaking the time barrier, this daunting prospect has caused some physicists to try and come up with ways to explain away Aspect's findings."

One of these physicists is David Bohm, who was one of Einstein's proteges from Birkbeck College at the University of London. Bohm stated that Aspect's findings implied that "objective reality really does not exist, that despite its solidity the universe is at heart a phantasm, a gigantic and splendidly detailed hologram."[5]

To understand what Bohm and others were talking about, we need to first understand what a hologram is.

Many of us have by now seen a hologram in real life or on the TV screen in science fiction programs. However, we have not yet managed to produce a walking, talking, and interactive hologram such as those seen on *Star Trek*. What we have managed to do is produce a 2-dimensional piece of film with a 3-dimensional picture on it. To make a hologram, a still object is flooded with light from a laser beam. Another laser beam is then brought into play, and it is the interference pattern, or convergence of the waves we discussed earlier, that reflect off the first beam, and this convergence is photographed and caught on film. The result is a totally obscure picture of light and dark images until the film is lit by another laser beam to reveal an amazing 3-dimensional image.

But now comes the amazing, peculiar, and profound element of holographic pictures: If we cut the picture into several small pieces, the whole picture will still be found within each of the smaller pictures! Every part of the hologram actually contains all the information of the whole picture.

This incredible outcome leads us now to the conclusion that we cannot reduce down the hologram into smaller parts, as each part is really just a smaller whole. No matter how small we go, the whole is still contained in each and every part. The explanation is that the subatomic particles that make up the picture are quantum entangled on the piece of film, and refuse to

be split up. Bohm believed that the reason for this was not that these particles were "sending a mysterious signal back and forth," but that they were instead falsely seen as being separate in the first place. He claimed all things were linked, and that separation was an illusion. As Talbot explains it:

According to Bohm, the apparent faster-than-light connection between subatomic particles is really telling us that there is a deeper level of reality we are not privy to, a more complex dimension beyond our own.... We view objects such as subatomic particles as separate from one another because we are only seeing a portion of their reality...and since everything in physical reality is composed of the "eidolons," the universe is itself a projection, a hologram.... If the apparent separateness of subatomic particles is illusory, it means that as a deeper level of reality all things in the universe are infinitely interconnected. The electrons in a carbon atom in the human brain are connected to the subatomic particles that comprise every salmon that swims, every heart that beats, and every star that shimmers in the sky.[6]

It is now virtually impossible to be correct in reducing down the universe or any part of it into smaller parts and to study them in isolation from the rest, as they are theoretically—and, with the hologram, evidentially—interconnected. In the same way, the fourth dimension we speak of as time (as we perceive it) is also connected, especially when we consider time's relationship with

gravity, as Einstein and others have proven. Time is now also part of the greater holographic universe, which is much more profound than that we have created on a piece of film. It is a holographic universe of four dimensions (and more, as we shall see), not just a 2-dimensional piece of film! In this way all things, from all the universes, past, present, and future, exist in all parts, no matter how small, of the universal hologram. Each piece contains every subatomic particle that has ever been or will be. It is the scientific explanation for the akashic records of the ancients. And *we* are little parts of the picture, so *we* contain *all*.

The next step comes when we discover that not only are we part of this holographic universe, but also that our own minds are also holographic, something Michael Talbot has called the "Holotropic Mind." This now explains many problems that psychologists, neuroscientists, and the general scientific community have had with our own brain functions. Problems such as, how can the brain cross reference and retrieve information at such incredible speeds—indeed at the speed of an entangled photon? Every piece of information in our brains seems to be checked for a given answer to a problem instantaneously, and we are given the response at the same time as asking the question. This is indicative of a holographic system. It also explains the issue of memory storage, as we have little or no idea where memory is stored in our brains—in fact, some believe it may have little to do with our physical brains at all. The problem was raised more seriously in the 1920s by the brain expert Karl Lashley, who found that no matter what portion of a rat's brain he cut out, he was in fact unable to take away

its memory. This implied that the memory was moveable, not in the brain at all, or something else entirely. This something else is now thought to possibly be the holographic and quantum-entangled state we have been discussing—the whole of the memory being in every part of the brain, similar to a hologram, and due to being quantum entangled.

In the 1960s Karl Pribram, professor of neuropsychology at Stanford University, claimed that this meant that the memory and other brain functions were not in the physical matter of the brain, such as the neurons, but in the nerve impulse patterns that criss-crossed the brain like a hologram. In this way, the energy impulses seen in the brain when the individual is concentrating are similar to the firing of the laser beam to retrieve the holographic picture in the pieces of film!

So, if the universe is a hologram and our brains are holograms, then there must be a method of seeing the whole in the part of the universe, and it seems that *frequency* has a lot to do with being able to shine the laser beam onto the hologram.

We have already seen in the course of this book that the body is receptive to a lot more senses than previously considered or believed. Astronauts on the space shuttle expeditions found that they could actually see cosmic radiation as little white flashes upon their eyes. Scientists have discovered that our visual systems are sensitive to sound frequencies, and we ourselves have noted how altered states of our very consciousness are capable through manipulating the dominant frequencies in our brain. I believe that it is this altering of our consciousness via the manipulation of frequencies that allows us to shine the laser beam onto the hologram. But more than that, we are a living, breathing part of this multidimensional holographic universe, and are therefore capable of affecting other parts of the hologram by just visualizing it. Now, the paranormal world becomes a distinct possibility, if not a stark reality.

Stanislov Grof, a trained Freudian psychoanalyst at Charles University and the Czechoslovak Academy of Sciences, explored the uses of LSD at the Psychiatric Research Institute in Prague until the mid-1960s. He is the author of dozens of books on the subject, and founded the International Transpersonal Association, which organizes international psychology meetings. Grof had one particular female subject who had been using LSD as a psychotherapeutic tool, and claimed that she had taken on the form of a prehistoric reptile—not an unusual occurrence when taking such drugs. However, without any knowledge on the subject of reptiles, the woman gave a detailed description of the reptilian form, and even noted that on the male anatomy of such reptiles there was an area of colored scales for sexual purposes. Grof checked out the story with a reptilian expert and found that there was indeed a species that had a colored area on the head, which played an important role in the sexual practices of the reptiles.

Grof went on to record many examples of such events and experiences, and covered most of the animals that evolutionists claim we evolved from—as if our minds had retained the memory. More than this, many patients also gave accounts of cultural acts from the past millennia, such as rituals and rites that we are only now discovering through anthropological and archaeological methods.

What Grof discovered was regression of the subjects to natal and prenatal periods, racial and ancestral experiences, and even consciousness of inorganic matter and a oneness with the "universal life." The subjects went so far as to show an intrinsic and "intuitive understanding of Universal Symbols—the Cross, Buddha, the Virgin Mother, et al." They showed "awareness of the chakras and kundalini energies" and "the acquisition of knowledge and information without objective means." In essence, they showed an awareness "of superconscious forces and cosmic mind, and a sense of the transcendental unity of all manifestations."[7]

How alike all of this is to the ancient experience of the mystics. The Kabbalists, for instance, insist that in "none of their systems did [they] fail to stress the interrelation of all worlds and levels of being. Everything is connected with everything else, and this interpenetration of all things is governed by exact though unfathomable laws. Nothing is without its infinite depths, and from every point this infinite depth can be contemplated." Indeed, "there was no contradiction between the reality of the spiritual world and its connection with the natural world.... In the chain of being, everything is magically contained in everything else.... It is in this sense that we must understand the statement often made by later Kabbalists to the effect that man's ascent to higher worlds and to the borders of nothingness involves no motion on his part, for 'where you stand, there stand all the worlds.'"[8]

The one common element to all of this was the transcending of the modern, evolved human consciousness; entering trance states as Gateways to the Otherworld—another world within the holographic universe, which transcends all borders, including space and time. In essence, these individuals were becoming aware of ancient history within their own genes—they were conscious of this history. The beauty of this is that it reveals the distinct possibility that we can be conscious of *all* that we are, not that which we are led to believe we are.

Time

Thomas C. Meseroll, of the Hughes Space and Communications Company in El Segundo, California, pointed out that if we concentrate on the entanglement principle of quantum mechanics, then what we discover is that communication of information is instantaneous, which is of course faster than the speed of light. "If a communication device utilizing this principle were to travel at a relativistic speed in relation to an integrally connected entangled partner communication device, it would be possible to communicate over temporal boundaries, i.e., with the future and the past."[9] Therefore, he says, by using communication devices that utilize quantum entanglement, and accelerating one of the devices, communication would in fact travel through time.

We have to raise the question, if it is possible to talk across temporal boundaries by using an electronic device such as a communicator, then what would happen if two minds were quantum entangled

within the greater holographic universe? Would they too be communicating in time? And because our thoughts are particles/matter, would they indeed be traveling in time? The answer, theoretically, is yes, the effect would be no different. Imagine then the response of the world of the psychic and mystic. They will react with the claim that they possibly entangle with the minds of those from the past, and via this entanglement could actually travel through the dimension of time—thus bringing messages to the present time through the "zero time." In psychologist David Loye's book *An Arrow Through Chaos: How we see into the Future,* he explains that this "time travel" is only possible because the mind is separate from the body, as I will show later in this chapter. To quote from Loye's book, specifically Appendix B: "Wolgang Pauli felt there could be a correspondence between the wave-particle mystery in physics and the mind-body problem in philosophy, the brain in this sense being 'solid' matter composed of particles, the mind being a flow of energy in waves.... The materialist view underlying science has been that out of matter comes 'mind.' The new psychophysical view is that, in transcendent ways, mind shapes 'matter.'"

This "time travel" using quantum methods is not the only unusual probability we find placed in our thought box. It appears that scientists have now even managed to tele-transport photons, as this extract from the California Academy of Sciences' *This Week in Wild* newsletter revealed in July 2004: "It's not exactly Star Trek, but physicists in the United States and Austria have independently teleported the properties of one atom into another."

In fact, just to take things a little further, it is even believed that the very structure of our physical reality may be only stable because of the probability wave, which has been generated by the consciousness or minds of billions of individuals. These have come together, or more correctly, formed, in time into the whole of which the physicists and even religionists speak. What is this collective mind other than what for thousands of years man has called god? *Christ is all and in all* is a line that has baffled many, until now. If, as we have shown in *The Shining Ones*, the Christ is really the inner sun, the illumination we each find locked away within our own minds, and if this "mind" is really connected to the greater whole of existence via quantum entanglement, then it is in effect a truth speaking to us across thousands of years—a truth that has been misinterpreted onto a literal left-brain level of reality.

Some have called this collective mind a "will" and, as Emma Heathcote-James put it:

This *will* provides a link to all other conscious entities that interact at any time physically. To use more graphic language, the will arises from the pool of all consciousness—a pool formed by small contributions of each without spatial or temporal bounds. This collective will has power to bring about events in the physical world that transcend the physical limits of information transfer or kinetic energy, suggestive of (but much more complicated than) the

ideas of omnipresence, omniscience, and omnipotence.... This shaping mind operates both on the subatomic or microcosmic level and on the level of everyday, macrocosmic reality we can see and feel.[10]

Conclusion

If it is true that the Great Pyramid—the fire in the middle—is truly a fantastic work of quantum engineering many thousands of years old and related to all manner of different opportunities that we can now see, from contact with the quantum field of the superconsciousness of mankind to the concept of god, then we have a lot to think about.

From the very early days of the tribal Shaman who was a guide to the hunter-gatherer, and on through the various human revolutions of the world and into the great civilizations, our humble and yet powerful guide has seen humankind through wave after wave of discoveries. It seems, after thousands—even millions—of years of humankind's so-called progress, we have completely lost the skills of times gone by.

We no longer understand our place upon this Mother Earth of ours; instead we get confused and upset when we are distanced from her, and wonder why—as we discovered with the NASA astronauts. We rape and pillage our natural resources as if some great benefactor will pop off his cloud and replace it all for us. We no longer respect our earth as we once did, and so how much less do we understand her.

I believe that the ancients not only respected the earth when they put back what they took out, but moreover, I believe that they understood her better. They had a firm grasp on the many cycles of the earth and the greater universe around her. They watched and understood the spirits of nature in the animal kingdom, and grew a great respect for their amazing ingenuity. They lived in unison with their surroundings, whereas we steal and destroy.

We no longer understand what we are doing to this only home we have. We put back filth from where we have taken goodness. We blow up, poison, and violate the very thing that gives us life. It will all come back upon us one day, as it may have done before. Just as the immune system within our bodies sends healing cells to cuts and bruises, so too will the earth heal those parts that are being damaged—by eradicating the cause. We do not send signals within our body consciously, and I am not saying that the earth shall do so consciously, but it is a natural effect, and we should be aware.

Ancient people understood and were in harmony with the earth, in ways that sound positively "New Age" to our modern, rationalistic, left-brain ears. They consciously conceptualized and materialized their beliefs in the images they carved and painted. They were at one with the resonance of a world at peace. But something changed. After millions of years of evolution, humankind began to wage war upon themselves as they overpopulated certain areas. They then waged war on the earth also. And now, in the 21st century, all we can say is that we are better at killing than ever before. How proud we are.

There is no wonder that people are attracted by the thought of life after death, because the life we have created has caused suffering and pain to countless and faceless millions. In an extension of our conscience we feel the suffering of the innocent inside our own minds as if it were us in pain, and we fear the unknown—death.

And yet, across the world, in every culture, creed, and religion; in every folklore, myth, and legend, the concept of death is to be rejoiced. It is and has been for thousands of years something humankind has hoped and longed for, and which has come through to us today in the Christian, Buddhist, and especially Islamic idea of paradise. But these are beliefs generated thousands of years ago from a basic core, and this core was more than belief—it was knowledge. It emerged from the actual ability to see for oneself the Otherworld.

We have found that people and the universe are interconnected through their biochemical and electromagnetic interactions. In a paper by Attila Grandpierre of the Hungarian Academy of Sciences entitled "The Nature of Man-Universe Connections," we have further backing for this hypothesis. Grandpierre is not alone in pointing out that there may be "possibilities of Man-Universe coupling with quantum-vacuum waves." This is no different in essence from the quantum entanglement now established to exist between two (or more) individuals—people who are basically on the same wave-particle length! It is postulated that cosmic radiation, neutrinos, and light actually contain biological information! Again, what difference is there here from the ancient concept of the akashic records? Or our concept of the collective superconsciousness? It is amazingly also postulated that we can receive this information through the many sensors and receptors we have. How much farther do we need to step to say that not only are we able to receive this information, but that by ignoring our modern world of illusions maybe we could actually *understand* this information? And then, how much farther a step is it to suggest that when the Shamans claimed to be able to manipulate this world of shadows, they were speaking the truth? As we have seen, even theoretical physicists postulate the theory of being able to manipulate matter with the mind alone. Lyall Watson, a well-known biologist and author of several books, described an encounter with a Shaman in Indonesia in which trees were made to disappear and then reappear with the use of a rhythmic tribal dance. The Shaman did this several times right in front of this respected scientist. It is believed that Shamans, understanding that what we perceive is nothing more than a holographic projection created from the collective superconsciousness of our own minds, do nothing more than delve into the hologram and adjust it.

One question did arise in my mind: How does the small brain that we have connect to the massiveness of space? Well, the answer is technical, but is there. As our Hungarian showed that "the application of the formula discloses the possibility of global-local information coupling between systems...a vital cosmic process between living organisms and the universe.... [T]here exist physical particles which may convey information from cosmic macrosystems to human brains."[11]

So, not only are we able to have a level of ESP through the recently discovered quantum entanglement, but now it is possible that we can indeed accept information from the universe. And, this, we must remember is a holographic, 11-plus-dimensional universe, with every scrap of information contained inside every particle in the entire universe! (Incidentally, we should also note that theoretical physicists are claiming this 11-dimension theory, which I do not intend to go into here, but I do want to note that this relates entirely to the ancient belief in the seven levels of heaven: 7 plus our four dimensions equals 11.)

The very methods of interaction between ourselves and the universe should not shock us, as they are no different from the methods with which cells pass on information, or any greater or lesser body to any other related body. It is a universal constant, and therefore following a greater universal law—*it has to be.*

❧❧❧

Following this law of constants to the nth degree brings us full circle to the beginning of my book and to the question I posed—is there life after death?

If you are prepared to accept that it will not be as you have been led to believe, and that almost nothing you can imagine will explain the reality, then the answer, in a way, is *yes.*

The universe, as we have shown, has constants—laws, even. These show that light from a distant sun cannot die or fade away. The fact that we no longer see it does not mean that it is not pushing at the edges of space somewhere, expanding

our universe—adding itself to the collective. I return to the Hungarian paper for more insight: Grandpierre theorizes that: "...the lost energy is transported by quantum-interactions [particle to particle] to the particle-reservoir of the whole Universe."[12] This energy is then passed back to the universe via further quantum interactions. This is the collective superconscious state, to where our quantum particles go, as they cannot die. Life after death is therefore a quantum field interaction of particles in a quantum reservoir—the Otherworld. In fact, Grandpierre's remarkable mathematical equations (Formula 4 in his paper) suggest that the human brain itself actually interacts with this vacuum through electromagnetic field quanta, and that our cells process the information through electron-vacuum wave interactions. We could theoretically contact or interact with the "energy" particles of the dead.

The vacuum waves interact with electromagnetic waves, which then interact with the waves of our brain—a kind of stepping down (or up), in the same way that a canal boat needs to in order to interact with the next level of the canal. Amazingly, the frequency of these vacuum waves observed in this interaction are "creative," in that they are the same as when cells divide, which is exactly what we have been saying—that this point is the creative principle, the point that makes the cycle begin! Not only that, but it also falls within the sphere of the Schumann Resonance we discussed earlier in the book. Nature gave us a way, and we lost it.

So, science and quantum theory are showing us that we can and do interact with the universe. It shows us that our thoughts are transferred into a quantum vacuum, and that they still exist after death!

But, I thought, this implies that the mind and the brain are separate entities—which is now known to be the case. Scientist Sir William Crookes, in experiments with psychic Douglas Home as early as the late 19th century, actually proved to the scientific establishment that the mind was separate from the brain by conducting reproducible experiments in his laboratory with a "materialization" medium named Florence Cook, who was there able to make a person appear out of nowhere, from the invisible part of the universe, on command. Indeed, this eminent scientist seriously believed that his methods proved beyond all doubt that not only was the mind separate from the body, but also that life existed after death. He was in fact knighted for his work, and made president of the Royal Society, as well as receiving the Order of Merit. Indeed, Crookes's experiments were even replicated by other scientists from France, Germany, Canada, and Ireland, all with the same conclusions.

"...[I]it is well established that at the time of death some vibration takes place, actuating something in nature, which occasionally gives information of the death to those who are sensitive." So said Richet in *Thirty Years of Psychic Research*. What exactly this "vibration" was that Richet observed during his 30 years of recording is unknown, but he certainly concluded that some kind of transference was occurring. The most incredible experiment that Richet noted was by a certain Dr. Dufay. The story goes that a prisoner strangled himself with a necktie, which the good Dr. Dufay managed to acquire. Putting the necktie into a piece of folded paper, Dufay handed it to a medium named Marie. The medium then went on to tell Dufay what was in the paper, and how the man had died. But she did not stop there. She went on to explain that the man had been charged with murder, and indeed that he was guilty of killing with a hatchet. She then told Dufay where he could find the hatchet—from where it was in fact later recovered. Vulliamy describes this as "pragmatic crypt-esthesia, or a sensibility to emanations from things, but the true meaning of such a phenomena is at present beyond our grasp. We ask ourselves whether the poor heathen, who believes that the ghostly essence of a man clings to his garments, is not just as near the truth as we are."[13]

At the same time as this discovery, a Harvard lecturer and psychologist by the name of William James was putting forward a theory that energy from some kind of external force was operating on the brain to enlarge its cerebral functions. This, he claimed, would thus explain away the seemingly spiritual answers that were the only recourse at that time. Others were of the opinion that consciousness in all likelihood pre-existed as an entity itself, and the various brains gave this consciousness individuality. Without modern scientific methodology and tools, these answers to very tricky and sometimes politically stressful questions, were a good shot in the dark.

In 2004 a Seattle doctor, Dr. Melvin Morse, believed he had found scientific evidence of life after death. To date, most scientists still believe that NDEs, or near-death experiences, are nothing more than the hallucinogenic result of a lack of oxygen to the brain. But Dr. Morse

once interviewed a 6-year-old boy who had just been resuscitated, and the boy had said, "That was weird; two guys just sucked me back into my body."

Although normally a skeptic, Dr. Morse was intrigued by the statement and decided to look deeper into the subject, finding another NDE experience in another youngster. This time the subject was a 7-year-old girl who was clinically dead, having spent 19 minutes under water. After her miraculous resuscitation she started drawing pictures, which Dr. Morse explained as a blow-by-blow, accurate description of her own resuscitation from a bird's-eye view. It seems, in her own explanation, that the girl had needed to return to her body in order to help her mother with her as yet unborn brother, whom she drew as a big red heart. It turned out that her brother was born several months later with a heart condition.

Dr. Morse then went on to carry out similar interviews with other children, and has come to the conclusion, with other medical experts, that at the moment of flatlining there is some kind of profound transference from the physical body into some other dimension—a dimension we have now scientifically explained.

One child told Dr. Morse that it was a light that had told her who she was and where she was to go, so Dr. Morse has made it his mission to contact that light, whatever it may be—but he does know or believe that through the rhythmic action of meditation or prayer (or even knitting), this element of the mind is brought into consciousness.[14]

Well, that is the precise conclusion of this book. On an extremely simplistic level

it is the meditation, hypnosis, rhythm, drugs, and any number of other tools that can be used in order to entrain the brain into the Holy Grail Frequency and experience the Gateway—the twilight zone in frequency. There are other elements also required, which can include the balancing between the left and right hemispheres of the brain, the magnification of the frequency through quartz, and most importantly, the entangling of photons.

It is a profound event in our lives when we decide to grapple with the unknown, when we take on the biggest issues, when we step outside of our own mental comfort zones and ask questions about life after death. It is much more profound when we discover that science is actually discovering that there is a kind of life after death, just not as we had been led to believe. It is also amazing to discover that our modern, theoretical quantum mechanics are just new ways of saying old things. Quantum theory is, in essence, the mystical world of the church of science. Electromagnetic manifestations of energy seen through the quantum entanglement of the particles in our mind is our complicated way of saying we have seen the spirits from the Otherworld.

I cannot place my hand on my heart and say that I believe every single psychic, scryer, and clairvoyant on the planet. I cannot say I believe any of them, no matter how heartfelt their work. But I can say that certain profound things are possible and seem to be, not only universal archetypes, but also evidently the most important element of life to humankind ever since we gained consciousness. We have hidden the whole gamut of our superconscious world within symbolism, myth, religion, and legend. We have hidden our journeys away from the public eye. But there is more than just the perception of this Otherworld; there is being completely conscious of it, being awake while seeing it and feeling it.

How much more profound is this whole scenario when we understand that Shamans claim to be able to control the world they see?

In the end, our search for the Gateway has truly led us full circle. We have traveled into the outside world in search of the physical portals built by ancient peoples. We have trawled through masses of documents in search of mythological maps. In truth we have found the physical manifestations of the Gateway, but in the end we must come to the stark reality that the Gateway is to be found inside of us. It is certainly true that "man" in general is completely unaware of the presence of an incredible and very human ability to access another dimension and energy source supposedly to be found deep within himself. This is why it is called the unconscious state, because we are simply not conscious of it. It can be disturbed in any ordinary person, leading to psychological problems or visions of heaven or hell in instances of near-death or even out-of-body experiences. It can even explain alien visitations. But we should be careful; we are told "it is important that the serpent should remain dormant, since it has a tremendous power when aroused. If disturbed, accidentally or by recourse to techniques ignorantly applied to awaken it, this force can prove very dangerous."[15] Apparently the serpent can rage unrestrained, causing strange and unusual desires and thoughts. This is the "bad landing" we spoke of earlier in the book. It is only the trained initiate who can achieve a good landing, so beware of experimenting with the serpent. Knowledge, strength, and will are much more important on the road to true wisdom and enlightenment.

We have seen now the way history, mythology, faith, and science can all come together and show us that there is a truth still to be discovered. It is a truth we are unconscious of, because something occurred to end our conscious connection. I hypothesize that ancient people were literally more in tune with this whole scenario, and that is why they could build such ancient wonders as the Great Pyramid and Stonehenge. Indeed, that is *why* they built

them—to reconnect and to take a journey through the Gateway to the serpent realm. However, in time this power was sent underground and hidden away from the people, giving rise to stories of great Underworld cities.

We see the sun cross the sky and say that it is taking a journey. But this is our perception of a real event—an incorrect perception. The Earth is moving, spinning, and the sun only appears to cross the sky; in reality, it is we that move. In the same way that our senses are misled, or rather, our senses mislead us, we now need to see the physical world in a different way. We now need to understand that there have been ways that people have in fact seen this hidden world—and more than that, they have understood it, and may have even manipulated it.

Conclusion
Time for Thought

 have learned so much during the process of researching and writing this and other books. And, with an almost deflated feeling, I have come to the end with the thought that what we have discovered had once already been known. It is this sad fact that surprises me the most: that people once had the knowledge and ability to perceive and access another dimension, which modern science and rationality is only now giving us glimpses of. It is a paradox that the same rationality and logic that destroyed our old perceptions of this very real Otherworld is now turning full circle and bringing us back once again to an understanding of what and where we are.

I decided to end the book with the thoughts of others. For throughout the course of human history there have been many individuals who did indeed perceive the Otherworld and what it truly meant for humankind. And so I will quote their words and leave it up to the reader to relate them to our modern scientific understanding, bearing in mind all that has been said before.

From the Bhagavad-Gita

When one sees Eternity in things that pass away and infinity in finite things, then one has pure knowledge. But if one merely sees the diversity of things, with their divisions and limitations, then one has impure knowledge.

The transmigration of life, takes place in one's own mind. Let one therefore keep the mind pure, for what a man thinks, that he becomes: this is the mystery of Eternity.

The Spirit without moving, is swifter than the mind; the senses cannot reach him: He is ever beyond them...the Spirit though one, takes new forms in all things that live. He is within all, and is also outside.

The Spirit that is in all beings is immortal in them all: for the death of what cannot die, cease thou to sorrow.

At the moment of death the sum of all the experiences of life on earth comes to the surface of the mind—for in the mind are stored all the impressions of past deads and the dying man then becomes absorbed in these experiences.

From the Tibetan Book of the Dead

First of all there will appear to you, swifter than lightning, the luminous splendor of the colorless light of Emptiness, and that will surround you on all sides.... Try to submerge yourself in that light, giving up all belief in a separate self, all attachment to your illusory ego.

Wonderful and delightful though they are, The Buddhas may nevertheless frighten you. Do not give in to your fright! Do not run away! Serenely contemplate the spectacle before you! Overcome your fear, and feel no desire! Realize that these are the rays of the grace of the Buddhas, who come to receive you into their Buddha-realms.... But if you miss it, you will next be confronted with the angry deities...threatening you and barring your passage.... All these forms are strange to you...and yet it is you who have created them. Do not give in to your fright.... They are but the contents of your own mind.... If at this point you should manage to understand that...and you will find yourself in a paradise among angels.

The mirror in which Yama seems to read your past is your own memory, and also his judgment is your own.

From Other Works

It is the ONE LIFE, eternal, invisible, yet Omnipresent, without beginning or end, yet periodical in its regular manifestations, between which periods reigns the dark mystery of non-being; unconscious, yet absolute Consciousness; unrealizable, yet the one self-existing reality; truly, "chaos to the sense, a Kosmos to the reason." Its one absolute attribute, which is ITSELF, eternal, ceaseless Motion, is called in esoteric

parlance the "Great Breath," which is the perpetual motion of the universe, in the sense of limitless, ever-present space.

—Madam Helena Blavatsky, *The Secret Doctrine*, 1888

When you speak, think that the World of Speech is at work within you, for without that presence, you would not be able to speak at all. Similarly, you would not think at all were it not for the world of thought within you. Man is like a ram's horn; the only sound he makes is that which is blown through him. Were there no one blowing the horn, there would be no sound at all.

—Maggid Devaraw Le-Ya'aqov

All these visibles and invisibles, movables and immovables, are pervaded by Me. All the worlds existing in the tattvas from Shakti to prithivi [earth] exist in Me. Whatever is heard or seen, internally or externally, is pervaded by Me.

—Sarvajnanottara, *Agama*, 2.9–11

...[T]he dust returns to the ground it came from, and the spirit returns to God who gave it.

—Ecclesiastes 12:7

For as the body without the spirit is dead.

—James 2:26

When God wished to create the world, He began His creation with nothing other than man and made him as a golem. When He prepared to cast a soul unto him, He said: If I set hom down now, it will be said that he was my companion in the work of Creation; so I will leave him as a golem [in a crude unfinished state], until I have created everything else. When He had created everything, the angels said to Him: Aren't you going to make the man you spoke of? He replied: I made him long ago, only the soul is missing. Then He cast the soul into him and set him down and concentrated the whole world in him. With him He began, with him He concluded, as it is written [in Psalm 139:5]: thou hast formed me before and behind.

—Yalkut Shimioni to Gen. No. 34, *On the Kabbalah and its Symbolism*

Therefore we do not lose heart. Even though our outward man is perishing, yet the inward man is being renewed day by day. For our light affliction, which is but for a moment, is working for us a far more exceeding and eternal weight of glory, while we do not look for the things which are seen, but at the things which are not seen are eternal.

—II Corinthians 4: 16–18

Verily I say, the human soul is exalted above all egress and regress. It is still, and yet it soareth; it moveth, and yet it is still. It is, in itself, a testimony that beareth witness to the existence of a world that is contingent, as well as to the reality of a world that hath neither beginning nor end.

—Baha'u'lla of the Baha'I Faith

There is surely a place of divinity in us, something that was before the elements, and owes no homage to the sun.

—Sir Thomas Brown, *Religio Medici*

We cannot be happy if we expect to live all the time at the highest peak of intensity. Happiness is not a matter of intensity, but of balance and order and rhythm and harmony.

—Thomas Merton

There is more to life than increasing its speed.

—Mahatma Gandhi

A man is what he thinks all day.

—Ralph Waldo Emerson

Life does not consist mainly, or even largely, of facts and happenings. It consists mainly of the stream of thought that is forever flowing through one's head.

—Mark Twain

...[R]ealize in your daily life that "matter" is merely an aggregation of protons and electrons subject entirely to the control of the Mind;

that your environment, your success, your happiness, are all of your own making.

—Robert Collier, business guru

Those people who think they can do something and those who think they can't are both right.

—Henry Ford

I think, therefore I am.

—Descartes

In the beginning.... The earth was without form, and void and darkness...on the face of the deep.

—Genesis 1:1 ("Was" between "darkness" and "on" has been taken out, because the words were a King James addition to the original text.)

When one separates from the body of flesh and blood, one possesses the form of the illusory mind, free from material existence and possessing two names.... Because liberation occurs through recognition of the manifestations as one's own projections, the illusion dissolves of itself.

—Giacomella Orofino, *Sacred Tibetan Teachings: On Death and Liberation*

What is a friend? A single soul dwelling in two bodies.

—Aristotle, *Diogenes Laertius*

In the beginning was the Word, and the Word was with God, and the Word was God.... And the Word was made flesh, and dwelt among us.

—John 1:1–14

To see a World in a grain of sand,
And a Heaven in a Wild Flower,
Hold Infinity in the palm of your hand,
And Eternity in an hour.
—William Blake, *Auguries of Innocence*

Not to be born is best. The second best is to have seen the light and then to go back quickly whence we came.

—Sophocles, *Oedipus at Colonus*

Non omnis moriar. (Not all of me shall die.)

—The opening words of Horace, Ode 3.30

In one fell swoop we have mastered the science of the day; we have journeyed from times hoary with age to the very future; we have seen the wonders of the ancients in their incredible buildings, built for a unique method of travel; we have spotted clues to the very real Atlantis; and we have come to our end. Can anyone now say that they do not believe in an afterlife? Can anyone say that there is not more to life than meets the physical eye? Can anyone of us now see life in the way we did before our journey?

If these few pages of investigation have altered our mindset in anyway, then all is well and good. For the Earth deserves better than what we are giving her. She deserves respect, for we are all one.

Appendix I
Material Locations of Gateways

 would urge the reader to take the time and go through this gazetteer of places, as there are many revelations included in each entry that needed the understanding gained from the main body of the text to clearly comprehend.

Aaru

In Egyptian mythology, Aaru was the heavenly Otherworld where Osiris ruled. It was also known as Yaaru, Iaru, or Aalu. Any souls weighed in the Hall of Maat that weighed less than a feather were allowed in Aaru. The specific location is unknown, but Aaru was believed to lie in the east, and was described as a series of islands covered in fields of wheat.

Abydos

This sacred place was the home of the Egyptian dead. No place on earth was more important as an entrance to the Underworld. Abydos was the cult center of Osiris, and the Underworld was situated between the hills of the desert just to the west. This in-between state is further evidence of the belief that the entrance to the Otherworld lay in the trance state, here manifested materially between two hills, which I believe to be symbolic of the Mother Goddess, with the cult of Osiris being the male element.

Today visitors are shown the main attractions of the temple complex erected mainly in the 14th century BC by Pharaoh Seti I. Along with the main Temple of Osiris are temples to Horus, Isis, Amon, Re-Harakhte, and Ptah. Another is dedicated to Seti himself.

Abu Simbel

This is the location of two large temples in Egypt, cut from rock by the workers of Ramses II (1279–1213 BC). Dating back much further in time, though, these great caves had previously been used for Hathor of Absek, but were rededicated to Amon-Re and Re-Horakhte. Located on the south side of the Nile in Nubia, the temples were moved upwards 200 feet in the 20th century due to flooding.

In front there are four colossal figures of Ramses himself, but it is inside where the true hidden reason for the temples resides. Going back 185 feet from the entrance there are a series of halls and rooms with rows of statues of the god Osiris, the god of the Underworld, revealing the true purpose of this entranceway to the Underworld. At the top of a pylon there is a row of baboons, or Watchers of the Dawn, who are seen with hands held aloft, adoring the rising sun god, and hence this is a place of rebirth from the Underworld.

What is strange, however, is the similarity (not just in the meaning of the temple tomb but also in a certain astrological effect) to Newgrange in Ireland: On February 22 and October 22, the first rays of the morning sun shine a path down the whole length of the temple, illuminating the very back wall of the most inner shrine and the statues of the four seated gods. This is illumination inside the cave or womb of Mother Earth, just like the illumination that Buddhists and others claim when inside caves. It is the outer sun illuminating the inner, and it is graphically seen in this amazing and ancient effect.

Annwyn

Specifically Welsh, this mythological Otherworld cannot be placed in any particular real location, although it was said that it could be entered by those still living if they could find the door. The door was believed to be at the mouth of the River Severn near Lundy Island or even Glastonbury Tor.

Athena Polias

Located near the Acropolis in Greece, and built upon a site of a much earlier goddess temple, this sacred place lies near an equally sacred cave, an ancient cairn, and a "natural" rock pillar—symbolizing the unity of male and female energies and bringing the materialization of the portal into our world.

Avebury

This is a huge British temple and stone monument erected circa 2000 BC in the shape of a serpent if seen from the sky. It was once known as *Abury*, which, according to Deane, is evidently *Abiri* or *Ab-ir* (after the Abiri people or Cabiri). Although some have argued whether it should ever have been *Abury* or *Aubury* ("serpent sun"), the fact remains that even as far back as the 17th century there was a Mr. Aubury who said that it should be pronounced and spelled *Aubury* (as found in the legier book of Malmesbury Abbey).

Of course, even as *Ave Bury* the *Ave* reverts back to the root of *eve*, which we know means "female serpent." (Deane also believed that the Kaaba or Caabir of the Muslims—which was a conical stone—resolved itself into *Ca Ab Ir*—the "Temple of the Serpent Sun"). The pathway of the Avebury serpent (Aub) passes through a large circular Temple of the sun (aur), emerging, winding again, and ending with an oddly, not-quite circular head—directly in line with Snakes Head Hill in Hackpen. The central circle is symbolical of the sun, which is the male principle in the creative process, and is symbolized elsewhere as a bull or lion. Once the serpent has passed through or around this sun circle it is recharged for new life. The archaeology of the area shows that people used to walk outside of the pathway of the serpent, leaving the inner pathway to the priests. In Egyptian hieroglyphs we can see the symbol of the snake going over the solar disc, emerging head erect. Overlaid onto Avebury it is the same image! Adding to

this that the snake is often depicted with the ancient Egyptian Ankh symbol dangling from its emergent neck (the Ankh being a symbol of new life), the great circle of Avebury simply has to be the solar disk and the pathway of the snake—thus illustrating in a painfully labor-intensive way the ritualistic path of the serpent-worshiper toward new life.

A past Vicar of Avebury remarked that the "mutilated figure" of a Druid in Abury Church, shown with winged serpents (dragons) biting his feet, symbolizes the victory of Christianity over Druidism—a religion that, as he says, venerated and worshiped serpents. After spending many hours sat in the cool, fusty air of the little church at Avebury, staring at the image, it is my view that the serpents "biting" the Druid's feet are actually subdued by the priest rather than attacking him. They are the energy lines of the dowser being controlled by the adherent.

Bath

The Roman baths in this aptly named English town were originally dedicated to the Celtic goddess Sul, which became Sulis Minerva once the Romans took up residence. It is believed that there once stood a Druid grove where now stands the Roman temple. Just as the Romans believed Minerva guarded the entrance to the Underworld, so too did the Celts of Sul. As water is worldwide seen as the entrance or Gateway to the Otherworld, there is no surprise that here the heated baths were also seen as a portal to the Otherworld.

Beit Guvrin

Located in the Holy Land, just west of Hebron, these incredible caves have been related to stories of giants from mythical times. Our esteemed academia has claimed that these caves were nothing more than quarries. However, there are problems with this hypothesis. It may be the case that the soft, chalky stone extracted from the site was used for building, but the symmetry of the "bell-like" shapes created in the inner cavern is a contradiction. The cavern is more than 65 feet in height to the very top, where a kind of chimney hole lies at the precise center of the cave. The theory states that the excavators dug down from this small chimney portal and opened the excavation out. However, this cannot make logical sense, to dig so deep and wide while lifting out chalk stone through a small opening. The normal and often-seen method would have been open-cast mining or tunneling, and certainly not in such a perfect fashion.

There are also spaces within the central locations that give the appearance of being "hidden" or "secret," where figures have been found carved into the chalk.

There are many tales of giants in relation to this series of caves, as well as the general locale. Often the inhabitants of the area would bring offerings to these "special" men of the past, whom I believe to have been the Egregor or Watchers spoken of in the book of Enoch and elsewhere.

These caves are another example of the true worship carried out in ancient times within caves and womb-like structures. The relationship between giants and caves is much more than a Northern European belief system; it is a worldwide phenomenon, as can be seen here, leading us yet again to the conclusion that the term *giant* is given to the men of old, the men of renown, who once walked the earth measuring the sacred energy currents of the globe and assigning specific locations for building and creating the sacred society of masons.

Black Madonnas

These are to be found across the world, but mostly on mainland Europe and France. Generally the stories relating to finds of this "Black Virgin" are associated with forests, woods, wells, water, serpents, dragons, and bushes, and the Black Virgins are then taken to the local parish church. They are also quite often seen as being taken from or cut from the trunks of trees, and often the tree itself is kept in a crypt. Also, churches were commonly built where the Virgins were found, regardless of the fact that many of these statues and figurines were really ancient Mother Earth goddesses such as Demeter and Cybele. With the association of black, which could be indicative of the "trance entranceway," I am sure that holy places are associated with this Virgin phenomena because of the very nature of accessing the Otherworld—it being a Gateway to "heaven." Following are a few examples of various locations of Black Madonnas with relevance that I could find to holy places, elements of related symbols, and possible "energy" points. (For further research on this subject I recommend a reading of Ean Begg's *The Cult of the Black Virgin*.)

Hu-la-Sarte, Belgium

Located on a hilltop near Meuse, this Black Madonna holds a Roman-styled scepter with the wings of Mercury, which is symbolic of enlightenment. The child holds a large, golden key near to the womb of the Madonna, indicating that the "Christ" or enlightenment is the key to the "womb," "tomb," or Otherworld.

Le Puy, France

This was a major Druid center in Roman and pre-Roman times, dominated by two rocky peaks, upon one of which stands the cathedral. In the locality there is a temple to Diana, as would be expected, and one to Mercury—both connected here (Mercury=serpent communication, Diana=Mother Goddess).

Originally the Black Madonna was said to have appeared in AD 46, when she told a widow to lie on top of a black rock or dolmen to heal a fever. The fever stone of the widow was even placed on the altar (now removed to the Golden Gate outside).

There is a "sacred spring" behind the altar, and a May Tree incorporated into the structure—the Gateway and World Tree or axis mundi together in one special place.

Liesse, France

There is a peculiar legend associated with this Black Madonna, which may tell us that the Templars were aware of the Black Madonna's significance. The legend goes that one day three knights of St. John serving under Foulques d'Anjou were caught and taken to Cairo. Here, with the aid of angels, they resisted attempts to make them Muslims. The angels also carved them a Black Madonna. The knights then converted the Sultan's daughter and returned back to their own lands. The Sultan's daughter was called Ismeria, which is a crossing of Isis and Mary—two of the characters we know to be associated with the Black Madonnas and implicated in our story on many occasions. The knights of St. John obviously understood the importance of the symbolism of the blackness, which is the Gateway, and the Mother Earth goddess, which is again the entranceway. The merging of the goddess Isis with Mary in Ismeria is a code of this importance. The angels or "Shining Ones" are the enlightened beings who are from the Otherside, and have made the knights a key to the Gateway.

Apparently when the knights were carrying the Black Madonna back to France, the load became so heavy when they reached a spring that they had to put it down, and built a church on the very spot. Charles de Gaulle found the location of special importance, and the Knights of Malta (part St. John and Templar) have a chapel in the church.

Luvigny, France

Here the Black Madonna (although denied to be so by the religious authorities) is said to resurrect dead children, who are then baptized in a local lake, which was previously a sacred Pagan site. This is the rebirth through the Gateway, as water (especially lakes, wells, and springs) was seen as a portal to the Otherworld—the symbol of childhood being the initiate who must die to him- or herself. Similar tales are found elsewhere, such as in Nanc, Prats-de-Mollo, and Orcival in France.

Mailhat, France

The original Black Madonna was stolen from the church in 1972, but the image remains a potent one. Nearby, the replica now in place is an image of a woman suckling snakes.

Malaucene, France

The name of this enigmatic and secretive location means "black earth," and the local legend explains why. The Black Madonna is thought to have been brought to the area by St. Eusebius in the fourth century, but the legend of the area states that rock "opens when the Gospel is read during Midnight Mass at Christmas to reveal gold behind." (*The Cult of the Black Virgin*, Ean Begg, Penguin.) The church itself was built by the Benedictines on the site of an ancient Pagan temple. This local legend must come from these ancient times, and indicates a belief in the Gateway phenomena, whereby the earth is opened to reveal the truth, or "gold." It is a literal and practical literary device for the opening of the "black earth" (possibly volcanic and electromagnetically charged) to reveal the Otherworld.

Mariazell, Austria

This is the religious epicenter of the old Austrian Empire. The Madonna currently in Mariazell was once painted black and carries a "Christ" child. Tradition states that Magnus (a Benedictine Monk) took this statue into the wilderness with him, which is an allusion to the emptiness we have spoken of in the main part of the book. His path to the wilderness was blocked (Shaman obstacles) by thickets or rocks, and the Madonna opened the way for him, hence the Black Madonna being the key to the Gateway—a female Shaman guide.

Mazan, France

This Black Madonna was supposedly found by some women who were weeding the fields in the 11th century. The church here was built on the site of a Pagan temple, and the belfry of the main church is built on a Templar tower. Also, on the town's heraldry (or coat of arms) is the hand of Fatima (*Fatima* means "the shining one"), the sun, and a crescent moon—coming from the Islamic incursions. Strangely, these items have remained on the arms, whereas the sword of Charlemagne has been removed by the religious authorities.

Metz, France

Metz means "mother of the middle," and implies the central way needed to access the Gateway. Metz was a very ancient center for Druidism, with a female leader called Arete, who was so inspired by a dream that she had a temple erected to the god Silvanus. There is a Merovingian and Templar association in the area, as well as the dragon that St. Clement called Graouly. St. Bernard, who helped to create the 12th-century incarnation of the Knights Templar, was familiar with the location, and preached the Second Crusade from here.

The cathedral actually had a statue of Isis right up until the 16th century. This must have been an important location for the ancient serpent-worshipers we have spoken so much of and indeed seen as a Gateway to the Otherworld.

Mondragon, France

The name (*Mondragon*="Dragon's Hill/Mound") implies strongly that this place had links with serpent worship and the enlightenment process. Again the Benedictines are here setting up their monasteries and churches. Unfortunately, its Black Madonna was whitened in the 19th century.

Myans, France

Here an avalanche was stopped by the Black Madonna. The monks who had fled to the church claimed to have heard the demons (who created the avalanche) say "Go on! Go on!" but they were answered by other demons that said, "We cannot, the Black One is stopping us." The Black One of course being the Madonna, who guarded the Gateway!

Najera, Spain

Legend states that St. Peter (the rock) brought this Black Madonna, but orthodox history claims something just as unbelievable. King Garcia VII of Navarre is said to have seen a shining light issuing from a nearby cave while out hawking, and so founded the place. Caves are symbolic of entranceways, and the shining light is indicative of enlightenment. A similar tale is told of Nuria in Spain, where a shining cave guides the way to hidden treasure, which consisted of a bell (to call to prayer), a cross, a cauldron, and the statue of the Black Madonna.

Palau del Vidre, France

Here the peculiar Black Madonna actually opens to reveal a bearded figure—a symbol of wisdom within.

Tarascon-sur-Ariege, France

This area was supposedly founded by Charlemagne after he came across an apparition of a "shining lady." The whole area is covered in Cathar and Albigensian history. It was to grottoes in the Tarascon region that the Cathars of Montsegur sent the "secret treasure" that they spirited away before succumbing to the death sentence of the Catholics. Many wonder why the area is so rich in spiritual beliefs—it may have something to do with the high levels of radiation caused by the uranium deposits, which are now mined at Sabart.

Bodh Gaya

This is the sacred location in India of the infamous Bo Tree of Buddha. Gautama (Buddha) sat cross-legged beneath this Bo (which means "enlightened") Tree or Pipal tree, and received illumination or enlightenment by meditation. The tree was then sanctified, and was even officially revered by the first Indian Buddhist emperor, Asoka. The tree that is currently on the site is thought to be descended from the

original, and nearby is a red sandstone "Diamond Throne" that marks the very spot that the Buddha is thought to have sat. It is the center of the universe for Buddhists.

The main attraction though is the Temple of Mahabodhi, which has a 150-foot pyramid spire where the original tree is thought to have been.

It is thought that this place simply must have some kind of earth energy associated with it, if not from the ground, then from the concentrated energy of the visitors.

Cahokia Mounds

A 2,200-acre site near St. Louis, Illinois, these are part of a once-great city, with complexes and burial mounds dating between AD 700 and AD 1500, although occupation of the site goes back to at least AD 300.

In 1971, researchers unearthed a small sandstone tablet with crosshatching on one side, indicative of a serpent's scales, and a depiction of a feathered or winged man on the reverse. It is similar to one found at Spiro Mound in Oklahoma, and leads some (namely Joseph Campbell) to assume that this is an American version of the feathered serpent of Central America from at least 1000 BC. This winged man is indicative of the Shaman and spirit flight to the Otherworld, indicating the objective of these mounds. It is the place of the serpent Gateway, with the wings of Shamanistic flight. There are other effigies found elsewhere in the United States with similar winged depictions.

One other peculiar effect is caused at the Cahokia Mounds: There seems to have been a problem with lightning strikes. In the southwest sector of one of the wood circles, archaeologists found that several of the posts had been replaced due to lightning damage. Ray A. Williamson, in his book *Living in the Sky*, said, "if the modern experience at Cahokia is any guide to the past, lightning damage appears to have been a particular problem." So there is a modern problem, implying that the current electromagnetic energy of the site is similar to its energy in ancient times. He continues, "In 1980, the observer's post was struck by lightning and shattered. The Winter Solstice post shows some signs of lightning damage as well."

If these areas are prone to lightning strikes, it proves that there is an attraction at this point, and I, as well as many others, believe that the ancients were capable of knowing this, through observation of the strike, or by manipulating the land in such a way as to cause the effect. There is no wonder now that poles and specific types of stones were dragged hundreds of miles and placed in specific locations such as the tops of mounds. Paul Devereux pointed out in *Secrets of Ancient and Sacred Places*, "And what more dramatic way could a link between heaven and earth be demonstrated to the populace than by a bolt from the sky linking with the sacred Omphalos?" A physical representation of the Gateway to the Otherworld. Scientifically, this effect is caused by the fact that the Cahokia Mounds are near to fault lines in the Earth's crust—namely the New Madrid seismic zone.

Now we can see folklore, archaeology, and scientific reasoning behind this cluster of mounds at Cahokia.

Caves

David Whitley, in *A Guide to Rock Art Sites: Southern California and Southern Nevada*, tells us, "Caves often served as vision quest locales because shamans believed the supernatural world lay inside or beyond them; the shaman entered the supernatural when the rocks opened up for him. Caves served as portals to the sacred realm."

Morris Opler in *An Apache Life-Way* tells us of this belief in a tale about an Apache Shaman: "...a spirit came to him and told him to go into that mountain [the holy mountain known as Guadalupe Mountain]...he heard a voice telling him to go into the cliff, he turned around and started to enter the mountain. The cliff opened like a door."

This strangely also relates to various claims that the Great Pyramid or "World Mountain" also had a stone swing door on the north face that opened to allow the priest in and out.

Beliefs such as this are universal. In Europe we have fairies and giants coming and going through openings in rocks or mountains; in Hawaii they are the "Little People." These openings have materialized as caves, fissures, and cracks. Many would see snakes and lizards entering and exiting these places, and this, in association with the vision of the particle-wave phenomena, gave rise to the belief in dragons and

serpent guardians. By following or defeating the serpent, the Shaman was able to enter into the other realm. We can see the most ancient tale of this when on Mount Mashu, the great Mesopotamian hero Gilgamesh becomes the "opener of the way."

This is the reason why some of the most amazing rock art to be found on the planet is hidden deep within caves or the Mother Earth's womb. We should therefore take note of the symbolism employed in these sacred locations. We should also note that many, if not most of these places are associated with the feminine principle as the Mother Earth's womb, and it is for this reason that we find the sibyls and female oracles situated within them. The Shaman, upon entering, enacts the male role when entering the womb, and brings the union. This is also why the sun entering the cave or mound at certain times of year is also important, as the sun is often the male principle.

In the Aboriginal creation myth of Australia (one of the oldest anthropological creation myths on the planet), the Father God instructs the Mother Goddess to create life. She proceeds to awaken the sleeping life form that resides deep inside her womb—the caves of the earth. This is an indication of the association with the caves and caverns of the world to the awakening or enlightenment process, which is the Gateway to the Otherworld.

Those who enter caves are often bestowed with great skills by the Underworld people, and often these skills are a musical ability, often used to open the portal

again. As we have seen with the particle-wave phenomena in the brain and the infrasound aspect of creating paranormal experiences, there is no wonder that music was seen as an opener of the way.

Hermits from across the ages have made it their passion to reside in caves, crevices, and fissures. They believed that they were closer to the gods, or god, being on the doorstep of the Otherworld. Here they could, like the Shaman, act on our behalf and deal with the deities and ancestor spirits. Here too, as in tales of the Buddha, the hermit or Shaman would gain his or her enlightenment. At Carn Ingli near Pentre Ifan in Wales, a hermit by the name of St. Brynach spent many years living on the summit. During this period he experienced a whole host of paranormal activity, including angelic visitations. This peculiar place is known to have a reversed electromagnetic field! These days the disturbance can be seen as fluctuating compasses, faulty electronic equipment, and "earth lights," or balls of light, in the locality. Also in the area were the "knowing ones," local people who gathered in the area, with arcane knowledge of herbs and healing—a kind of retinue of Witches or Shamans.

Chartres Cathedral

Located in the small town of Chartres in France just outside of Paris, this cathedral is one of the most enigmatic and mysterious Christian buildings on the planet. Building began in the 12th century on much older and sacred Pagan ground, and continued into the 13th. The previous site was sacred to the Druids and even had a

Neolithic mound, according to Louis Charpentier. In *The Mysteries of Chartres Cathedral*, Charpentier tells us of the Notre Dame de Sous-Terre, an underground Mother Earth effigy:

The statue, carved in the hollowed-out trunk of a pear tree and very ancient, represented the Holy Virgin, seated with the Infant God on her knees. Age had blackened it, for it was made, not by Christians but before the birth of the Savior by the Druids, pagan priests to whom a prophetic angel announced that a Virgin would give birth to a God; and it was thus that they portrayed her, as she was to be, with great devotion and on the pedestal they wrote, in fine Roman lettering the words "Virigini pariturae," meaning, "The Virgin who will give birth to a child." When the first Christians came to Chartres they found this statue and were amazed.... Generations and generations before them came to mediate in the grotto where a Virgin Mother reigned, a Black Virgin who was named Isis perhaps, or Demeter....

There has to have been something here at Chartres that drew in the religious across the ages. Could there be a clue in the name of the ancient tribe, the Carnutes? Their name means "guardians of the stones," and as Charpentier pointed out, the place of the stone was Chartres, which he also stated was once known as "the place of the strong." Whatever this stone was, it could be that it had strong electromagnetic properties and probably brought on altered states of consciousness, as did the

granite of Machu Picchu and the Great Pyramid. This is the reason that the entry point to the Gateway, namely the black of the Mother Goddess, is worshiped here.

Cloch a Bhile

This is a large, megalithic stone found at Lough Gur, County Limerick, and which looks remarkably like a tree trunk, giving rise to the concept that it was an axis mundi and called the Stone of the Tree. It is believed that this tree stone was where the ancients could access the Otherworld, and if one were to climb up (or down) the branches, one would access the varying levels of the Otherworld.

Delphi

Located in Greece, this ancient center for oracular prophecies is where the infamous omphalos is located, thought by many to be a pattern of the energy (electromagnetic grid) of the earth as designed by the ancient Greeks and by others to be a pyramid shape and equal to the Egyptian ben ben stone.

Delphi is called the navel of the earth, the center point, and Plutarch told us that Zeus sent out two eagles to the extremes of the earth, and where they crossed was at Delphi. This, I and others believe, should be interpreted as a crossing of the electromagnetic currents of the earth, as in feng shui. In another legend a herdsman discovered the oracle in a chasm or fissure in the earth where fumes emanated from the abyss. These fumes were said to cause the

animals and all those in the vicinity to behave oddly, and some have taken this to explain the prophecies of the oracle. However, one thing is sure, where faults such as this occur, electromagnetic phenomena are not far behind.

Dupath Holy Well and Dunloe Circle

Located in Cornwall, this Holy Well is infamous for its healing ability. But what are really interesting are the deposits. Apparently, pilgrims used to visit the well, and one of the customs was to bring offerings of quartz crystal and deposit them in the well. This caused such a buildup that Aubrey Burl noted in *A Guide to the Stone Circles of Britain, Ireland and Brittany* that "bits of quartz can still be found near Dupath holy well east of Callington." Nearby is Dunloe, which is a megalithic circle consisting of eight large, shiningly white quartz stones, the largest of which weights 12 tons.

Fairy Mounds

These are ancient mounds, burial chambers, and cairns found across Europe and associated strongly in Celtic legends to the fairies of the Otherworld. Malcolm Fergusson in *Rambles in Breadalbane* said, when speaking of Ireland's fairy heritage:

If all the tales one hears related by old natives of Rannoch could be fully relied on, Schiehallion in days of yore used to be a

favourite resort of the fairy folks, and more especially once a year, when all the various tribes throughout Glenlyon, Rannoch, Strathtummel, etc. congregated. Here they used to assemble in large numbers and hold their annual convocation, presided over by the beautiful and accomplished Queen Mab [Mebd], gorgeously arrayed in her favourite green silk robes, with her abundant crop of beautiful golden-yellow hair waving in long ringlets over her shoulder down to her waist. It is said that there are a long series of mysterious caves, extending from one side of the mountain to the other.

Here we will linger a while on some Irish fairy mounds, suffice it to say that I could literally fill an entire encyclopedia with fairy mounds, should I wish.

Cnoc Firinn

Located at Knockfierna in County Limerick, it is the home of the fairy king, Donn, the god of the Underworld.

Mullachshee

Located near Ballyshannon, County Donegall, this was the home of the fairy king Ilbreac, the son of Manannan Mac Lir.

Oweynagat, Cave of Cruachain

Located at Rathcroghan in County Roscommon, Ireland, the cave of Cruachain is a limestone cave that has been modified at some time in the past and is thought to be an entrance to the Otherworld and home of Queen Mebd.

The entrance itself leads to a man-made stone passage of orthostats, dry stone walls, and lintels connecting to the cave inside.

There are many caves in the area, mostly not much more than potholes; however, there is Uamh Tom a'Mhor-fir, which is where the fairies are said to dwell, and its name means, "cave of the great man of the bushes." This may come from the legends that mortals were sometimes said to go and dwell with the fairies in the caves and lurking under bushes.

Rath Cruachan/Rathcrigham

Located in County Roscommon in Connaught, this is believed to be an entrance to the Otherworld, and is now known as the Cave of the Cats. Feidelm came out of this mound from the Otherworld to warn Queen Mebd that she would have an army covered in blood should she continue her quest for the Brown Bull of Cuailgne.

Sidh-ar-Femhin

Located on the plain of Cashel, this was where the king of the sidhe (pronounced "shee") resided. One day a harpist by the name of Cliach gained access to the Otherworld by playing music near the entrance. This is a clear allusion to the fact that rhythm and music can bring one into alpha-theta mode and entrain the brain into the trance state.

Sliabh Fuaid

Located near Tara in County Meath, it is the mound where the fairy lord Aillen Mac Midhna would emerge from the Otherworld every Samhain to cause havoc. This fairy lord was said to cause warriors to sleep whenever he played his mystical music—yet another allusion to the power of music and rhythm. It was also the place where Lir, the father of four swan children, was said to reside during the time of the Tuatha De Danaan.

Slieve Gallion

Located near Armagh, this is the place that Culann, the smithy of the sidhe, lived. His hound (of the Otherworld and therefore the Shaman hound) was killed by Setanta, who then promised to protect Culann. Setanta was then named Cuchulainn or the "hound of Culann."

Fairy Rings

These are circles of mushrooms growing in the grass where fairies are thought to gather. Place one foot inside the fairy ring, and you will be able to see the fairies, as you will be half inside their world. Place both feet in and you will be trapped inside the world of fairies forever. This is an obvious allusion to the dangers of straying too far, mentally, into the sleeping state, which modern psychologists believe to be a dangerous state where people do actually get trapped.

Another tool used to enable ordinary folk to see fairies is elderberry wine. At Beltane, for instance, the elder twigs can be woven into a garland and worn around the head to give the wearer second sight. In fact, green elder wood is toxic and can bring on trance states and was used by Witches and Shamans for just such a purpose.

Fudarakuzan Rokuharamitsuji (Chinkoji)

Otherwise known as the Temple of the Six Perfections, this fantastic complex is located in Kyoto, Japan, and comes to life (or death) in August when the souls of the dead are welcomed back to the earth. For more than a week they are allowed to wander freely with family and friends, being fed and entertained before returning to the Underworld. The portal is opened, and indeed the souls are forced back into the Underworld via a unique bonfire burning, which encircles the town.

There is an old neighborhood called Rokudo, where this returning of the souls to the underworld still remains a strong belief. Here, at a small temple called Chinkoji, it is believed lays the entrance to the Underworld. Between the seventh and 10th of August many make pilgrimages to this sacred place to call upon the ancestors. Lanterns, incense, and altars are sold from temple stalls, with earthenware dishes being popular for placing food on to feed the dead.

Glastonbury Tor

According to stories related to Saint Collen, the entrance to the Otherworld was to be found in the side of the hill at Glastonbury, much like the sidhe (Tuatha De Danaan or Shining Ones) who came and went through the sides of hills.

Golgotha

Otherwise known as Calvary, this special place was where the Bible tells us that Christ was crucified. Its name meaning "place of the skull," Golgotha is no different from a cave in meaning, and is the place where Jesus goes through his death trial on the cross before entering the womb/tomb to visit the Otherworld. Here too Adam was said to have been created, and indeed buried. Some say that traditions state Golgotha to be the entrance to the Underworld, the center of the world, and the highest point. Obviously Golgotha is not the highest point, and this can only be symbolical. An inscription in Adam's Chapel at the foot of the hill reads *topos kraniou paradeisos gegonon*, or "Golgotha has become paradise."

In Cyprus and elsewhere I have seen many orthodox depictions of Golgotha with the crucifixion above a tomb, which holds a skull. In many, the tomb or cave is associated with the Vesica Piscis image, which we now know to be symbolic of the entrance to the Otherworld or heaven. Golgotha was therefore associated with the entrance to the Otherworld.

Hal Saflieni

Located on Malta, this temple complex runs to at least three levels underground and is where the remains of more than 30,000 people have been discovered. Inside there is an oracle chamber, from where the soothsayer would emit great prophecies through a small aperture. These were soothsayings from the Otherworld, and the oracle was seen to be in touch with the ancestors or deities. Hal Saflieni, then was an entrance into the Otherworld itself.

There are numerous legends that the tunnels emanating from Hal Saflieni emerge on other sides of the island, and indeed many "Underground" theorists believe they spread across the globe. I visited the sites across Malta, including many catacombs, and can vouch for the amazing extent to which the tunnels reach. It is a work of truly breathtaking scope that took hundreds of years to complete, right up into the Christian period. The catacombs are a mysterious and eerie place to be, and it can easily be seen how a belief in an underground world developed in time.

Howling Caves

Located at Delphi near the ancient Oracle in Greece, this vast limestone cave complex descends into the bowels of the earth and was believed to be an entrance to the Underworld. The whistling wind was believed to be the sound of the souls of the dead wailing.

Kiva

Although not a specific place, a kiva is a location of sorts. It is the Hopi word for "ceremonial room," and the Anasazi kivas

were underground chambers or caves. It seems the Anasazi used them to conduct all manner of rituals, including healing and drawing down rain from the gods. They were also places of gathering for the community. Often there were roof beams and mud walls covering the site, and the only way in was normally via a wooden stepladder through the hole in the center of the covering. More importantly though, there was a symbolic hole in the center of the floor, which was the entrance to the Underworld and was called "sipapu." This hole was understood to be in the "roof of the Underworld."

La Caune

Located near the infamous Rennes le Chateau in the Languedoc region of France, this cave lies on the slope of a large hill. It is an immense subterranean cavern lit by an 18th-century opening in the ceiling, which allows natural light to stream in and was created by seismic activity. Inside there are many stalagmites and stalactites as well as Neolithic inscriptions, which were discovered along with statuettes and pottery. Many believe that this place served as a sacred sanctuary serving a form of primitive initiation. Others believe that this was the cave identified by Ramon de Perillos as the entrance to the Underworld.

In the language of the area, Occitan, *cauna* is a feminine word, and means, quite simply, "cave." In the 18th century, the local priest, Laborie, declared that he had seen the image of the Great Bear constellation engraved into the walls above the

coupe recipient de la saincte csene de nostre seigneur Jesus, or the "recipient cup of the Holy Communion of our Lord Jesus." This has obviously been associated with the Holy Grail, especially with its location being so close to the infamous Rennes. The relationship of the Great Bear can be seen to be associated with the Roussilon region, which gained its name from the first "lords of the region" Orseolus, which is obviously taken from the name for the Great Bear itself. This also relates to an earlier name of the cave written by Laborie himself as *Oursus*, who seems to have named the cave after his vision of the Great Bear. The Roussilon family crest incorporates the bear as a totem animal flanking a central blazon incorporating the Holy Grail itself. I was not surprised to find that the Grail is associated with caves, as readers will recognize the correlation between cave and Grail.

Some researchers have noted how the easiest path, which leads into the cavern, meanders like a "serpent" and resembles initiation pathways seen elsewhere. Once at the end of this path we see another straight path, which runs between two rocks, like Joachim and Boaz, and which leads into increasingly darkened areas, where the first inscriptions are found. These inscriptions are faint crosses encircled or partly encircled.

Amazingly, there was also a Black Madonna found in this cave near the cross engravings. This suggests to many that this chapel area was seen as the "holy of holies," the sacred center and connection point to the Otherworld. The presence of the Black Madonna is itself very telling, as we have already noted in earlier chapters. However, there were also earlier (and later) "offering" statuettes of female anthropomorphic figures discovered in the same area, suggesting a strong Mother Goddess/Earth link to this "womb" cavern.

Most important is the discovery of a piece that suggests strong associations with the Ubaid figures of serpent people from Sumeria some 6,000 years ago. Many have described these figures as "aliens" due to their stretched eyes and cranial features; however, with the knowledge of the serpent worship I have gathered throughout the years it is beyond doubt that this discovery implicates this cave in the European serpent worshiping past, and was therefore a place of the Shining Ones or serpent priests and an entrance to the Otherworld.

Ley Lines

Although ley lines are a disputed subject, there are certain elements that I cannot ignore. It is a fact that ancient sites, such as megalithic monuments, appear to have been created to align with each other—not just in Europe, but across the world. Lines such as those near Weris in Belgium are in fact acknowledged by archaeologists to have been deliberately planned, and I believe that this one alignment cannot have been in isolation, nor could it have had no purpose. The fact that many Christian monuments, churches, and establishments such as monasteries were built over preexisting Pagan sites is not a problem: It is now well-known and accepted that Christianity stamped its mark upon the Pagan world by taking over sacred sites and building upon them, often with the same alignments to celestial bodies that were already there. I now know this to be a simple marketing technique of the new emerging cult of Christ, and to have been a continuance of the old sacred ways. Unfortunately, the "power" or "energy" of these lines has, in my opinion, been upset by the Christian buildings on the sites, although there are many Christian buildings that do seem to reflect the knowledge of the earth's magnetic signature.

I am of the opinion, following my researches into such sites, that many of these ley lines were specifically created to magnify the resonance of the earth and/or those of the individual using them. The use of granite is a good indicator of this understanding, as well as the building of sites on fault lines and places of ideal telluric energy. Another factor I found was the presence of the Black Madonnas on many ley lines. Admittedly, these may be in their locations due to the presence of the Christian churches; however, it is also a fact that the traditions that surround these enigmatic symbols of the "trance" were found in their place before a church was built—many churches having been built after the discovery of the Black Madonna.

I will now outline a few ley lines that I believe to be important Gateways using the earth's resonance to magnify energy to enable the individual to attain the perfect balance for travel. In each case, modern dowsers have registered their abnormal recordings of energy at each site.

Belgium

The Weris alignment is to be found approximately 2 miles outside of the town of Erezee in Belgium, and begins with three menhirs, which I noted were at right angles to a nearby "passage grave" (called such due to the dead gaining passage to the Otherworld through it). The next point finds us at another menhir, which today is to be found actually built into a wall. Next we arrive at a dolmen, and following that, more menhirs.

Boyne Valley

Situated in the most holy places in Ireland, taking in Newgrange, Knowth, and Dowth, this is one of the most important leys in relation to our work here. I already knew that these chambers were Gateways, and to find that they too stood upon an ancient ley line was double confirmation. In fact, two leys cross Newgrange directly upon the central chamber, a confirmation of the importance of the center point we have discussed.

Bristol and Wells

A modern ley line in England, this one has supernatural qualities and ancient associations. According to Danny Sullivan in *Ley Lines*, "there is a folk tale attached to a length of the old coach road from Bristol to Wells that runs between Bedminster Down and East Harptree, suggesting that the route has a corresponding equivalent in the Otherworld." The story goes that a 19th-century woman by the curious name of Molly N. was so exhausted on her journey that she cried out for a horse. Suddenly a white pony appeared to take her to her destination. However, at Mollybrook Stream the horse came to a sudden halt and threw her to the ground, knocking her unconscious in the process.

This story is a sorry tale full of difficult symbolism. She came to rest, unconscious at the stream of living water that bore her name. She was spirited by an Otherworldly white horse. The whole journey passes through equally difficult place names such as Dundry Hill, Pagan Hill, and Wriggleswell. *Dun* is an ancient fort on a hill, *Pagan* speaks for itself, but *wriggle* must come from the serpentine nature of the spirits or deities that were said to guard the sacred waters of wells, streams, and lakes. In essence, they were guarding the route to the Otherworld. With a stone circle and holy wells along the journey, there are reasons to believe that this peculiar folk tale is derived from a much older and Pagan concept. Molly, incidentally is a nickname for Mary (of the sea or water—*mare*, which is also a female horse).

Camac

Located in the Breton region of France, this beautiful and enigmatic row of megalithic stones shares a name with the Temple of Karnak in Egypt, and relates to the etymology for serpent. At Kermario (its name meaning "place of the burning") we find the largest row of stones, which once had cromlechs at either end. Cromlechs are in fact open passageways for rituals of Otherworldly travel, and probably developed from passage tombs or fairy mounds.

Again at le Menec nearby there are 12 rows of stones, which in this instance go in between two cromlechs of egg-shape design (the egg being symbolic of new life born from the Other realm).

Dartmoor

The whole of Dartmoor, in England, is literally strewn with Neolithic monuments and rows of stone. It is a special place, with a lot of supernatural or paranormal activity being recorded throughout the years, and has one particular enigma that has been, until now, difficult to understand. One row has a cairn at the end, another a stone block. Some have suggested that these were ritual pathways with astronomical alignments, but no one has taken this seriously, because there are strange blocking stones along the paths, which would serve to stop the procession in its tracks. However, I believe that these stones were purposefully erected on these locations. The stones are granite, with quartz veins obvious to the eye. I believe that just as Jacob rested his head upon a granite stone, otherwise known as Jacob's Pillar, in order to ascend to heaven (through the Gateway), these Dartmoor stones were for the same purpose. These stones are not symbolic devices (other than also being the Shaman obstacles of the mind), nor were they accidentally placed. They were stages on the road to trance, on the pathway to the Otherworld.

The same is true of the various cists that can be found here. These are sunken holes in the ground, often stone lined, but more often capped with a large granite block. These were more than burial chambers for the dead. They were instead Shamanic man-made caves where none naturally existed. They were Gateways, with the profound properties of quartz, in order to guarantee the passage of the dead into the Otherworld.

Devil's Arrow

This particular site in Yorkshire, England, is what my long-suffering wife called "just another load of big stones," and are the megalithic remains of what was probably a great ancient alignment. The stones' alignment can still be seen today meeting nearby mounds and circles. There are Neolithic ceremonial avenues, henges, and one cursus (taken from William Stukeley's idea that the ditch near Stonehenge was a Roman race circuit) was found to pass directly beneath the middle henge—showing that center point yet again. There are, not surprisingly, many burial mounds clustering around the ley lines and the henges, as this area was without doubt seen as a portal into the Otherworld.

Fairy Steps

Located in Cumbria, England, this ley line, similar to many others, is famous for its paranormal activity. This particular phenomenon is often found around ancient sites and may be due to the atmosphere of the place creating images in the subconscious mind, which then emerge into the conscious. However, the proliferation of such activity at these places could also be an indication of the resonance activity or

ELF signals that are magnified by the natural and man-made erections through time—thus bringing on a glancing vision into the energy signatures of the Otherworld. At the Fairy Steps ley in particular, the "supernatural" occurrences are said to happen specifically on the corpse road or death way—an ancient procession of the dead or funeral path.

The road or pathway runs from an ancient tower now called Hazelslack Tower Farm, through a series of stone steps, until it arrives at the Fairy Steps. These are rock-cut steps from antiquity used traditionally for the processional route to achieve the high place.

Gozo

Located on the beautiful Maltese island of Gozo, this remarkably old alignment runs through dolmens, the megaliths of Tal Qighan, Qala menhir, the Ggantija Temple, and even Xewkija Church (which has the third largest dome in Christendom—a symbol of the womb).

With a peculiar prehistoric past on the Maltese Islands, this alignment seems to date from at least 3800 BC, and predates most of those in mainland Europe (although there are many in Scotland dating from 4000 BC). Strangely, in around 2500 BC, the temple builders of Malta disappeared, and no one is quite sure where they all went or who replaced them. What is sure is the fact that at the same time the megalithic building projects of mainland Europe were seriously underway.

The Hurlers

Near the moorland village of Minions in the UK, lies this Bronze Age stone temple known as The Hurlers, consisting of three large stone circles aligned from NNE to SSW, and built between the River Fowey and the River Lynher. It is not unusual for stone circles to lie near rivers in this fashion. The religious authorities of the day would have been acutely aware that trade would have used the rivers like a great prehistoric motorway, and built their impressive structures at such locations.

The largest circle at the center is egg-shaped, and was in fact once linked to the northern circles by a granite pathway along their axes. Indeed, a scattering of quartz crystals in the central circle was found, which some believe to have come from shaping the stones with hammers, although it is possible that quartz was used in a ritual fashion, especially given the location of the quartz at the center.

Sligo

Located in County Sligo, Ireland, this Fairy Ley Line was noted by Paul Devereux in The Ley Hunter no. 119, and starts with a Fairy Fort or rath. It then runs straight through various other raths and toward Benbulbin Mountain, thought to be inhabited by fairies. The association with these locations and fairies is obvious, as fairies are beings from another dimension or the Otherworld. The locations where fairies are found are therefore Gateways to the Otherworld.

Logan Stones

Not located in any one place, Logan stones are to be found across the British Isles. It was said that to touch a Logan stone nine times at midnight would make a woman turn into a Witch—and what is a Witch, but one that can access the Otherworld?

Logan stones were formed through the weathering of various layers of rock. There is often a soft lower layer that is worn away by the elements until only a thin neck remains and leaves behind a large "head." Before the 19th century, many believed they had been constructed by the ancient Druids, or even the devil himself. They had, and seem to continue to have, a supernatural association, and this made them a focus for Witchcraft. Rocking the stone near Nancledrea in Cornwall could only be achieved at midnight when Witches were abroad—the in-between hour. One at Land's End was said to have been put there by a giant who rocked himself to sleep on it.

The origin of the word *Logan* is in the English word "log," which means "to rock."

It may be that the stones were seen as the very rock emerging from the womb of the Otherworld, like the head of a baby as he or she emerges from the womb. One thing they do show, which has relevance to the whole scheme of things, is balance. Unfortunately, because of this precarious balancing act, many puritanical Christians actually rocked the stones from their pinnacles, and so the nation lost a dynamic archaeological heritage.

Although the origin of the term *Logan stone* is in Britain, the stones are to be found all over the world as natural creations, and are now being termed *Logan stones* in several countries, from Thailand to Canada.

Machu Picchu

This is a great Inca citadel near Cuzco in the Andes, located on a geological fault that has given rise to peculiar magnetic anomalies, such as floating lights and even perceived alien visitation. We have here a location high in the mountains, on a fault line and built from granite, which we have previously discovered has radioactive and electromagnetic properties due to its quartz crystal content. People have seen visions of ancestors or "guardian spirits of light" walking around these ancient ruins, and this could be brought on by the accumulation of these factors on the human mind—linking into the "quantum mind of the universe." Indeed, the Dragon Project of Paul Devereux found that people exposed to this natural radiation (such as at Machu Picchu) spontaneously went into altered states of consciousness! In addition, Villoldo and Stanley, in *Healing States*, tell us, "The shamanic legends say that when one touches one's forehead to the stone, the Intihuatana opens one's vision into the spirit world." In order to test the theory the two authors visited the site, and Villoldo laid down on one of the stones to rest. About 10 minutes later he walked away from the stone, turned around, and saw his own body still lying there.

Minehowe

The world was shown Minehowe in 1999 when it was discovered on the Orkney Islands off Scotland. However, it was first excavated in 1946. It is a subterranean chamber held within a large man-made earthen mound. The only way in seems to be via a steep staircase. When I went I was first led down into a narrow landing, which then branched out into two chambers at right angles. Further down still I ended up at the lower chamber, which was believed to be a well by the 1946 excavators. Julie Gibson, one of the archaeologists who worked on the site in the late 1990s, said, "This thing is extraordinary and is definitely of international significance." She suggested that it must have had a ritualistic importance even as a Gateway or Portal to the Otherworld and a place of commune with the spirits.

Mountains

The World Mountain or Cosmic Mountain is central to a belief in the Otherworld and was seen as a method of gaining access. This is the reason that building the Tower or World Mountain of Babylon was seen as building towards the gods. Probably the most amazing of all is the Great Pyramid, which we have discussed in detail elsewhere. But there are other places and natural mountains, which are also important.

Mount Meru

This is the mythical center of the universe in the Hindu cosmology, and has many interpretations. Some say Mount Meru is in the Himalayas, and others that it is made of pure gold and reaches 160,000 leagues into the sky. It is the axis mundi, the backbone of the world, the place of ascension. Apparently the ancient immortals dwelled at Meru due to the emanating vibrations or resonance, enabling them to converse with the humans on earth. Chinese images of Mount Meru show it as an antenna, and this is because it was believed to pick up the signals of the immortals or deities.

Mount Tabor

This is a mountain in Galilee, which by tradition was the location of the transfiguration of Christ where the face of Jesus "shone like the sun" (Matthew 17:1–9)—an indication of the electromagnetic energy signature. Here, Jesus conversed with Moses and Elias, the spirits of the dead (mystics), just as did any number of Shamans before and after have claimed to do—via the Gateway. It was at this point of conversation that god said he was "well pleased" with his son, an indication of achievement in the mystical powers.

Another interesting and very telling text comes from the *De Vitae Moysis* (*Life of Moses*) by St. Gregory of Nyssa, written in the fourth century. Peculiarly, Gregory states that Elias was in fact hidden in the

same "cleft of rock" that the Lord had hidden Moses. This is a strange thing to say, considering the current Christian and Jewish belief that the Lord took them both to heaven. As Moses and Elias may never actually have existed as real, singular people, it could be that this was a revealing statement. It could be that this was an indication that the likes of Moses and Elias—and now, of course, Jesus—were to be found in caves upon mountains, or more telling that these shining beings were believed to come and go through these Gateways. God said in Exodus 33, "Here is a place beside me. You must stand on the rock, and when my glory passes by, I will put you in a cleft of the rock and shield you with my hand while I pass by." Here we see a direct allusion to the place any mystic needs to be in order to see the glory or shining of god.

We find elsewhere in the Old Testament that when God reveals himself there is a rushing of wind, an earthquake, and fire—are these indications of energy signatures caused by locations where faults lie? We also find that the shekinah, or presence of God, is seen as a bright or shining cloud that puts the three prophets (Moses, Elias, and Jesus) in darkness—the location of the Gateway. This cloud aspect is seen as a pillar of cloud leading the people out of Egypt, and with the image of the hand of God descending from a cloud in various iconographies. It is, in this respect, no different from the "smoke hole" of the Shaman, which was the Gateway to the Otherworld. Indeed, whenever Moses entered the Tabernacle (*skene martyriou*), the people saw a pillar of cloud descend and stand at the entrance. The word *shekinah* comes from the root *sakan*, which means "pitched

tent," and this is an indication that the Tabernacle, with the Holy of Holies within it, was seen as a mobile Gateway (for more on this see *Tabernacle*).

Similar claims for mountains can be made for Mount Sinai, where Moses "talked with God" and received the Ten Commandments; Mount Choreb; and Mount Hermon. Connection on top of the mountain to the ancients or deities is a long-standing belief, as can be seen when Moses receives the Ten Commandments from the Lord on top of a mountain. These mountains are often associated with the Shining Ones or Lords of Time, and often the great secret groups are to be found on top of them, such as the Great White Brotherhood and the Tibetan Lamas.

They are often the place of solitude, reflection, and enlightenment, as connecting to the Otherworld in this place brought on visions and prophecies. Jesus himself was said to go to the mountains and receive wisdom, as did Buddha and other great avatars. It was a Shamanic journey, and was materialized in the building of massive mountain-like monuments and pyramids. It is my belief that mountains acted as more than spiritual isolation locations. I believe they also play a part as massive antenna for the "earth energies" or ELF frequencies we have discussed in the book. Other imitations include the omphalos, which has already been seen as mirroring the energies of the earth.

There are many folk legends of "mountains opening up" and releasing captured mortals from the Otherworld, and being a doorway to the Underworld. All of these are related to the same natural phenomena we have discussed in the book.

Newgrange

Located in County Meath in Ireland, this amazing UFO-shaped mound has been known by many names: Brug Maic Ind Oc, the home of the youthful hero; Brug Oengusa, the mansion or home of Oengus; Bru Na Boinne, the house or home of Boyne or the palace of the gods. Most telling though is the title Sid in Bruca, the entrance to the Otherworld. *Bru*, which as we can see translates as "mansion," also means "womb" and relates to the layout of the mound, which many authors have claimed resembles the layout of the female productive organs.

Built around 3200 BC, Newgrange predates Stonehenge and even the Great Pyramid—as far as standard archaeological beliefs go. Standing approximately 40 feet tall with a diameter of more than 330 feet, it stands on top of a slightly sloping natural hill above the River Boyne. The passageway is 60 feet long and leads to the inner chamber area at the center of the mound. All around, and especially prominent on the entrance stones, are whirls, spirals, and serpentine shapes. A small opening above the entrance allows the sun's rays to penetrate the passageway on Winter Solstice, illuminating the very inner chamber. Surrounding this incredible feat of human engineering were once 39 megaliths, of which now sadly only 12 remain.

Newgrange appears to have been the center of a prosperous society, with trading known to have existed all along the Atlantic coastline. It is possible also that this was a center for pilgrimage, as we have found elsewhere. Legend states that it was the now infamous Tuatha De Danaan that built Newgrange—lending a supernatural air to the monumental task. To the Celts in later years, these became merged with the sidhe or Shining Ones. These were the Lords of Light, the masters of illumination and enlightenment, and it is therefore only fitting that they should build their beliefs in a material fashion. The sidhe were guardians of the entrances of the Otherworld.

Legend goes on to tell us that Dagda, the great horned god of the Celts, also known as Cernunnos, took Newgrange from the Tuatha De Danaan and married Boand, the goddess of the River Boyne, there. Boand would later emerge in Christian legends as St. Bridgid/Bridget, and is intimately linked with serpent worship. Bridgid was guardian over the entrance to the Otherworld, a smithy, and always associated with water serpent deities. She is also especially associated with the cult of the Black Madonnas through the feast of Imbolc or Candlemas.

Who were the settlers that built Newgrange, and what beliefs did they import?

With no signs of battles or warfare, it may be that people who already followed similar beliefs welcomed them. From the archaeological evidence it appears that the settlers were Eastern Beaker people—the same as the ones who built Stonehenge. The chamber within the tomb is in a cruciform shape, like so many others, such as the West Kennet Long Barrow. And within one of the chambers there are three small recesses; within each of these is a basin of stone. No one has any idea what these basins were used for, although it is postulated that they were for the drying-out of human remains prior to burial. What is clear is that they were definitely placed to be kept dry and away from humidity.

Maybe the legends of Dionysius will give us a clue: A container called the cista, used in the rituals of the cult, was supposedly used for carrying "secret" implements. What these implements were nobody knows. What is known is that wherever we see depictions of this cista they are like baskets with serpents rising out of them. On certain sarcophagi the cista is shown being kicked open by the Horned God—an allusion to the fact that the Horned God could reveal the secret of the serpent from the cista. The basins in Newgrange have spirals on the outside, and we know that these spirals relate to serpent worship and indeed earth energies. These cista are shown on coins and on ancient sarcophagi where the cista is being kicked open by Pan, the Greek horned god who is basically the same as the Dagda, whom we know is associated with Newgrange. Is this part of an ancient and secret ritual that has altered over time? Are these basins, baskets, and cups all related? They are certainly related in the symbolism of the snake.

The passageway was also built to allow a single beam of light to enter from the rising sun on the Winter Solstice, which illuminates the basins. This time of year is said to be the "time of the serpent days." Early Irish legends say that the mound was built as a tomb for the high kings of Tara, and there have been burials and the remains of cremations found within the tomb. These high kings of Tara are the same ones in the same legends said to have descended from the Gadelius or Gaythelos (husband of the daughter of the ancient Egyptian pharaoh, Akhenaton, and said by many to have been a Scythian), and is therefore connected with serpent worship in legendary lineage. Also found inside were several beads and marbles, said to be "serpent stones"—healing stones created by legendary serpents.

Nibiru

Nibiru is a Sumerian word for a star that is at the center of heaven, among other meanings, which all relate to one thing—Gateway. In the Chicago Assyrian Dictionary we find that the word translates as "crossing," "crossing marker," or "crossing point"—where energies converge or where we cross over. We can see in the picture of an Akkadian Seal (2340–2180 BC) found in the British Museum that this Gateway is surrounded by wavy lines, which I believe to be the ELF electromagnetic signature picked up while in the correct state of mind as we have discussed throughout the text.

Much of the controversy concerns which star this Nibiru is, as it seems to move. It could be that the Gateway is in many places. The ark, for instance, was a mobile Gateway. Often the word *nibiru* has a "d" placed before it to render it "doorway of the deity," or something similar. This "d" or delta symbol was a triangle, and is often associated with the shining aspect. It is also related to "can" or "kan," the serpent of various languages. Other elements of the word *nibiru* also have interesting associations:

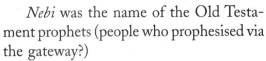
Nebi was the name of the Old Testament prophets (people who prophesised via the gateway?)

Nob is "serpent" or "sun."

Nebo is the mountain of the sun serpent and was the place that Moses died.

Nebu-chadnezzar was the king of Babylon, and he opened up the fiery furnace for the three biblical mystics.

Nabu was the title given by the followers of John the Baptist to the saint.

Omphalos

This is another Gateway object that can be seen all over the world. The superstition of the omphalos was widespread, similar to the serpent belief, from India to Greece. It is a boss or orb with spiral lines thought to represent serpents coiled or the electromagnetic energy encircling the globe. There are similar markings on ancient stone monuments across the world—especially at Newgrange in Ireland. Quintus Curtius also pointed out that in Africa there were such stones with spiral lines drawn, said to be a symbol of the serpent deity. According to Herodotus, a sacred serpent was fed honey cakes once a month at the Acropolis in Athens. These honey cakes were marked with the omphalos.

To the Etruscans, the omphalos was seen as a route to the Underworld. It was placed in a trench called a *mundus*, and the first fruits were offered into the trench, which was then covered by a huge stone. The entire city was centered on this spot, with all roads leading to and from it.

Onuphrius

Although not a specific location, other than generally in and around Egypt, St. Onuphrius is important because of the folklore that surrounds him. Otherwise known as Humphrey, Onofre, Onofrio, Onophry, St. Abu-Nofer, Anupras, or Onuphrius of Egypt, this peculiar and probably nonexistent hermit was said to have lived in the desert for 70 years (hence as precessions of the zodiac) near Thebais in Upper Egypt in the fourth–fifth century AD. He supposedly gained fame for the solitude and harsh way in which he lived, following the biblical pattern of St. John the Baptist.

It was said that an angel brought him food, and that he also lived from the dates of a palm tree (Tree of Life) that miraculously grew outside his cave. He dressed in nothing but his long, white hair, and a loincloth, and is represented with a crown at his feet or two lions—both of which are indicative of light.

His cult became popular throughout Christendom, both east and west, from the Middle Ages onward, beginning with monks, and later the general population, who began naming their children Humphrey in his honor.

Apparently the abbot and saint Paphnutius decided to find out for himself whether the eremitical life was for him, and visited Onuphrius. Paphnutius saw that this strange hermit had a countenance of light and illumination following his many years in the desert and living in a cave. The hermit informed the abbot that his arrival now meant that he could die, and the next day,

he did. The abbot then buried Onuphrius in a cave or rock opening, which immediately closed up, and then the palm tree died.

This story of the peculiar hermit can be nothing more than a folk memory of the Shining Ones or Shamans who dwelled and worshipped in the caves and earth. The illumined aspect of Onuphrius and his living off the tree are indicative of this fact. There is no literal truth in his life, other than him being the amalgamation of beliefs in the ancients.

Pentre Ifan

Located near Newport in Wales, this cromlech has a special place in the hearts of the locals, with links to hermits and Otherworldly visitations. Julia Murphy of the University of Wales has stated in print her theory that it was more than a mere burial chamber and was in fact also an initiation center for entrants into the Otherworld—in other words, Shamans. As Michael Howard pointed out in his paper "The Womb of Ceridwen," "...the cromlech was always the haunt of the...Welsh fairy folk. In the 18th century people...saw them dancing around the stones. They took the form of small figures...in red coats and pointed caps. Psychic observations at the site in recent years suggest the Little People are still...in occupation today."

Could this be an indication that the earth currents or ELFs are still in operation at the site? Howard also points out that the cromlech is also known locally as the "womb of Ceridwen." This is the link with Ceridwen's cauldron or womb, as the potion was said to be brewed within it. Some of the local people who have lived in the area for generations are said to have strong psychic powers and practice Witchcraft.

Penwith (Land's End, England)

A long-standing area of human habitation and mineral resources, this still-magical location demonstrates some of the most interesting energy sources, as Paul Devereux pointed out in *Secrets of Ancient and Sacred Places*. He wrote that mysterious lights are still seen in modern Penwith, giving the example of a research psychologist who had seen "tiny pricks of light, like stars" and "thin spirallic filaments" inside the granite stone of the underground chamber. Archaeologist John Barnatt and photographer Brian Larkman also saw the strange lights underneath the capstone.

Devereux goes on to explain that granite is prevalent in West Penwith, which means that the levels of background radiation are fairly high—especially in dolmens and fogous. In fact, he found the levels inside such structures, for example Boleigh and Chun Quoit, were strikingly similar to those inside the King's Chamber in the Great Pyramid at Giza. He noted even higher readings at the Sancreed Holy Well, where visitors often feel tired after gazing at the surface of the water. Devereux suggests that this site was utilized for ritual sleep.

Psychro

This sacred Minoan cave on Crete is probably one of the most important caves on the island. For more than 6,000 years caves have been used for religious purposes, and this one is no different. Scholars have called this cave the Diktaian Cave, where Zeus was born (the solar deity born from the Underworld). It is also, and not surprisingly, connected to the myths of Epimenides the seer, who slept here to reveal prophecies.

Sacred Stones

There are many sacred stones around the world, but I wanted to look at those of special importance to my story here, such as the meteorites that fell from the sky, like the Kaaba at Mecca, or Witness Stones.

Jacob's Pillar or Pillow is one such Witness Stone, and is of immense importance. This matstsebah or beth-el (house of shining) was the very pillow stone that Jacob is said to have rested his head upon in order to take his mystical journey to the seven levels of heaven. All of this happened at a place between Haran and Beer-sheba, and became known as Bethel, interpreted as the House of God, although *el* is Semitic for "shining." Either way, this was the place of connection. Laying his head upon a stone, which as we know was probably granite, and being transferred to the Otherworld in such a way has obvious interpretations for us now, as the granite block may have aided the balancing of the internal ELF or Holy Grail Frequency needed to achieve the trance state or key

to the Gateway. People would not have rested their heads upon a hard stone otherwise.

In Turkey, a meteorite was actually regarded as the personification of Cybele, whom we know to be the queen of the Underworld. This stone, according to Adrian Gilbert, was even seen as the Philosopher's Stone by Maier. In fact, several meteorites have been important to many cultures, including the Egyptians and Muslims. It may be that there is some kind of radioactive charge in these rocks that aids the process—I simply cannot say.

Often, rocks are related to the Otherworld portal, especially those on mountains and hills, and this gives rise to such stories as those of the Rock Babies or People. Some even believe that certain Shamans can pass freely through rock, which is an allusion to them being able to pass into the Otherworld—or maybe they capacity to alter the material world.

In Venezuela there is a tale told by the Yupa Indians of a woman who found a red rock one day by a river. Because it shone so brightly, she decided it would be a good idea to paint herself with the same color. She crushed the rock into powder and mixed it with water, and then painted herself with the mixture. Standing alone, she sang with joy, and the rock she stood upon opened up and swallowed her. People still claim to hear her singing. In essence, there may be a truth in this little story. We have a woman painted with what could be a narcotic substance, and we know that such a practice was prevalent as a method of taking in drugs into the body. She also sang a song of joy, a musical device we have spoken of elsewhere, and which is a mythical representation of initiation into the mysteries of the Otherworld. Thus she became a true female Shaman and entered into the Otherworld.

Sardinia

There are some enigmatic archaeological remains in Sardinia that need further investigation, namely the 7,000-plus stone towers known as Nuraghi after the Nuragic people. These conical towers are believed to be the primary dwelling places of the Bronze Age inhabitants (2000–1000 BC) who were settled farmers. The same is true of the *di gigantic*, or "giants tombs," which are contemporary with the thousands of towers. What has been discovered is a very peaceful society, no weapons having been found in the graves, nor deaths by violence. I believe that these giants tombs were simple passage graves to the Otherworld, and there are many ley lines seen across the island running through them.

Local legend has it that these tombs were made by the giant inhabitants of the past, and at more than 7 meters in length we can see why. Also discovered at some sights were remains that suggested gatherings such as ritual activity occurring at the entrances.

Sheela-na-gig

These weird sculptures and images can be seen in many locations across the British Isles. To be graphic, they are images of open-legged females, often holding open their vaginas with both hands. Amazingly,

these images are to be found on churches, cathedrals, convents, and all manner of religious establishments. It is quite remarkable that the puritanical Protestants of reformed England deemed it fit to destroy images of idolatry such as the fully clothed Mary (and often Jesus), and yet left behind not just Green Men and other Pagan images, but also this most obscure of erotically symbolic devices.

It will probably be apparent to all now that this symbolizes the opening of the Gateway by the Mother Goddess to the Otherworld. Most people believe that these images date from the Middle Ages, but there is no literature that survives to enable us to date them specifically. Christians often claim them to be images of the whore of Babylon, but the symbolism of this, in my opinion, would have been lost on the masses—and anyway, Babylon is the Gateway. Instead, I already knew that the Middle Ages was still rife with beliefs in the Pagan past, and the "popular" masses would certainly have understood the meaning of the portal phenomena, the yearly processes of cyclical supernatural activity being something that was deeply embedded in the mindset of the population. This cyclical element explains the often quoted explanation of the Sheela-na-gigs being fertility symbols, as all of this was tied up in one great mystery tradition. The masses, and more especially the Masons, employed to destroy the idolatry of the Catholic churches would have left well enough alone for fear of upsetting the true Mother Earth. And this is the truth of the Sheela-na-gig: she represents the opening of the portal into the womb of her earth. She is in fact no different from the depictions of the

Vesica Piscis, the almond symbol that reflects the shape of the vagina.

There is one Sheela-na-gig in Derbyshire, England, at the village church of Darley Dale, 3 miles from Haddon Hall. Here, the Sheela holds her legs high in the air, revealing her sexual organs to the world—a strange sight at a village church. Close by in the graveyard I found a strange gravestone with the peculiar un-Christian markings of a pentagram and a Star of David or Seal of Solomon, revealing that the church was built upon ancient and sacred ground, and I could not help but think that there was some ancient Gateway here. My compass did indeed go wild at the spot, and there are stone circles in the area.

Smoo Cave

Located in Durness, Scotland, this wonderful sea cavern is accessible by boat and is a true sight to behold. The word *smoo* comes from the Norse *sumvya*, and means "cleft" or "creek." The cleft drops some 25 meters into a secondary chamber, the Falis Smoo (Chimney Cleft). Inside is a deep pool, which after heavy rains turns into a torrent creating a roaring sound giving rise to tales of dragons. Local folklore tells us that this place is an entrance to the Otherworld. In one tale a piper enters the cave playing his pipe and is never seen again—thus involving the opening of the portal with music again. Another tale involves a local wizard known as Lord Reay who goes to study the black arts or alchemy in Rome. One day upon his return this wizard goes exploring in the cave with his pet dog (the Shaman dog), which runs ahead

into the cavern. Moments later a loud yelp is heard and the dog comes running back hairless. Knowing this to be the work of the devil, the wizard accepts his fate, knowing that the devil wants his soul. However, just before he could give himself up sunlight filters into the cave, a cock crows, and the devil, accompanied by three witches, blows out of the roof of the cave to escape the new dawn. This hole is now where the water cascades down as a waterfall.

The Tabernacle

How could it be that a mobile tent could be the Gateway if it needed to be a cave, tree, rock, or other symbolic (and scientifically proven) device to bring on the trance states required? According to Hebrews 8:5, the contents of the Tabernacle mirrored what was in heaven, making the Tabernacle a heaven on earth (1 Cor. 6:19–20, Acts 2:3, Eph. 2:21–22, 2 Peter 1:13–14). Hebrews 9:1–5 tells us the specifics:

Then verily the first covenant had also ordinances of divine service, and a worldly sanctuary. For there was a tabernacle made; the first, wherein was the candlestick, and the table, and the shew-bread; which is called the sanctuary. And after the second veil, the tabernacle which is called the Holiest of all; Which had the golden censer, and the ark of the covenant overlaid round about with gold, wherein was the golden pot that had manna, and Aaron's rod that budded, and the tables of the covenant; And over it the cherubims of glory shadowing the mercy-seat; of which we cannot now speak particularly.

The candlestick and shewbread can be discounted here as inessential. What cannot be discarded is the Ark of the Covenant, which held the Rod of Aaron—the serpent staff—and the altar, which was, according to some, made from stone. The powers attributed to the Ark in particular must indicate a supernatural affect caused by it or its contents—the Rod of Aaron and the Ten Commandments of stone taken from God by Moses on Mount Sinai. The top of the Ark was called the Mercy Seat, between two solid gold cherubim, where it is said the cloud also appeared—in the center.

The ark was also very powerful, as we can see in II Samuel 6:6–7: "And when they came to the threshing floor of Nacon, Uzzah put out his hand to the ark of God and took hold of it, for the oxen stumbled. And the anger of the LORD was kindled against Uzzah; and God smote him there because he put forth his hand to the ark; and he died there beside the ark of God."

Teotihuacan

This is a massive urban and religious complex northeast of Mexico City, Mexico. Following a heavy rainstorm in 1971, a great depression was discovered in front of the Pyramid of the Sun, located there. Beneath it there was discovered a large cave, which is believed to represent the emergent place of the legendary Chicomoztoc—the origin of the Aztecs from the Otherworld. The layout,

looking something like a four-leaf clover, is similar in design cairns and burial chambers elsewhere in the world, including Malta, and corresponds to the four cardinal points or the four-fold cosmos. The cave was heavily embellished as a sacred cave, and must be the reason for the pyramid built above it. According to Paul Devereux in *Secrets of Ancient and Sacred Places*, "It was also, perhaps, where shamanic initiation was conducted. The Pyramid of the Sun and the axial plan of the city seems to have evolved from this holy spot. It seems therefore, that the axial arrangement of Teotihuacan echoes both subterranean and celestial configurations at the site. A marriage of heaven and earth."

There were great statues that once adorned the pinnacle of the pyramids here, and as we can see at Cahokia Mounds, poles on top of mounds attract lightning strikes. It could be that with the electromagnetic properties of pyramids having peculiar properties that this addition also brought down the shining god to earth. Indeed, in 1906 archaeologists discovered a thick sheet of mica on top of the fifth level of the Pyramid of the Sun, which suggests, because mica has electrical insulating properties, that the ancients were using the pyramid as an energy source. This could now also explain the great obelisks of Egypt—lightning conductors with their gold tops.

Trigrad Gorge

This amazing place has long held the tradition that it is truly an entrance to the Underworld. Located in Bulgaria, its sheer

walls oversee the River Trigradska, from which it derives its name. Following a 150-meter tunnel, the thunderous water falls into the cavernous space to disappear beneath the earth. Anything swept into the cave is never seen again. Legend has it that Orpheus used this as an entrance to the Otherworld.

West Kennet Long Barrow

Located near Avebury in England, this 4,500-year-old burial chamber has long been seen as an entrance to the Otherworld. Measuring approximately 100 meters in length, this mysterious place held a series of 46 burials at one end of the internal chamber and was used for more than a thousand years. Terrence Meaden, in *Stonehenge: The Secret of the Solstice*, noted that the forecourt "entrance to the chambered barrow or passage grave was modelled on the womb-opening which leads to a vault chamber, the place of rebirth or regeneration for the souls of the dead." It was therefore a passageway to new life, like so many other mounds and burial chambers across the world that mirrored the rebirthing in the World Mother's womb. Modern folklore claims this place to be haunted by the spirit of a Druid or lord of the Underworld.

West Kennet is a small but magical place, built like Newgrange in a cruciform shape, looking like the Cross of Lorraine from the air. Archaeologists also discovered that there was a semicircular ceremonial area at the top of the T-cross, forming an Ankh if viewed from above.

Another strange coincidence that struck me, and one that I later confirmed against other sites, was the layout of the interior of the tomb. Imagine an upright with two parallel horizontals at equal distances apart, and you have the Cross of Lorraine. This would not really have struck me had it not been for the blatant fact that the Cross of Lorraine was a symbol for poison, the trinity, and a symbol used by the Templars. These relationships should have nothing to do with each other—but for the fact that the thread of the snake connects all these areas. Add into this the fact that no one is sure where the Lorraine symbol originated and why, then we indeed have a mystery. Taking a look at other burial mounds viewed from above, they often look just like the cross, as if the bodies and ceremonies were being somehow played upon this sacred shape. It is a shape that is hidden beneath the ground and not a shape seen openly—as if this were the 3-dimensional aspect of the symbol, a stairway to the Other realm. In fact, many of the actual stairways from the period that I know of were in this very shape, indicating a kind of copycat symbolism—from reality into mystery.

Appendix II
A Timeline of Serpent Worship

Creation

🐍 Most creation stories relate how it was a serpent that was the creator, or at least a serpent is always involved. For instance, in Egypt, the sun god Amun-Ra emerged from the water as a snake to inseminate the cosmic egg. All life on earth came from this one egg, but it was through the medium or Gateway of the water that Amun-Ra emerged.

🐍 There is a remarkable tradition across the globe that there were great wars in heaven, which involved the serpent deities. All of this points back to an original and primary serpent cult, which spread in a migratory pattern across the globe, leaving its traces as it went in the belief in the Gateway.

160000 BC

🐍 The earliest known remains of primitive man from this time were discovered in Ethiopia in 2003. Two shattered skulls, which were strangely highly polished (reminding me of the crystal skulls), have been given the name Homo Sapiens Idaltu, and are said to be modern humans with some primitive features. The fact that the heads were polished indicates to scientists that there was some form of ancestor worship in operation—a peculiar and ancient head worship that seems to have remained with us. Professor Tim White of the University of California said, "They show Africa was inhabited by human ancestors from 6 million to 160,000 years ago." They also show a very ancient understanding of the importance of the head in relation to the spirit world.

The Flood

- In antediluvian times, the pole of the heavens was said to be the constellation Alpha Draconis. In fact, it was the pole star 4,800 years ago, but the idea that it was Alpha Draconis points to the belief in the serpents' rule before the flood. In astronomical temples, the dragon is the ruling constellation at the pole, matching the Greek myth of Draco, who is found around the North Pole.

45000–50000 BC

- Ayers Rock in Australia is said to be archaeological evidence proving that humans have worshiped there for 5,000 years. There are many images upon this rock that might prove that the worship of the snake (and other symbols associated with it), go back before the end of the last ice age (approx. 10800 BC). There are images of peculiar "Snake People," pictured alongside ordinary humans and ordinary animals. There are many spirals, circles, and snake images. It can be said that these are universal patterns within each one of us, and could therefore emerge anywhere at any time. And indeed there is evidence that people from Australia were part of a trade network around 5000–4000 BC. It also shows that the worship of the serpent is very ancient indeed, and is from the same time period as the emerging serpent-based beliefs of the West. However, civilization according to standard history did not emerge until the Sumerian times, and therefore pre-civilization records are incomplete on the subject. It is

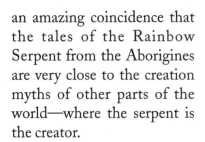

an amazing coincidence that the tales of the Rainbow Serpent from the Aborigines are very close to the creation myths of other parts of the world—where the serpent is the creator.

9850 BC

- The Turin Papyrus (a list of kings dated to 1300 BC) records the installation of the next series of Egyptian kings in 9850 BC—close to Plato's dating for Atlantis. The third on the god-king list from Turin Papyrus is Agathodaemon or Su—the good serpent.

9000 BC

- Old Europe, Anatolia, and Minoan Crete display Goddess-centered worship. The Minoan matriarchal goddess is linked with snakes and dowsing. This is at the same time that standard history tells us that cultivation of wild wheat and barley, domestication of dogs and sheep, and the change from food gathering to food production, began.

6000 BC

- The earliest evidence of village-level civilization at Mehgarh,

125 miles west of the Indus valley. There is evidence of crop farming, producing Asiatic wheat. The site also shows domestication of animals and trade with the west, including copper and cotton, as far away as Arabia. This idea of international trade is almost ridden over by many. The very idea that ancient peoples traded with each other for wealth and products begs the question—did these traders also take religious systems with them? It must be that the ancient priesthood of the serpent worshipers were traveling with these trade routes, and at present nobody is quite sure just how far the traders reached. Indeed, the evidence states that the slightly later Harappan cultures were extremely advanced in comparison to other cultures at the time, and were a great seafaring people. If the worship of the serpent was being spread from anywhere at this time, then it may be from here. By 5000 BC the site changed from semi-permanent structures to mud brick and large housing. This culture is thought to have evolved into the Harappan culture.

5000–3000 BC

- Beginnings of the Indus-Sarasvati civilizations of

Harappa (approx. 4000 BC) and Mohenjo-daro (approx. 2500 BC) with densely packed villages, extensive irrigation, and a wide variety of crops being planted, covering more than half a million miles of northern Indian subcontinent. They are classed as highly artistic and skilled with images of snakes, unicorns, and other animals seen in their art for religious and serpent-worshiping purposes. The swastika, thought to be overlapping snakes in the symbol of eternity, is also seen. Earliest signs of Shiva worship (as Pashupati)—Shiva being linked with the snake.

Pashupati is the horned god of the Indus civilization of the great Harappan city, which developed from a culture at this time in northern India and Pakistan. At its peak this civilization covered an area twice as large as that of the Egyptian kingdom and four times that of Sumer and Akkad. There is strong archaeological evidence for the worship of the horned god and a mother goddess at this time. The horned god is symbolic of the enlightenment of the Shaman. Pashupati is seen as the prototype for the god Shiva, who is linked with serpent worship and Shamanism. In the Skanda Purana, Shiva says, "As I reside here in the forest of Sleshmanta in the form of a beast, My name will hence be known as the Pashupati the world over," indicating a wide knowledge of the horned god. Pashupati means "Lord of the Animals," and there is an undeniable link between Pashupati and Cernunnos, the horned god of the Celts seen on the Gundestrup cauldron associated with the serpent. As the Gundestrup Cauldron is dated between the fourth and first centuries BC, this shows the long-standing belief in this Lord of Animals and his links with the resurrection of the dead in the cauldron—the cauldron being a symbol of the Gateway.

The first evidence of martial arts is found in the Indus civilization, especially among the Northwest Frontier Province, by Ahmad Hasan Dani and Durrani, who found evidence of it predating 3300 BC. This particular martial art was based upon the movement of the snake. The first martial arts priest was called Kana Mor Vac, and his art was said to be made up mainly of wrestling, although weapons such as the slingshot were used. This style of snake martial art is said to have moved into Babylonia and Egypt with various invasions, becoming Hikuta in Egypt.

Yoga is also said to derive directly from the Indus snake period.

4000 BC

- 🐍 The period of the rising of Wadjet in Lower Egypt.
- 🐍 A Mesopotamian libation vase depicting the caduceus was discovered dating from around this time, relating to the god Ninazu, who was the Lord of Healing and the father of Ningizzida, who in turn is the progenitor of Thoth. Professor Frothingham, in a presentation to the Philological Association and the Archaeological Institute back in the 19th century, said that the caduceus of the Hittites and Babylonians was also taken away by the Etruscans, explaining some of the serpent symbolism in Italy. There are also strange similarities between the tale of Ninazu and the Christian world. In a balbale to Ninazu (7–15) we find the words, "May he make the way straight for you as far as the ends of heaven and earth..."—sounding remarkably similar to the idea that the Baptist would make the way straight for Jesus. There are many such similarities; the snake in the Garden of Eden

and whole of Genesis are originally Mesopotamian epics. There are also remarkable links in symbolism between Sumeria and the Templars.

3100 BC

- 🐍 Aryan people inhabit Iran, Iraq, and the western Indus-Sarasvati valley, although some experts say the first wave was 2000 BC. These Aryans are described as a culture of spiritual knowledge, and probably inherit the serpent worship beliefs of the Indus civilization.
- 🐍 The first known incarnation of Stonehenge in England.
- 🐍 A stele of the Serpent King from this period found in Egypt has a bas-relief of a falcon in profile above a nearly abstract stroke of a snake (now in the Louvre, Paris).

3000 BC

- 🐍 There is evidence of serpent worship in China from this period. The Manchurian goddess temple shows fragments of a bear-dragon statue. This confirms that the culture of the serpent with other beasts was already in place, and therefore serpent worship in China *must* be older.
- 🐍 Newgrange in Ireland is built.

2700 BC

- The worship of Shiva is indicated on seals of the Indus-Sarasvati valley. The Indus-Sarasvati civilization spreads from Pakistan to Gujurat, Punjab, and Uttar Pradesh, largest of the world's civilizations, with strong links to Mesopotamia, Minoan Crete, Afghanistan, Central Asia, and Karnataka.

- Hindu beliefs, in which the snake is central, are said to emerge at this time, as the mixture of Indian and Aryan culture creates new beliefs. Besides Vishnu, snakes are commonly associated with Shiva (previously Pashupati). Priests in the modern era still wear the serpent across their chests as the sacred thread Upanayanam, which is a symbol of initiation and second birth (and the night before receiving this "second birth" is spent in isolation, similar to Jesus). Coiled serpents adorn the hair, neck, and arms. Offerings to snakes are made in holes; milk and blood are offered. Could this be what the worldwide phenomenon of cup and ring marks were for? These cup and ring marks range from 30 centimeters in diameter down to 1 centimeter. They are often seen in association with horseshoe shapes and spirals—solar symbols. They are often circular, depicted as rings within rings, a cup being at the center. These shapes and patterns can be shown to have remarkable astronomical associations, as well as cyclical and fertility-related meanings. The concept that these markings must be for one purpose only is just not tenable. This was a time of religion, when everything was interrelated. There was no great difference between the snake that crawled on the floor and the one that was envisaged in the sky.

2500 BC

- Arbor Low in England construction begun with a mound said by some to be a serpent.

- Avebury Serpent in England constructed.

- In the Middle East, Dumuzi (or the son of the abyss) emerges as the prototype of the resurrected savior (also called the shepherd), the ever-reviving Sumerian god of vegetation and the very first known green man. Dumuzi is known for his horned crown of the moon and is both the son and husband of the goddess Gula-Bau. She is seen sitting in front of the serpent in

a relief from 2500 BC called "Goddess of the Tree of Life." Dumuzi is Tammuz, the equivalent of Osiris (born from the mouth of the snake). Osiris is seen as Dionysius in the Greek tongue, and Bacchus in Rome, thus proving the ancient link of the serpent with healing and the Otherworld. He was originally the son of Ningishzida, the serpent god of Mesopotamia entwined about an axial rod as a pair of copulating vipers, and hence one of the oldest images of the caduceus. His dual counter part, Gula, the earth goddess, sits below ground (in the Otherworld), where the cosmic serpent begins to rise (the sun). She is the patroness of herbs, healing, and life. From the very beginning, the serpent deities are involved in the most important aspects of ancient man's life: fertility, creation, healing, and immortality.

2100 BC

- The second stage of Stonehenge with bluestone granite from Wales is moved 135 miles. A total of 90 bluestones are set up in a horseshoe pattern—a perfectly shaped receptor of wave-energy.

2000 BC

- World population is 27 million, of which India is 5 million, making it 22 percent of the world's population.

- Approximate dating for Stonehenge's third phase, with the familiar topped caps (trilathons).

- Stone construction takes place at Arbor Low in England. At Carnac in France, another ancient stone walkway is built, which actually means "snake," as in the Egyptian Karnac.

- Silbury Hill near Avebury in England is constructed. It is the largest prehistoric mound in Europe, more than 130 feet high, built in three phases and thought not to be a burial mound, although the purpose is still unknown.

- There is continual improvement to Stonehenge up until 1500 BC.

- Cylinder Seals from Mesopotamia show the goddess Ishtar, the Tree of Life, and the serpent.

1600 BC

- The period of the Minoan snake goddess.

975 BC

- The fabled King Hiram of Phoenicia trades with the equally fabled King Solomon, and with the port of Ophir (*oph*="serpent"), some say near Bombay in India, which would make sense, as India is a center of serpent worship.

- According to Eusebius, the Phoenicians were among the earliest serpent worshipers, in this period. In fact he even names the originator of the belief as Taautus (Thoth).

920 BC

- According to William Harwood in *Mythologies Last Gods: Yahweh and Jesus*, this is the time that the myths of Adam and Eve were laid down as the Genesis story we know today.

- Solomon's policy of religious toleration allowed the raising again of the asherah tree—the Mother Goddess symbol so important to the story of the Gateway. The use of the tree of knowledge is clear evidence of the appearance of the Goddess in her "traditional" form of the serpent.

725 BC

- King Hezekiah, famous for destroying the brazen serpent of Moses that was in the Temple (2 Kings 18:4), also cut down the asherah. However, in Isaiah 37:14–16 there is a peculiar mention that Hezekiah worshiped the "God of Israel, that dwellest between the cherubim [that is Ark]." This is peculiar because what "dwellest in the Ark" was the Rod of Aaron, which had turned miraculously into a snake and was itself a symbol of the age old serpent worship at the very time of Moses, who had erected the Brazen Serpent and therefore definitely links the continued worship of the serpent even under the supposed oppression of Hezekiah. It is also enlightening, as god was said to only be where the Ark was; he dwells there—in the center, which we know to be the location of the Gateway. It is, strangely, after this time of Hezekiah that the Ark is lost to history, never to be seen again. The serpent worship is obviously being sent underground in favor of a one-god system, Yahweh, and the Ark was sacred to the serpent gods. Whoever took the Ark may

very well have had the safety of it in mind and the secrecy of it would be paramount. Hezekiah's son, Manasseh (687–642 BC) went on to bring condemnation upon himself with "graven images," erecting more asherah groves and much wickedness. The graven image of the grove that 1 Kings 21:2–7 speaks of is in fact the image of asherah again, and according to Hancock, the Ark was removed at this time to enable the graven image to be installed, although there is little evidence of this.

700 BC

❦ The Tower of Babylon to the god Bel is said to have been built around this time. According to many sources, it was built on a spiral pattern upward toward god—a truly serpentine Gateway. Bel may very well come from Ob-El, or serpent shining god, and in the Greek he is said to be Beliar (Bel Aur the solar deity). This is therefore highly likely to be the dragon of Babylon spoken of in the Bible. It was indeed the opinion of John Bathurst Deane in *Worship of the Serpent Traced Throughout the World,*

that "live serpents were kept at Babylon as objects of adoration; or at least, of veneration, as oracular or talismanic." As these practices were common in Egypt and Greece at this time (and prior), then there is little wonder that the practice should also be found in Babylon.

❦ The Assyrians are said to have given their dragon standard to the emperors of Constantinople in this time, the same standard also borne by the Parthians, Scythians, Saxons, Danes, and Chinese. No wonder that the Pendragon (*pen*="head," *dragon*="serpent") title was passed to Arthur. The Persians also venerated the serpent and held dragon standards similar to the Assyrians. Indeed, Eusebius says, "they all worshiped the first principles under the form of serpents, having dedicated to them temples in which they performed sacrifices, and held festivals and orgies, esteeming them the greatest of gods, and governors of the universe." These first principles that the Persians worshipped under the form of serpents were Ormuzd and Ahriman, the good and evil deities of the Zoroastrian faith.

640 BC

 The king Josiah "desecrates" the Temple with the image of Astarte—the tree. Because of this, writes Graham Hancock in *The Sign and the Seal*, the Ark of the Covenant was removed and the laity not informed.

628 BC

 Josiah purged the Temple again of all graven images, and had the asherah burned in the river Kidron (2 Kings 23:6). Although Ezekiel then goes on a century later to blame Josiah for actually having the walls painted in idolatrous images, which in *Peake's Commentary on the Bible*, he "sees mural paintings containing pictures of 'creeping things' and other mythological scenes...which seem to point to syncretistic practices of Egyptian provenance." Egypt, of course, having the serpent central to its doctrine.

600 BC

 The Tower of Babylon said to have been built.

520 BC

 The Persians, the world's first Indo-European nation, conquered Babylon. They rebuilt temples, including the Temple of Jerusalem. Although it is said in the *Elephantine Papyri* that "they knocked down all the temples of the gods of Egypt, but not one did any damage" to the Jewish Temple. The religious influence of this Persian/Indian invasion must have also had its influences, especially Zoroastrianism and the fire (enlightenment)/snake worship that this implies.

500 BC

 World population is 100 million, India being 25 million, or 25 percent.

4 BC

 The birth of Apollinus of Tyana—possibly the true Christ who went to India to learn from the King Serpents and was taught in the Temple of Aesculapius, the serpent god of healing.

 The supposed birth of Jesus.

AD 70

- The Temple of Jerusalem sacked by the Romans. The Ark that was there at the time was said to have been full of stones and some Badger skins dyed purple. This could not have been the real Ark that is said to have contained the Rod of Aaron, or if it were, then the contents had already gone.

AD 100

- Pliny points out that the serpent was a symbol of health for one reason only—that the flesh of the creature "is sometimes used in medicine" and that this is *the* reason of his consecration to health. Indeed there was a proverb at the time "to eat of snakes" denoting that man ate of what gave him vigor. This vigor was given by the practical snake in venom and blood.

- Coptic texts, translated from Greek from around this time, were discovered at Nag Hammadi in Upper Egypt toward the end of the Second World War. These included fragments of the Gospels of Thomas and the Gospels of Philip and Mary. They make it plain that the Virgin Birth and Resurrection were very much symbolic. They also point out that the serpent from the Garden of Eden was wise in giving the fruit of knowledge to Adam and Eve.

AD 400

- The Emperor Theodosius bans many Pagan rituals, including tying ribbons to trees—the same emperor who had his sight restored by a grateful serpent that laid a precious stone upon his eyes.

AD 500/600

- The time of Arthur. Albert Pike, the Masonic historian, says that the lost word of Masonry is concealed in the name of Arthur: *Pendragon* means "head dragon."

AD 1150/1200

- A branch of the Templars builds round churches in Bornholm. In the 12th century the Sword Knights, a branch of the Knights Templar, was established by the Cistercian friar Theoderik, in Riga. These Sword Knights were later to become the Teutonic Knights in Germany. The round churches of Osterlers, Nyker,

Olsker, and Nylars were said to have been built defensively, although there is some debate as to against what, as the buildings were certainly not built to aid very many people in that case. According to Erling Haagensen in *Bornholms Mysterier*, all these sites were built upon the familiar Templar sacred geometry, and hence location points of Gateways. On the wall in Nyker church there is the Templar symbol of the Agnus Dei, the Lamb of God, with blood pouring from his wound into the chalice. Inside Olsker church on the north side there is an image presumed to be St. Olaf (also thought to be Thor) surrounded by a circle and 12 stars, and holding a serpent in his hand. Surely this is the image of the healing god in the sky, Ophiucus, Aesculapius, and is an image of the portal? There are also many images of heads or green men similar to those at Rosslyn, especially seen at Osterlers.

AD 1140

- *Secretum Secretorum*, a psuedo-Aristotlean translation of *Kitab Sirr al-Asrar*, a book of advice to kings (translated into Latin by Hispalensis and Philip of Tripoli in 1243) is written. It is thought to be the first showing of the Emerald Tablet of Hermes.

19th Century

- Colonel Meadows Taylor in the Indian Dakkan tells of contemporary accounts that the locals, worshipping the Nagas, looked to the snake for healing of cholera, disease, and pestilence.

AD 1896

- A census shows more than 25,000 Naga forms in the northwest province of India, with 123,000 votaries of the snake god Guga, and 35,000 votaries of snake gods in the Punjab.

Notes

Chapter 2

1. The light in this instance is perfectly natural. Trees were placed on mounds to attract lightning strikes—this being a connection of earth with the heavens in the brightest light known to ancient man.

2. The fact also remains that Leonardo da Vinci himself depicted man encompassed by the pentacle—the Vitruvian Man. This was a hidden icon though, in that da Vinci left space above the head of the man for the point of connection to the divine, showing that the true "head" of man in esoteric terms is in the emptiness.

3. Castaneda, *Teachings.*

4. See *Det Norske Pentagram*, by Harald Boehlke.

Chapter 3

1. *www.case.edu/univlib/preserve/ Etana/hibbert_lectures_1887/ appendix4p1.pdf.*

2. Churchward, *Origin.*
3. Roberts, *Antiquity Unveiled.*

Chapter 4

1. Encarta Encyclopedia, "Quantum Theory," 1997.
2. Gordon, "Paranormal."
3. Fenwick, "Neurophysiology."
4. Krishna, *Wonder.*
5. Altman, "Neuropharmacology."
6. Krishna, *Real Nature.*
7. Ramachandran, *Phantoms.*

Chapter 5

1. Jennings, *Ophiolatraea.*
2. Bonwick, *Irish Druids.*
3. Stephen, "Hopi Tales."
4. Leone, *Totality.*
5. Taken from a paper in *New Energy News (NEN) Fusion Information Center, Inc.*

Chapter 6

1. Loye, *An Arrow Through Chaos.*
2. See *www.emergentmind.org* for updates on latest testing and theories.
3. Powell, Dr. Andrew, "Consciousness."
4. Schwartz, *Living.*
5. King, *Instant Healing.*

Chapter 7

1. Budge, *Book of the Dead.*
2. The story is related in *The Holy Land of Scotland: Jesus in Scotland and the Gospel of the Grail* by Barry Dunford, and comes by way of George Sandwith, a professional surveyor.
3. Wylie, *History.*
4. Coles, *Field Archaeology.*

Chapter 8

1. Peniston, "Peniston-Kulkosky."
2. Amos, "Organ Music."

Chapter 9

1. Bray, "HAARP Project."
2. Miller, "Schumann Resonances."

Chapter 10

1. *Sappir* is rendered *sapphirus* in many ancient texts (see the works of Josephus), but the stone may not have been the modern sapphire. Theophrastus and Pliny described the sapphirus as a stone with golden spots, and may have been indicating the lapis lazuli or Philosopher's Stone, which has elements of pyrites with a golden sheen.

  The lapis lazuli was called *chesbet* by the Egyptians, and was obtained from some of the oldest mines in the world, dating from as early as 4000 BC. It was used to make magical amulets and figurines worn by the Egyptian high priests.
2. Epstein, *Kabbalah.*
3. Schaya, *Universal Meaning.*
4. Fortune, *Mystical Qabalah.*
5. Low, "Necronomicon."

Chapter 11

1. Redway, *Book of Ceremonial Magic.*
2. Jones, *Dictionary.*
3. One could always circumnavigate paying with a coin by offering a Golden Bough (see *The Golden Bough* by Sir James Frazer).
4. Dakaris, "Dark Place."
5. *Trail of the Serpent.*

Chapter 12

1. Tesla, "Transmission."
2. According to author Alan Alder, who claims to have spoken directly to several Egyptologists and archaeologists who told him that it was for stability, and yet architects refute this, saying they have no point and would not have worked anyway (from a conference at the Folklore Society London, England, October 2004).

Chapter 13

1. Powell, Dr. Andrew, "Consciousness."
2. Ibid.
3. Ibid.
4. Talbot, *Holographic Universe.*
5. Ibid.
6. Ibid.
7. Zollschan, *Exploring,* 100–101.
8. Scholem, *On the Kabbalah,* 122.
9. Meseroll, "Instantaneous Data Transfer."
10. Heathcote-James, *They Walk.*
11. Grandpierre, "Nature."
12. Ibid.
13. Vulliamy, *Immortality,* 191–192.
14. "Is There Life After Death?"
15. Walker, *Hindu World.*

Bibliography

Abdalqadir as-Sufi, Shaykh. *The Return of the Kalifate*. London: Madinah Press, 1996.

Ableson, J. *Jewish Mysticism*. London: G. Bell and Sons Ltd., 1913.

Altman, Christopher. "Neuropharmacology of the Mystical State: Entheogenic Tradition and the Mystical Experience." *http://altman.casimirinstitute.net/mysticism.html* (accessed October 2007).

Amos, Jonathan. "Organ Music 'Instills Religious Feelings.'" BBC News Online, September 8, 2003. *http://news.bbc.co.uk/2/hi/science/nature/3087674.stm* (accessed October 2007).

Andrews, R., and P. Schellenberger. *The Tomb of God*. London: Little, Brown and Co, 1996.

Appollodorus. *The Library: Greek Mythography*. Second century BC.

Ashe, Geoffrey. *The Quest for Arthur's Britain*. London: Paladin, 1971.

Baigent, Michael. *Ancient Traces*. London: Viking, 1998.

Baigent, Michael, and Richard Leigh. *The Dead Sea Scrolls Deception*. London: Arrow, 2001.

———. *The Elixir and the Stone*. London: Viking, 1997.

———. *The Temple and the Lodge*. London: Arrow, 1998.

Baigent, Michael, Richard Leigh, and Henry Lincoln. *Holy Blood, Holy Grail*. London: Jonathan Cape, 1982.

———. *The Messianic Legacy*. London: Arrow, 1996.

Balfour, Mark. *The Sign of the Serpent*. London: Prism, 1990.

Balfour, Michael. *Megalithic Mysteries*. London: Parkgate Books, 1992.

Barber, Malcolm. *The Trial of the Templars*. Cambridge: Cambridge University Press, 1978.

Barrett, David V. *Sects, Cults and Alternative Religions*. London: Blandford, 1996.

Barrow, John D. *Theories of Everything*. London: Virgin, 1990.

Basham, A.L. *The Wonder that was India*. London: Fontana Collins, 1954.

Bauval, Robert. *The Orion Mystery*. London: Heinemann, 1995.

Bayley, H. *The Lost Language of Symbolism*. London: Bracken Books, 1996.

Beatty, Longfield. *The Garden of the Golden Flower*. London: Senate, 1996.

Begg, E. *The Cult of the Black Virgin*. London: Arkana, 1985.

Begg, E., and D. Begg. *In Search of the Holy Grail and the Precious Blood*. London: Thorsons, 1985.

Blaire, Lawrence. *Rhythms of Vision*. New York: Warner Books, 1975.

Blavatsky, H.P. *Theosophical Glossary*. Unknown city: R.A. Kessinger Publishing Ltd, 1918.

Bonwick, James. *Irish Druids and Old Irish Religions*. London: Griffith Frran, 1894. *http://www.sacred-texts.com/pag/idr/index.htm* (accessed October 2007).

Borchant, Bruno. *Mysticism*. Centennial, Colo.: Weisner, 1994.

Bord, Janet, and Colin Bord. *Earth Rites: Fertility Practices in Pre-Industrial Britain*. London: Granada Publishing, 1982.

Bouquet A.C. *Comparative Religion*. London: Pelican, 1942.

Boyle, Veolita Parke. *The Fundamental Principles of Yi-King, Tao: The Cabbalas of Egypt and the Hebrews*. London: W & G Foyle, 1934.

Bray, William J. "Re: The HAARP Project." MadsSci Network, October 1998. *http://www.madsci.org/posts/archives/1998-10/909512898.Es.r.html* (accessed October 2007).

Brine, Lindsey. *The Ancient Earthworks and Temples of the American Indians*. London: Oracle, 1996.

Broadhurst, Paul, and Hamish Miller. *The Dance of the Dragon*. UK: Mythos, 2000.

Bryant, N. *The High Book of the Grail*. Cambridge: D.S. Brewer, 1985.

Bryden, R. *Rosslyn: A History of the Guilds, the Masons and the Rosy Cross*. Edinburgh: Rosslyn Chapel Trust, 1994.

Budge, E.A. Wallis. *An Egyptian Hieroglyphic Dictionary, Volume 1*. Mineola, N.Y.: Dover Publications, 1978.

———, trans. *The Book of the Dead: The Papyrus of ANI, 240 BC. http:// altreligion.about.com/library/ bl_bookofthedead8.htm* (accessed October 2007).

Butler, E.M. *The Myth of the Magus*. Cambridge: CUP, 1948.

Callahan, Philip S. *Ancient Mysteries Modern Visions: The Magnetic Life of Agriculture*. Austin, Tex.: Acres U.S.A., 2001.

———. *Nature's Silent Music*. Austin, Tex.: Acres U.S.A., 1992.

———. *Paramagnetism: Rediscovering Nature's Secret Force of Growth*. Austin, Tex.: Acres U.S.A., 1995.

Campbell, Joseph. *Transformations of Myth Through Time*. London: Harper and Row, 1990.

Cantor, N.F. *The Sacred Chain*. London: Harper Collins, 1994.

Carpenter, Edward. *Pagan and Christian Creeds: Their Origin and Meaning*. London: Allen and Unwin Ltd, 1920.

Carr-Gomm, Sarah. *Dictionary of Symbols in Art*. Winchester, UK: Duncan Baird Publishers, 1995.

Castaneda, Carlos. *The Teachings of Don Juan: A Yaqui Way of Knowledge*. New York: Pocket Books, 1974.

Cavendish, Richard. *Mythology*. London: Tiger, 1998.

Ceram, C.W. *Gods, Graves, and Scholars: The Story of Archaeology*. London: Victor Gollancz & Sidgwick and Jackson, 1954.

Chadwick, N. *The Druids*. Cardiff, UK: University of Wales Press, 1966.

Childress, David, ed. *Anti-Gravity and The World Grid*. Kempton, Ill.: Adventures Unlimited Press, 1987.

Churchward, Albert. *The Origin and Evolution of Religion*. Bensenville, Ill.: Lushena Books, 2003.

Churton, Tobias. *The Golden Builders*. Lichfield, UK: Signal Publishing, 2002.

Clarke, Hyde, and C. Staniland Wake. *Serpent and Siva Worship*. London: R.A. Kessinger Publishing Ltd, 1877.

Coles, John. *Field Archaeology in Britain*. London: Methuen, 1972.

Collins, Andrew. *From the Ashes of Angels, The Forbidden Legacy of a Fallen Race*. London: Signet Books, 2001.

———. *Gateway to Atlantis*. London: Headline, 2000.

———. *Gods of Eden*, London: Headline, 1998.

———. *Twenty-First Century Grail: The Quest for a Legend.* London: Virgin, 2004.

Cooper, J.C. *An Illustrated Encyclopaedia of Traditional Symbols.* London: Thames and Hudson, 1978.

Croker, Thomas Crofton. *Legend of the Lakes.* N.p., 1829.

Crooke, W. *The Popular Religion and Folk-lore of Northern India.* Whitefish, Mont.: Kessinger Publishing Ltd., 1997.

Cumont, F. *The Mysteries of Mithra,* London: Dover Publications, 1956.

Currer-Briggs, N. *The Shroud and the Grail; A Modern Wuest for the True Grail.* New York: St. Martin's Press, 1987.

Dakaris, Sotirios. "The Dark Place of Hades." *Archaeology* 15, no. 2 (1962).

David-Neel, Alexandria. *Magic and Mystery in Tibet,* London: Dover Publications, 1929.

Davidson, H. R. Ellis. *Myths and Symbols of Pagan Europe.* Syracuse, N.Y.: Syracuse University Press, 1988.

Davidson, John. *The Secret of the Creative Vacuum.* London: The C.W. Daniel Company, Ltd., 1989.

Davies, Rev. Edward. *The Mythology and Rites of the British Druids.* London: J. Booth, 1806.

De Martino, Ernesto. *Primitive Magic.* Dorset, UK: Prism Unity, 1972.

Devereux, Paul. *Places of Power: Measuring the Secret Energy of Ancient Sites.* London: Blandford, 1999.

———. *Secrets of Ancient and Sacred Places: The World's Mysterious Heritage.* Beckhampton, UK: Beckhampton Press, 1995.

———. *Shamanism and the Mystery Lines.* London: Quantum, 1992.

———. *Symbolic Landscapes.* Glastonbury, UK: Gothic Image, 1992.

Devereux, Paul, and Ian Thompson. *Ley Guide: The Mystery of Aligned Ancient Sites.* London: Empress, 1988.

Dinwiddie, John. *Revelations: The Golden Elixir.* Self-published by iUniverse and Writers Club Press, 2001.

Dodd, C.H. *Historical Tradition of the Fourth Gospel.* Cambridge: Cambridge University Press.

Doel, Fran, and Geoff Doel. *Robin Hood: Outlaw of Greenwood Myth.* Nottingham, UK: Temous, 2000.

Duckett-Shipley, Eleanor. *The Gateway to the Middle Ages, Monasticism.* Ann Arbor, Mich.: University of Michigan Press, 1961.

Dunford, Barry. *The Holy Land of Scotland: Jesus in Scotland and the Gospel of the Grail.* Perthshire, UK: Sacred Connections, 2001.

Dunstan, V. *Did the Virgin Mary Live and Die in England?* Rochester, N.Y.: Megiddo Press, 1985.

Eliade, Mircea. *Shamanism: Archaic Techniques of Ecstasy.* Princeton, N.J.: Princeton University Press, 1951.

Ellis, Ralph. *Jesus, Last of the Pharaohs.* Cheshire, UK: Edfu Books, 2001.

Epstein, Perle. *Kabbalah: The Way of the Jewish Mystic.* Boston: Shambhala Classics, 2001.

Ernst, Carl H. *Venomous Reptiles of North America.* Washington, D.C.: Smithsonian Books, 1992.

Evans, Lorraine. *Kingdom of the Ark.* London: Simon and Schuster, 2000.

Feather, Robert. *The Copper Scroll Decoded.* London: Thorsons, 1999.

Fedder, Kenneth L., and Michael Alan Park. *Human Antiquity: An Introduction to Physical Anthropology and Archaeology.* Mountain View, Calif.: Mayfield Publishing Company, 1993.

Fenwick, Dr. Peter. "The Neurophysiology of the Brain: Its Relationship to Altered States of Consciousness (With Emphasis on the Mystical Experience)." A Wrekin Trust lecture. *http://www.scienceandreligion.com/b_myst_2.html* (accessed October 2007).

Ferguson, Diana. *Tales of the Plumed Serpent.* London: Collins and Brown, 2000.

Fergusson, Malcolm. *Rambles in Breadalbane.* N.p., 1891.

Fontana, David. *The Secret Language of Symbols.* London: Piatkus, 1997.

Ford, Patrick K. *The Mabinogi and other Medieval Welsh Tales.* Berkeley, Calif.: University of California Press, 1977.

Fortune, Dion. *The Mystical Qabalah.* New York: Weiser Books, 2000.

Foss, Michael. *People of the First Crusade.* London: Michael O'Mara Books, 1997.

Frazer, Sir James. *The Golden Bough.* London: Wordsworth, 1993.

Freke, Timothy, and Peter Gandy. *Jesus and the Goddess.* London: Thorsons, 2001.

Gardner, Laurence. *Bloodline of the Holy Grail.* London: Element, 1996.

Gardiner, Samuel R. *History of England.* London: Longmans, Green and Co., 1904.

Gascoigne, Bamber. *The Christians.* London: Jonathan Cape, 1977.

Gerber, Richard. *Vibrational Medicine.* Santa Fe, N.M.: Bear & Company, 2001.

Gilbert, Adrian. *Magi.* London: Bloomsbury, 1996.

Goldberg, Carl. *Speaking With The Devil.* London: Viking, 1996.

Gordon, Stuart. *The Paranormal.* London: Headline, 1992.

Gould, Charles. *Mythical Monsters.* London: Senate, 1995.

Grandpierre, Attila. "The Nature of Man-Universe Connections." *The Noetic Journal* 2, no. 1 (1999): 52–67. *http://www.konkoly.hu/staff/grandpierre/noetic.html* (accessed October 2007).

Graves, Robert. *The Greek Myths: 2.* London: Pelican, 1964.

Gray Hulse, Tristan. *The Holy Shroud.* London: Weidenfeld and Nicolson, 1997.

Guenther, Johannes Von. *Cagliostro.* London: William Heinemann, 1928.

Hagger, Nicholas. *The Fire and the Stones.* London: Element, 1991.

Hanauer, J.E. *The Holy Land.* London: Senate, 1996.

Hancock, Graham. *The Sign and the Seal.* London: Arrow, 2001.

Halifax, Joan. *Shaman: The Wounded Healer.* London: Crossroad, Thames, and Hudson, 1982.

Harbison, Peter. *Pre-Christian Ireland.* London: Thames and Hudson, 1988.

Harrington, E. *The Meaning of English Place Names.* Belfast, UK: The Black Staff Press. 1954.

Hartmann, Franz. *The Life of Jehoshua The Prophet of Nazareth: an occult study and a key to the Bible.* London: Kegan, Trench, Trubner & Co, 1909.

Harvey, Clesson. "The Great Pyramid Texts." *http://www.pyramidtexts.com.*

Heathcote-James, Emma. *They Walk Among Us.* London: Metro, 2004.

Hedsel, Mark. *The Zelator.* London: Century, 1998.

Howard, M. *The Occult Conspiracy.* Rochester, N.Y.: Destiny Books, 1989.

"Is There Life After Death?" NBC 10 news story, April 30, 2004. *http://www.nbc10.com/news/3253894/detail.html* (accessed October 2007).

James, E.O. *The Ancient Gods.* London: Weidenfeld and Nicolson, 1962.

Jean, Georges. *Signs, Symbols and Ciphers,* London: Thames & Hudson, 1999.

Jennings, Hargrave. *Ophiolatreia.* Whitefish, Mont.: Kessinger Publishing Ltd., 1996.

Johnson, Buffie. *Lady of the Beasts.* San Francisco: Harper and Row, 1988.

Jones, Alison. *Dictionary of World Folklore.* New York: Larousse, 1995.

Josephus, Flavius. *Antiquities. http://www.indypublish.com.*

Kauffeld, Carl. *Snakes: The Keeper and the Kept.* London: Doubleday and Co., 1969.

Kendrick, T.D. *The Druids.* London: Methuen and Co., 1927.

King, Serge Kahili. *Instant Healing: Mastering the Way of the Hawaiian Shaman Using Words, Images, Touch, and Energy.* Los Angeles: Renaissance Books, 2000.

Knight, Christopher, and Robert Lomas. *Uriel's Machine: Reconstructing the Disaster Behind Human History.* London: Arrow, 2004.

———. *The Second Messiah.* London: Arrow, 1997.

Krishna, Gopi. *The Real Nature of Mystical Experience.* Toronto, Canada: New Age Publishing, 1979.

———. *The Wonder of the Brain*. Ontario, Canada: Institute for Consciousness Research, 1987.

Laidler, Keith. *The Head of God*. London: Orion, 1999.

Laidler, Keith. *The Divine Deception*. London: Headline, 2000.

Lapatin, Kenneth. *Mysteries of the Snake Goddess*. Boston: Houghton Mifflin Company, 2002.

Larson, Martin A. *The Story of Christian Origins*. London: Village, 1977.

Layton, Robert. *Australian Rock Art: A New Synthesis*. Cambridge: Cambridge University Press.

Leakey, Richard, and Roger Lewin. *Origins Reconsidered*. London: Doubleday, 1992.

Le Goff, Jacques. *The Medieval World*. London: Parkgate Books, 1997.

Lemesurier, Peter. *The Great Pyramid Decoded*. London: Element, 1977.

Leone, Al. *The Totality of God and the Izunome Cross: Unlocking the Secret Riddle of the Ages*. Unpublished, at *http://www.gizapyramid.com/ Leone1.htm*.

Levi, Eliphas. *Transcendental Magic*. London: Tiger Books, 1995.

Lincoln, Henry. *Key to the Sacred Pattern*. Gloucestershire, UK: The Windrush Press, 1997.

Low, Colin. "The Necronomicon Anti-FAQ." *http://www.digital-brilliance.com/necron/necron.htm*.

Loye, David. *An Arrow Through Chaos: How We See Into the Future*. Santa Fe, N.M.: Inner Traditions International, 1983.

Lyall, Neil, and Robert Chapman. *The Secret of Staying Young*. London: Pan, 1976.

Maby, J.C., and T. Bedford Franklin. *The Physics of the Divining Rod*. London: Bell, 1977.

MacCana, Proinsias. *Celtic Mythology*. New York: Hamlyn, 1970.

Mack, B.L. *The Lost Gospel*. London: Element, 1993.

Maclellan, Alec. *The Lost World of Agharti*. London: Souvenir Press, 1982.

Magin, U. *The Christianisation of Pagan Landscapes*. In *The Ley Hunter No. 116*, 1992.

Mann, A.T. *Sacred Architecture*. London: Element, 1993.

Maraini, Fosco. *Secret Tibet*. London: Hutchinson, 1954.

Matthews, John. *The Quest for the Green Man*. Newton Abbot, UK: Godsfield Press, 2001.

———. *Sources of the Grail*. London: Floris Books, 1996.

McDermott, Bridget. *Decoding Egyptian Hieroglyphs*. Winchester, UK: Duncan Baird Publishers, 2001.

Meseroll, Thomas C. "Instantaneous Data Transfer Over Temporal Boundaries: A Method for Communicating With the Past and

Future." El Segundo, Calif.: Hughes Space and Communications Company, 1999. *http://www-ssc.igpp.ucla.edu/meseroll/Quantum.pdf* (accessed October 2007).

Milgrom, Jacob. *The JPS Torah Commentary: Numbers.* New York: Jewish Publication Society, 1990.

Miller, Richard Alan, and Iona Miller. "The Schumann Resonances and Human Psychobiology." *Nexus Magazine,* 2003.

Moncrieff, A. R. Hope. *Romance & Legend of Chivalry.* London: Senate, 1994.

Morgan, Gerald. *Nanteos: A Welsh House and its Families.* Llandysul, UK: Gomer, 2001.

Morton, Chris, and Ceri Louise Thomas. *The Mystery of the Crystal Skulls.* London: Element, 2003.

Muggeridge, Malcolm. *Jesus.* London: Collins, 1975.

Nilsson, M.P., *The Minoan-Mycenaean Religion and Its Survival in Greek Religion.* London: Lund, 1950.

O'Brien, Christian, and Barbara Joy. *The Shining Ones.* London: Dianthus Publishing Ltd., 1997.

Oliver, George. *Signs and Symbols.* New York: Macoy Publishing, 1906.

Oliver, Rev. George. *The History of Initiation.* Whitefish, Mont.: Kessinger Publishing Co., 1841.

O'Neill, John. *Nights of the Gods.* N.p., n.d.

Oppenheimer, Stephen. *Eden in the East.* New York: Phoenix Mass Market Publications, 1952.

Orofino, Giacomella. *Sacred Tibetan Teachings on Death and Liberation.* London: Prism-Unity, 1990.

Pagels, E. *The Gnostic Gospels.* London: Weidenfeld and Nicolson, 1980.

Paterson Smyth, J. *How We Got our Bible.* London: Sampson Low, 1895.

Peniston, Eugene O. "The Peniston-Kulkosky Brainwave Neurofeedback Therapeutic Protocol: The Future Psychotherapy for Alcoholism/PTSD/Behavioral Medicine." The American Academy of Experts in Traumatic Stress, Inc., 1998.

Pennick, Nick. *Sacred Geometry.* Chievely, UK: Capall Bann, 1994.

Picknett, Lynn, and Clive Prince. *The Templar Revelation.* London: Corgi, 1998.

Piggot, Stuart. *The Druids.* London: Thames and Hudson, 1985.

Pike, Albert. *The Morals and Dogma of Scottish Rite Freemasonry.* London: L.H. Jenkins, 1928.

Plichta, Peter. *God's Secret Formula.* London: Element, 1997.

Plunket, Emmeline. *Calendars and Constellations of the Ancient World.* London: John Murray, 1903.

Powell, Dr. Andrew. "Consciousness That Transcends Spacetime: Its Significance for the Therapeutic Process." *http://www.rcpsych.ac.uk/pdf/powell_CTTS.pdf* (accessed October 2007).

Powell, T.G.E. *The Celts.* London: Thames and Hudson, 1989.

Rabten, Geshe. *Echoes of Voidness.* London: Wisdom Publications, 1983.

Radin, Dean. *The Conscious Universe.* London: Harper Collins, 1997.

Ramachandran, V.S., and Sandra Blakeslee. *Phantoms in the Brain.* London: Fourth Estate, 1998.

Randles, Jenny, and Peter Hough. *Encyclodepia of the Unexplained.* London: Brockhampton Press. 1995.

Read, Piers Paul. *The Templars.* London: Phoenix, 1999.

Redway, George. *The Book of Ceremonial Magic.* London: William Ryder & Sons, Ltd., 1911.

Rees, Alwyn, and Brynley Rees. *Celtic Heritage.* London: Thames and Hudson, 1961.

Reid, Howard. *Arthur: The Dragon King.* London: Headline, 2001.

———. *In Search of the Immortals: Mummies, Death and the Afterlife.* London: Headline, 1999.

Richet, C. *Thirty Years of Psychic Research.* New York: Macmillan, 1923.

Rinbochay, Lati, Locho Rinbochay, Leah Zahler, and Jeffrey Hopkins. *Meditative States in Tibetan Buddhism.* London: Wisdom Publications, 1983.

Roberts, Alison. *Hathor Rising: The Serpent Power of Ancient Egypt.* London: Northgate, 1995.

Roberts, J.M. *Antiquity Unveiled.* New York: Health Research, 1970.

———. *The Mythology of the Secret Societies.* London: Granada, 1972.

Robertson, J.M. *Pagan Christs.* London: Watts, 1903.

Rohl, David. *A Test of Time: The Bible—From Myth to History.* London: Arrow, 1995.

Rolleston, T.W. *Myths and Legends of the Celtic Race.* London: Mystic P, 1986.

Russell, Peter. *The Brain Book.* London: Routledge, 1980.

S, Acharya. *The Christ Conspiracy: The Greatest Story Ever Sold.* Kempton, Ill.: Adventures Unlimited Press, 1999.

Schaya, Leo. *The Universal Meaning of the Kabbalah.* Baltimore, Md.: University Books, 1987.

Schele, Linda, and Mary Ellen Miller. *The Blood of Kings: Dynasty and Ritual in Maya Art.* New York: George Braziller, 1992.

Scholem, Gershom G. *On the Kabbalah and Its Symbolism.* London: Routledge & Kegan, 1965.

Schonfield, Hugh. *Essene Odyssey.* London: Element, 1984.

———. *The Passover Plot.* London: Hutchinson, 1965.

Schwartz, Gary, and Linda Russek. *The Living Energy Universe.* London: Hampton Roads Publishing, 1999.

Scott, Ernest. *The People of the Secret.* London: The Octagon Press, 1983.

Seife, Charles. *Zero: The Biography of a Dangerous Idea.* London: Souvenir Press, 2000.

Seligmann, Kurt. *The History of Magic.* New York: Quality Paperback Book Club, 1997.

Sharper Knowlson, T. *The Origins of Popular Superstitions and Customs.* London, Senate, 1994.

Simpson, Jacqueline. *British Dragons.* London: B.T. Batsford and Co., 1980.

Sinclair, Andrew. *The Secret Scroll.* Edinburgh, UK: Birlinn, 2001.

Smith, M. *The Secret Gospel.* London: Victor Gollancz. 1999.

Snyder, Louis L. *Encyclopaedia of the Third Reich.* London: Wordsworth, 1998.

Spence, Lewis. *Introduction to Mythology.* London: Senate, 1994.

———. *Myths and Legends of Egypt.* London: George Harrap and Sons, 1915.

Stephen, Alexander M. "Hopi Tales." *The Journal of American Folklore* (January/March 1929).

Stone, Nathan. *Names of God.* Chicago: Moody, 1944.

Sullivan, Danny. *Ley Lines.* London: Piaktus, 1999.

Talbot, Michael. *The Holographic Universe.* London: Harper Collins, 1991, 1996.

Taylor, Richard. *How to Read a Church.* London: Random House, 2003.

Temple, Robert. *The Crystal Sun.* London: Arrow, 1989.

———. *Netherworld: Discovering the Oracle of the Dead and Ancient Techniques of Foretelling the Future.* London: Century, 2002.

Tesla, Nikola. "The Transmission of Electrical Energy Without Wires." *Electrical World and Engineer,* March 5, 1904. *http://www.tfcbooks.com/tesla/1904-03-05.htm* (accessed October 2007).

Thiering, Barbara. *Jesus of the Apocalypse.* London: Doubleday, 1996.

———. *Jesus the Man.* London: Doubleday, 1992.

Toland, John. *Hitler.* London: Wordsworth, 1997.

Trail of the Serpent. Unknown author and publisher, 1940s.

Tull, George F. *Traces of the Templars.* London: The Kings England Press, 2000.

Villanueva, Dr. J.L. *Phoenician Ireland.* Dublin, The Dolmen Press, 1833.

Villars, de, Abbe N. de Montfaucon. *Comte de Gabalis: discourses on the Secret Sciences and Mysteries in accordance with the principles of the Ancient Magi and the Wisdom of the Kabalistic Philosophers*. Whitefish, Mont.: Kessinger Publishing Ltd., 1996.

Vulliamy, C.E. *Immortality: Funerary Rites & Customs*. London: Senate, 1997. Previously *Immortal Man*, published by Methuen, 1926.

Waite, Arthur Edward. *The Hidden Church of the Holy Grail*. Amsterdam: Fredonia Books, 2002.

Wake, C. Staniland. *The Origin of Serpent Worship*. Whitefish, Mont.: Kessinger Publishing Ltd., 1877.

Walker, Benjamin. *The Hindu World: An Encyclopedic Survey of Hinduism in Two Volumes*. London: Frederick A. Praeger, 1968.

Wallace-Murphy, Hopkins. *Rosslyn*. London: Element, 2000.

Waters, Frank. *The Book of the Hopi*. New York: Ballantine, 1963.

Watson, Lyall. *Dark Nature*. London: Harper Collins, 1995.

Weber, Renee. *Dialogues with Scientists and Sages: Search for Unity in Science and Mysticism*. London: Arkana, 1990.

Weisse, John. *The Obelisk and Freemasonry*. Whitefish, Mont.: Kessinger Publishing Ltd., 1992.

Williams, E.R. "The Schumann Resonance: A Global Tropical Thermometer." *Science*, 1992.

Williamson, A. *Living in the Sky*. Norman, Okla.: Oklahoma Press, 1984.

Wilson, Colin. *The Atlas of Holy Places and Sacred Sites*. London: Doring Kindersley, 1996.

———. *Beyond the Occult*. London: Caxton Editions, 2002.

———. *Frankenstein's Castle: The Double Brain—Door to Wisdom*. London: Ashgrove Press, 1980.

Wilson, Hilary. *Understanding Hieroglyphs*. London: Brockhampton Press, 1993.

Wise, Michael, Martin Abegg, and Edward Cook. *The Dead Sea Scrolls*. London: Harper Collins, 1999.

Wood, David. *Genisis*. London: Baton Wicks Publications, 1985.

Woods, George Henry. *Herodotus Book II*. London: Rivingtons, 1897.

Woolley, Benjamin. *The Queen's Conjuror: The Science and Magic of Dr. John Dee, Adviser to Queen Elizabeth I*. London: HarperCollins, 2001.

Wylie, Rev. J.A. *History of the Scottish Nation, Volume 1*. N.p., 1886.

Zollschan, Dr. G.K., Dr. J.F Schumaker, and Dr. G.F. Walsh. *Exploring the Paranormal*. London: Prism Unity, 1989.

Dictionaries

Dictionary of Beliefs and Religions. London: Wordsworth, 1995.

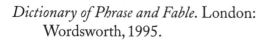

Dictionary of Phrase and Fable. London: Wordsworth, 1995.

Dictionary of Science and Technology. London: Wordsworth, 1995.

Dictionary of the Bible. London: HarperCollins, 1974.

Dictionary of the Occult. London: Geddes and Grosset, 1997.

Dictionary of World Folklore. London: Larousse, 1995.

Religious texts consulted

The Apocrypha, Talmud, Koran, Bible, Dead Sea Scrolls: Damascus Document, The Community Rule, War of the Sons of Light with the Sons of Darkness, Messianic Rule of the Congregation, Temple Scroll. The writings of Pliny the Younger, Flavius Josephus, Pythagoras, Plato, Hippolytus of Rome, Ephraim the Syrian, Carl Jung, Jeremiah Creedon (Guardian). The Foundation for the Study of Cycles, The I Ching (Richard Wilhelm Translation), New Scientist, Nag Hammadi Gospel of Truth, Gospel of Mary, Gospel of the Egyptians.

Index

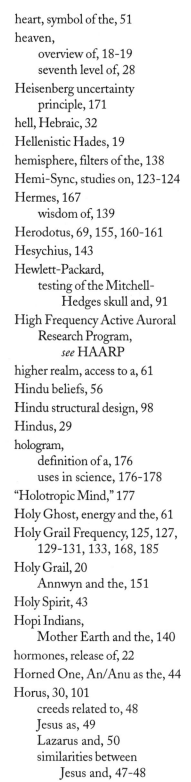

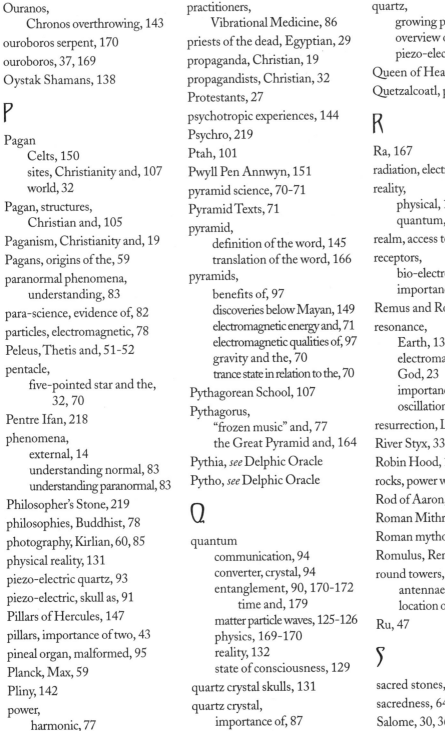

About the Author

Philip Gardiner is the best-selling author of
Gnosis: The Secret of Solomon's Temple Revealed;
The Ark, The Shroud, and Mary;
The Serpent Grail;
and *Secrets of the Serpent*.
He lectures around the world, from Australia to Europe, and is an
award-winning filmmaker.

His Website is *www.gardinersworld.com*.